IMAGES
of America

LOST ORLANDO

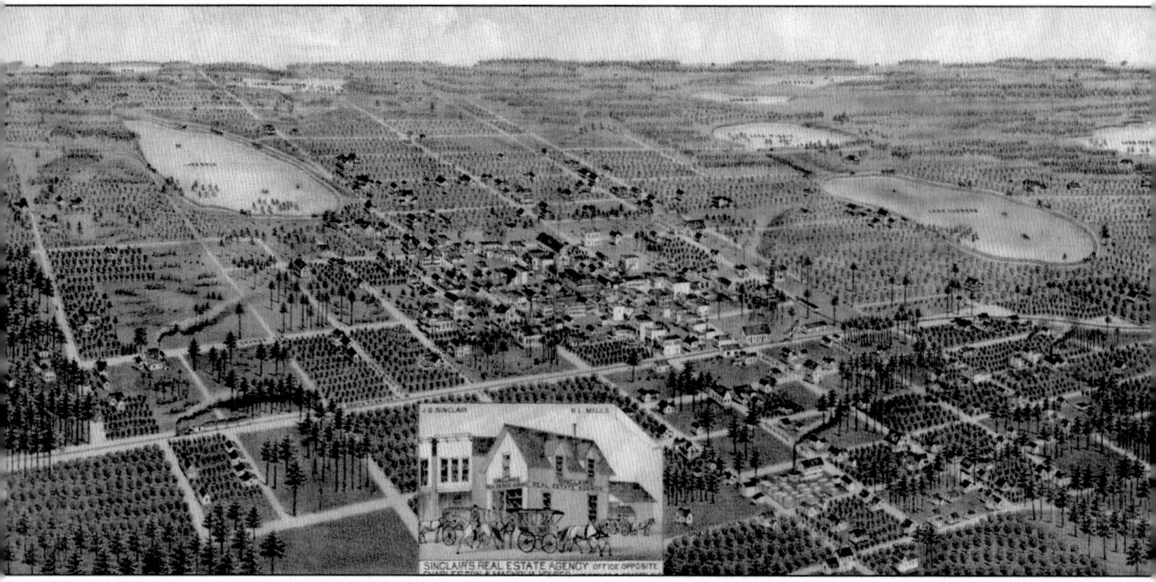

This map, entitled "1884 Birds Eye View of Orlando, Florida," shows lakes, streets, and buildings in a unique perspective, adding a visual dimension to the city's history. Important structures cluster near the center of the city, surrounded by residential areas amid the numerous lakes and remaining pine forest. Much has changed over the years, but the downtown area still follows the plan laid out by early settlers. (Courtesy of the Orange County Regional History Center.)

On the Cover: Orange Avenue in downtown Orlando is barely recognizable in this 1920s photograph taken from Church Street. Much of Orlando's architectural history exists only in images, as old buildings have continually given way to modern construction. As a result, many people do not fully realize the depth of Orlando's history. These photographs help showcase the city's vibrant past before theme parks made it a world-class destination. (Courtesy of the Orange County Regional History Center.)

IMAGES
of America

LOST ORLANDO

Stephanie Gaub Antequino and Tana Mosier Porter
on behalf of the Historical Society of Central Florida

ARCADIA
PUBLISHING

ISBN 978-0-7385-9173-5

Published by Arcadia Publishing
Charleston, South Carolina

Printed in the United States of America

Library of Congress Control Number: 2011942698

For all general information, please contact Arcadia Publishing:
Telephone 843-853-2070
Fax 843-853-0044
E-mail sales@arcadiapublishing.com
For customer service and orders:
Toll-Free 1-888-313-2665

Visit us on the Internet at www.arcadiapublishing.com

To the men and women who braved the unknown
and made Orlando what it is today

Contents

ACKNOWLEDGMENTS

We would like to express our appreciation to the Historical Society of Central Florida for years of collecting and preserving an amazing repository of information and photographs that document the history of Orlando and Central Florida. A special thank you goes out to volunteer Clayton Phillips for his assistance with challenging historical research. All images appear courtesy of the Orange County Regional History Center.

INTRODUCTION

Today, Orlando is a city of glass and steel, but here and there, among the downtown skyscrapers, an occasional older brick or stone building still stands as a reminder of an earlier Orlando. A few frame Victorian houses survive on the edges of the downtown, and many of the 1920s bungalows line the streets of the residential neighborhoods surrounding the city. The old houses, churches, and commercial structures offer physical evidence of the city's history. Their sizes, styles of architecture, and construction materials, as well as their locations, delineate a pattern of growth and development.

Unfortunately, too few of the old buildings survive to complete the tapestry, and modern structures have taken their places. One-story frame houses and stores gave way to larger and taller brick commercial structures as the downtown first prospered in the 1880s, while prominent citizens built more pretentious houses only a block or two away from the expanding business district. The process repeated itself over the years with steel replacing bricks and commerce replacing residential mansions. The cycle continues today with the demolition of steel and glass structures built in recent decades on the sites of earlier landmark structures. The buildings they replaced became history long ago, and now the new construction itself will be history. Several older buildings have thus far escaped demolition, but at least two of them will soon join the list of structures lost to Orlando.

When a building is demolished, destroyed by a fire, or just falls from neglect, more is lost than an old building. A part of the city's history, and with it, some sense of its identity, disappears with the structure. Progress seems too often to involve loss, and the loss of so many landmarks robs any place of a consciousness of its past. Often, surviving photographs provide the only record of houses, churches, courthouses, and other buildings, and those photographs can help to reconstruct history. Arranged chronologically and identified with locations and dates of construction and demolition, photographs of some of Orlando's lost buildings can rekindle a sense of place. The history, so often dismissed as nonexistent, emerges from the images of proud families on the front porches of their houses and from pictures of solid commercial buildings along streets busy with vehicles and pedestrians. Photographs bring the city's past into focus.

No photographs exist to document Central Florida's settlement years, and historians are forced to rely on eyewitness accounts of life in the frontier wilderness. The area's recorded history begins in 1838, when the US Army built Fort Gatlin just south of what is now downtown Orlando. At the conclusion of the Second Seminole War, the government offered homestead land to individuals willing to occupy the region around the abandoned military forts and to act as citizen soldiers in the event of Indian attacks. Brothers Aaron and Isaac Jernigan arrived with their families in 1842 and took up homesteads near Fort Gatlin. A post office opened in Aaron Jernigan's house in 1850, and the Fort Gatlin settlement became known as Jernigan.

An 1856 county election chose the Fort Gatlin settlement as the seat of Orange County government, but new settlers arriving during the previous decade had established their homes and businesses farther to the north, causing the center of the population to shift away from Jernigan and Fort Gatlin. After some debate about exactly where to place the county seat, B.F. Caldwell, a land speculator, settled the question. He gave the county four acres of land for a courthouse, situated north of Fort Gatlin in what is now downtown Orlando. Under the circumstances, a new name seemed in order for the new community, and after some discussion, Orlando was chosen.

The first courthouse in Orange County's new county seat was an old, abandoned log cabin out in the pinewoods near the present-day Church Street Station. It had no windows and a dirt floor. The courthouse occupied one of the two rooms in the log cabin, while the other was used for a school and for church services. Near the courthouse, the county built a jail from native pine logs. Caldwell's donation of a building site in Orlando determined the future location of a permanent courthouse, and businesses and houses began to cluster along what is now Magnolia Avenue in anticipation of the commerce that government would bring. John R. Worthington erected the first log building in downtown Orlando, where he sold merchandise shipped by boat south on the St. Johns River from Jacksonville and then hauled 34 miles from Lake Monroe to Orlando by ox team.

Orlando grew slowly in part because of the difficulty of getting to Central Florida. The lack of rivers and passable roads also discouraged shipment of building materials, so settlers in need of places to live used the pine trees growing everywhere. Sawmills, brought to Orlando in pieces and reassembled, made construction of larger and better buildings possible. John Worthington built the first frame house in 1857, using pine boards from William A. Lovell's steam sawmill on Lake Eola. Logs seldom lasted long in Florida's damp climate, and the wood frame structures that replaced the log cabins shared their vulnerability to termites, rot, and fire.

In 1863, Orange County built a two-story frame courthouse on the property known as the Courthouse Square. Three years later, according to one eyewitness, Orlando consisted of four houses, four stores, a saloon, and the courthouse. Log cabin dwellings dotted the pine forest. John Worthington, reasoning that lodging would be needed for people coming into town for court, constructed the first hotel in Orlando, a large frame building on Magnolia Avenue adjacent to the courthouse. This changed hands several times, and finally became Lovell's Hotel, later described as a frame building with five rooms and a lean-to kitchen.

Orlando's economy centered on the cattle industry, and the cow hunters who came into town from the surrounding open range gave it the atmosphere of a Wild West cattle town. In 1868, on the eve of a contentious cattle rustling trial, the courthouse burned, taking with it most of Orange County's early records. The jail burned with the courthouse, forcing the county to build a new jail to contend with the general lawlessness, which included the murder of the county sheriff in 1870 and a family feud that took several lives. Completed in 1873, the log jail had stout planks inside to secure the prisoners.

Orlando's population stood at 85 when the city incorporated in 1875. The 22 eligible voters platted the city in a square with the four-acre Original Town and the Orange County Courthouse at its center. By 1880, two hundred people lived in the city of Orlando, though trees still grew in the streets and cows grazed at large. Mahlon Gore, who later became mayor, recalled finding four stores, one hotel, a blacksmith, a wagon shop, and a livery stable surrounding the Courthouse Square when he arrived in 1880. Gore also saw new sawmills and planing mills providing lumber for more construction. A year later, the South Florida Railroad began service to Orlando, enabling the more affluent to build with bricks.

As the town grew, the commercial center became less desirable for home building and more in demand for business expansion. Sometimes, private homes were converted into shops, but more often, new construction better suited to business or manufacturing replaced them. The well-to-do citizens moved a block or two out from the center of the town and built larger and more stylish houses as evidence of their success. As the growth continued, these houses also fell to commercial needs, and the families moved farther from the central city. Government buildings, businesses, and institutions, such as churches and schools, remained in the downtown area, where property became too costly for residential use. The pattern of growth, construction, and demolition established at that time has prevailed for over a century.

The South Florida Railroad brought Orlando's first boom. By 1884, businesses lined Orange Avenue and Church Street, and the population reached 1,666. The streets remained unpaved, though the city had begun to remove the stumps that obstructed the roadways. A few board sidewalks resulted from a city ordinance requiring them, and garbage collection began. After a disastrous fire in January 1884 that destroyed several buildings between Pine Street and Central Boulevard and Court Street and Magnolia Avenue, threatening much of the downtown, Orlando organized a fire department in 1885. The city's recommendation that all new commercial construction be made of brick became a law in 1912, when a city ordinance required that all one-story, frame buildings in the business district be demolished and replaced with brick.

By 1886, with a population of about 2,000, Orlando called itself "The Phenomenal City." The Orlando Street Railway provided mule-drawn rapid transit on Orange Avenue, and the newly franchised Orlando Water Works promised 45 fire hydrants. The South Florida Gas & Electric Light Company built its gasworks, and the city planted 400 oak trees along downtown streets to replace the hundreds of trees they had cut down earlier in order to plat regular streets and straight lot lines. A large number of hotels and boardinghouses shared the downtown with stores and other businesses, but Orlando did not look like a city. Residences tended to be scattered, with undeveloped land in abundance. Many people lived outside the corporate limits, especially along the shores of the lakes south of the downtown, but some of the more impressive houses remained in or near the business district. Houses tended to be large to accommodate boarders and servants.

Orlando's first economic boom ended with the Great Freeze of 1894–1895. The unusually low temperatures that winter extended south as far as Key West and destroyed Central Florida's citrus industry. The first cold snap in December 1894 killed the fruit on the trees. The second hard freeze followed in February 1895, killing citrus trees to the ground. Faced with starting over, some grove owners abandoned their properties. Banks failed. During the 15 years required for the citrus industry to recover, Orlando's population dropped from 2,856 in 1890 to 2,481 in 1900. The city annexed its first addition in 1904 on the north side of Marks Street, the same year a numbering ordinance required that the buildings be numbered beginning at the intersection of Orange Avenue and Central Boulevard. In order to comply, existing building numbers changed, confounding researchers to this day. Streets paved with clay gave way to brick streets beginning in 1907 with the bricking of Orange Avenue, Central Boulevard, and Pine and Church Streets. The Phenomenal City became "The City Beautiful" in 1908.

Tourists and the recovering citrus industry brought prosperity back to Orlando by 1910, and the city began to grow again. The population more than doubled between 1910 and 1920. New commercial buildings appeared downtown, and the wealthier class began to build ostentatious houses farther from the central city. A few of the mansions built between the 1890s and the 1920s survive today as reminders of an era of conspicuous consumption, but most were lost in street realignments and expressway construction south of the downtown.

The popularity of automobiles and the national prosperity of the 1920s brought people to Florida in unimaginable numbers, and the automobile changed tourism. The traditional tourists, usually financially secure, arrived on the steamships and, later, the trains to spend the season at one of Florida's fine hotels. The new middle-class tourists drove to Florida in their automobiles and toured the state, stopping to see interesting places before moving on. Highways improved to accommodate the greater number of automobiles, and roadside attractions multiplied. Tourist homes opened to offer overnight lodging.

Some of the visitors liked what they saw and decided to buy property, build houses, and stay. In the resulting real estate frenzy known as the Great Florida Land Boom, Orlando added area and residents. The city's population increased three-fold, from just over 9,000 in 1920 to more than 27,000 in 1930. Business, especially construction, flourished. Developers platted more than a dozen new subdivisions in outlying areas of the city between 1924 and 1926 alone. Built for sale to the middle-class, bungalows and small Mediterranean-style houses predominated, their cement-block and stucco construction especially well suited to the subtropical climate. Institutions opened offices outside the business district, and churches and schools were built in residential neighborhoods. New hotels and office buildings went up downtown, and with less land available downtown, architects designed taller commercial buildings. Some existing stores and hotels added stories.

The citrus industry returned to dominate the city's economy, and Orlando became the most important citrus shipping center in Florida. Twelve packinghouses belonging to different growers and shippers lined the railroad in downtown Orlando in the 1920s. In 1926, as much as three-fourths of Florida's citrus crop was marketed through Orlando. Agriculture, citrus fruit in particular, figured importantly in Orlando's economy through the opening of Walt Disney World in 1971. By the 1980s, the land had become too valuable for agriculture, and the growers did not replant after the second of the devastating freezes of 1983 and 1985. Housing developments replaced acres of citrus groves.

Orlando's housing supply expanded during World War II to accommodate Army Air Corps personnel at Central Florida air bases and again after the war when many airmen who had trained in the area returned to live in the city. The small, affordable, ranch-style houses, usually frame, lined the streets of new subdivisions farther and farther from the business city. New roads, hotels, hospitals, banks, and shopping centers followed. Schools and hospitals multiplied. Remaining old downtown residences and commercial buildings were demolished to make space for parking lots near the stores, but downtown shopping could not compete with the new shopping centers that opened in the 1950s. With the loss of residents, institutions, and shopping, Orlando's downtown declined.

Evidences of blight in the downtown area led to revitalization projects that usually included the demolition of older buildings. Many of the bungalows in the first tier of annexations and much of the postwar tract housing remain standing, but the downtown suffered serious losses. The city allowed the demolition not only of most of the historic downtown properties, but also of structures only two or three decades old. Old buildings were razed to construct new, and new buildings were demolished to build newer. The process continues, threatening more of the few remaining historic properties. With the building, demolishing, and reconstruction, the city reinvented itself as modern with innovative glass and steel architecture, but the historical Orlando has been lost, recovered only in photographs.

One

1857–1875

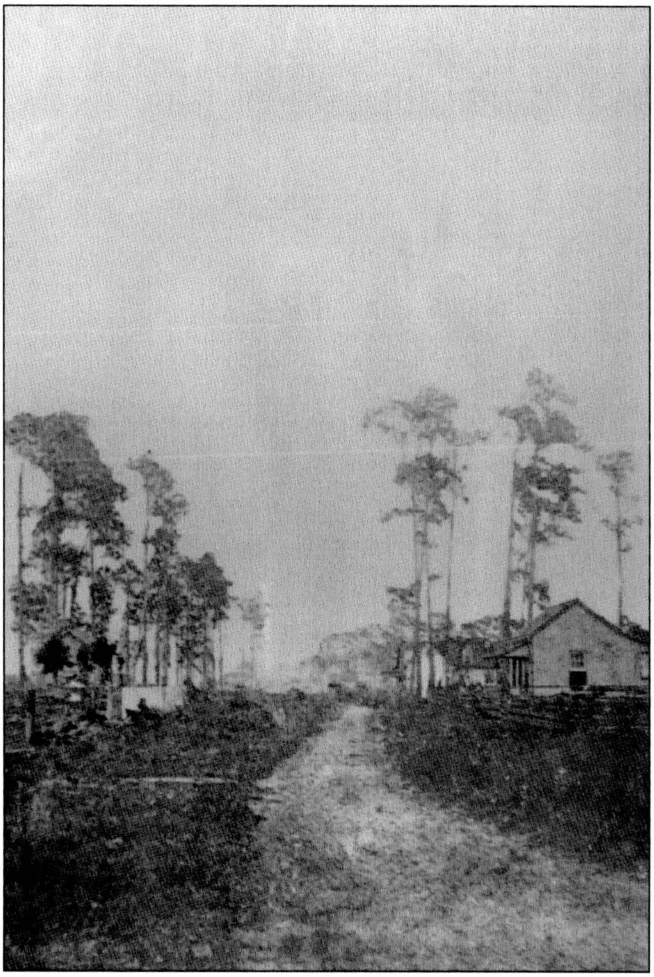

The years 1857 to 1875 mark Orlando's early settlement period. In its infancy, the city consisted more of pinewoods and sand streets than of city blocks. Unrecognizable to today's residents and visitors, early street views, such as this one of Church Street taken around 1875, illustrate just how rural Orlando once looked.

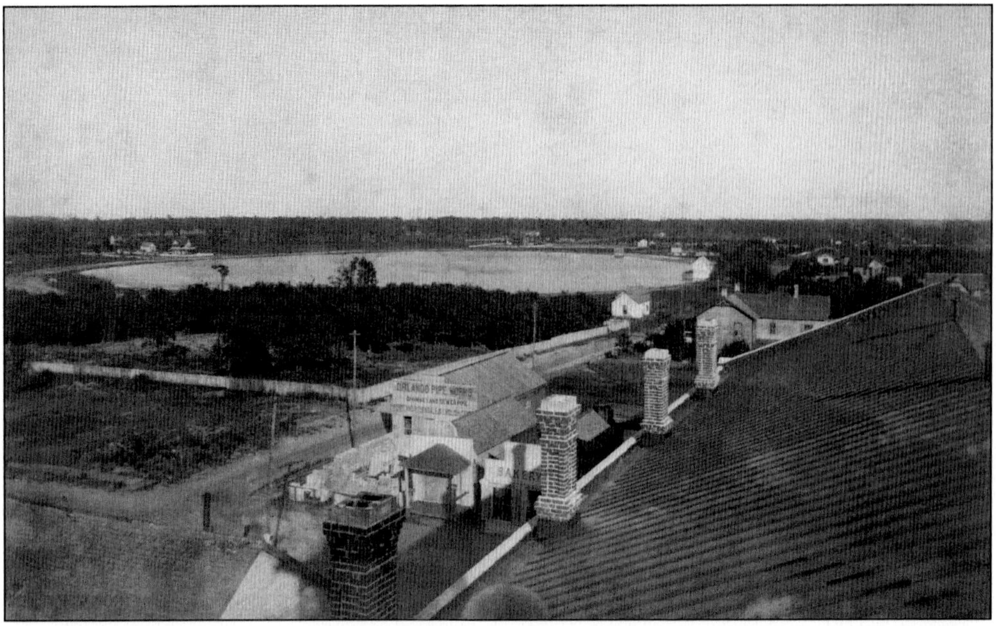

This photograph of the Orlando Pipe Works was taken from the roof of the Armory building around 1886. First mentioned in 1866 as "the old pipe works," it continued in business until at least 1887, making chimney and sewer pipes in the building near the corner of Magnolia Avenue and Central Boulevard.

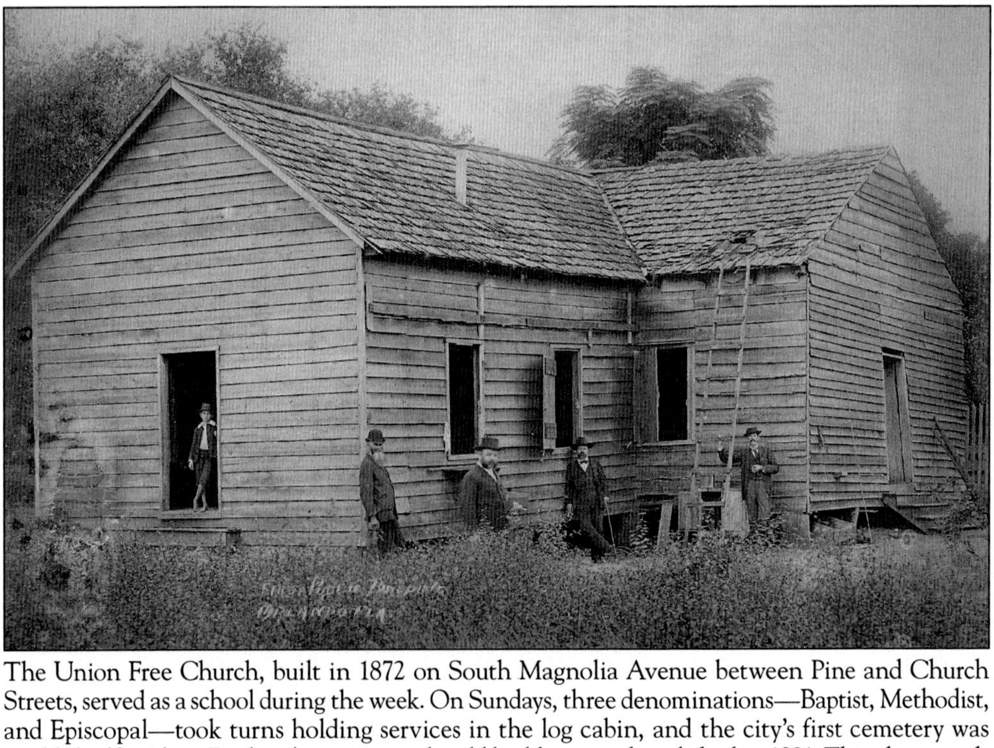

The Union Free Church, built in 1872 on South Magnolia Avenue between Pine and Church Streets, served as a school during the week. On Sundays, three denominations—Baptist, Methodist, and Episcopal—took turns holding services in the log cabin, and the city's first cemetery was established beside it. Declared a nuisance, the old building was demolished in 1891. This photograph was taken shortly before the structure's demolition.

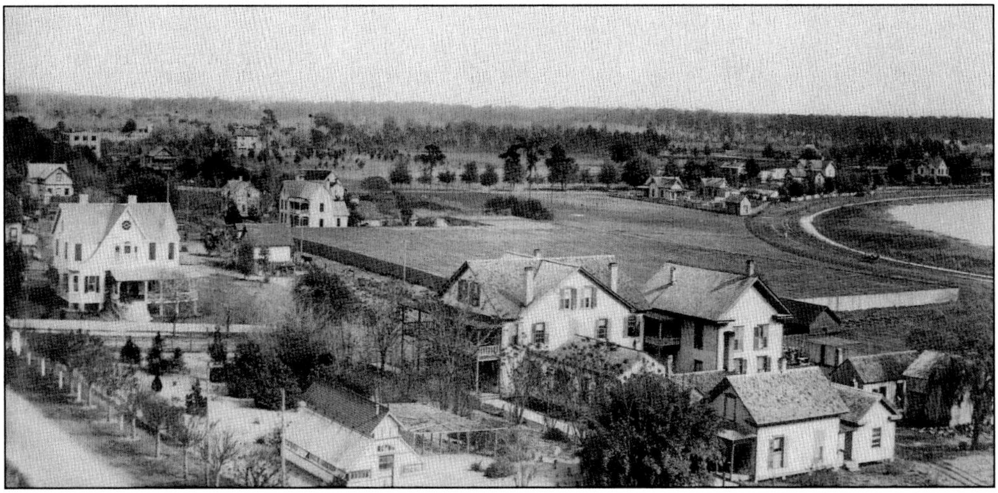

The large house Jacob Summerlin built in 1874 on Main Street was moved to face Washington Street and remodeled into a hotel around 1880. The Summerlin Hotel, seen in the center of this c. 1890 photograph, became Orlando's most fashionable place to stay. It remained open as a boardinghouse until 1941 or 1942. Southern Bell Telephone bought the property in 1953, and the hotel was demolished by 1955.

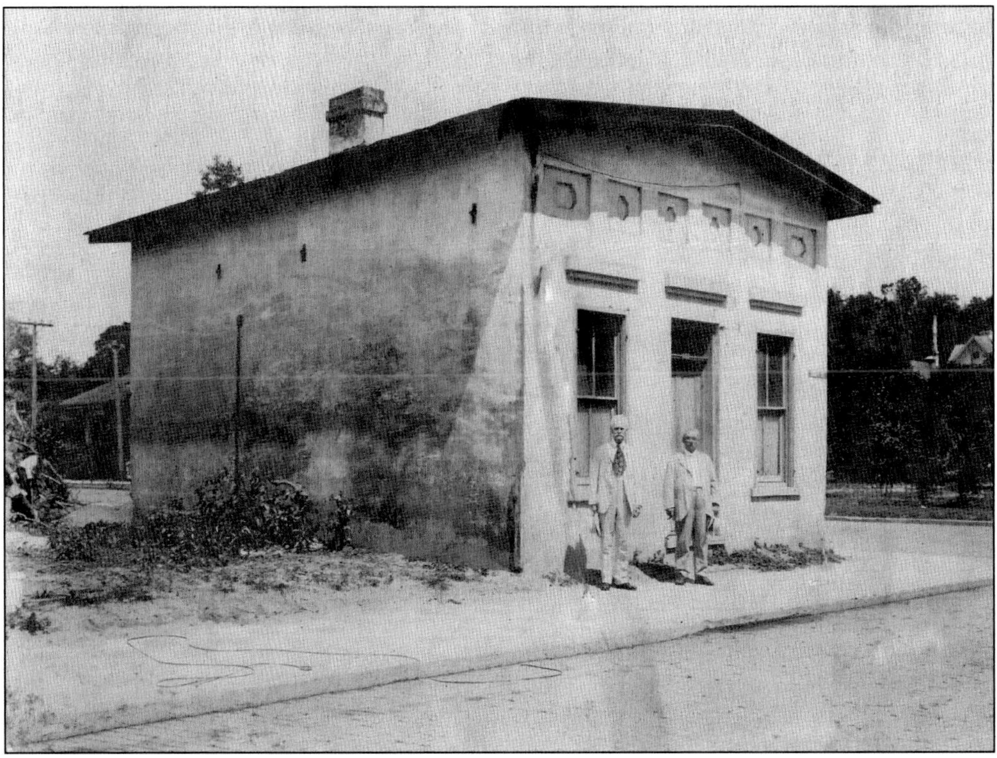

The concrete Abstract Office at the corner of Wall and Court Streets dated to the days of the wooden courthouses, when it served as a storage vault for Orange County records. In 1892, the county constructed its first brick courthouse and rented the building to various abstract companies. Orange County demolished the building in 1917 to construct a new jail. Today, the site is part of Court Street.

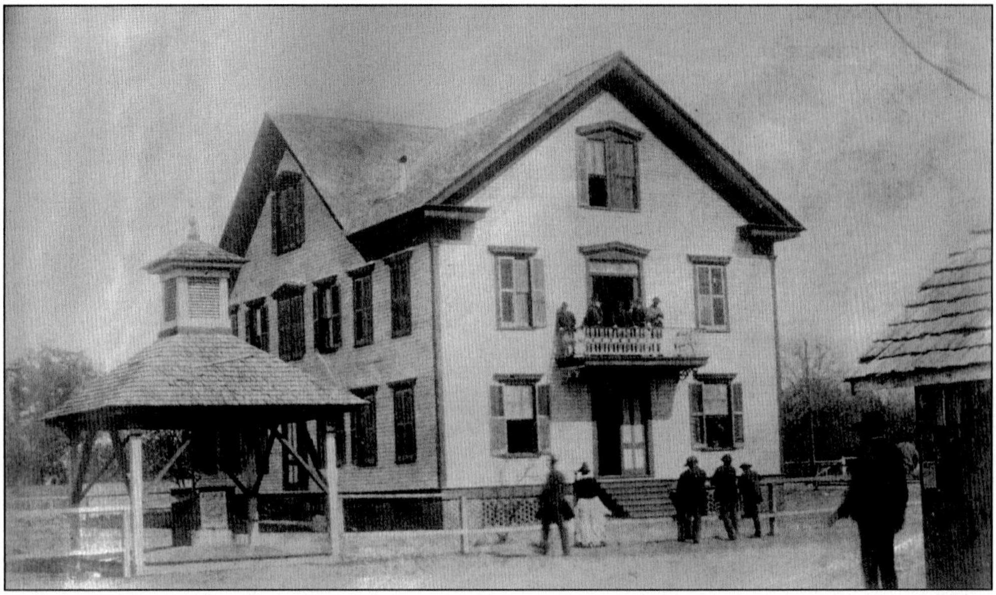

Forestalling Henry Sanford's effort to move the county seat to Sanford, Jacob Summerlin promised $10,000 to build a new courthouse if Orlando remained the county seat. Orange County built the larger wooden courthouse, the city's fourth, in 1875 the city's fourth at a cost of $7,800. A well on the corner in front of the building had a shingle roof and a watering trough for horses and oxen.

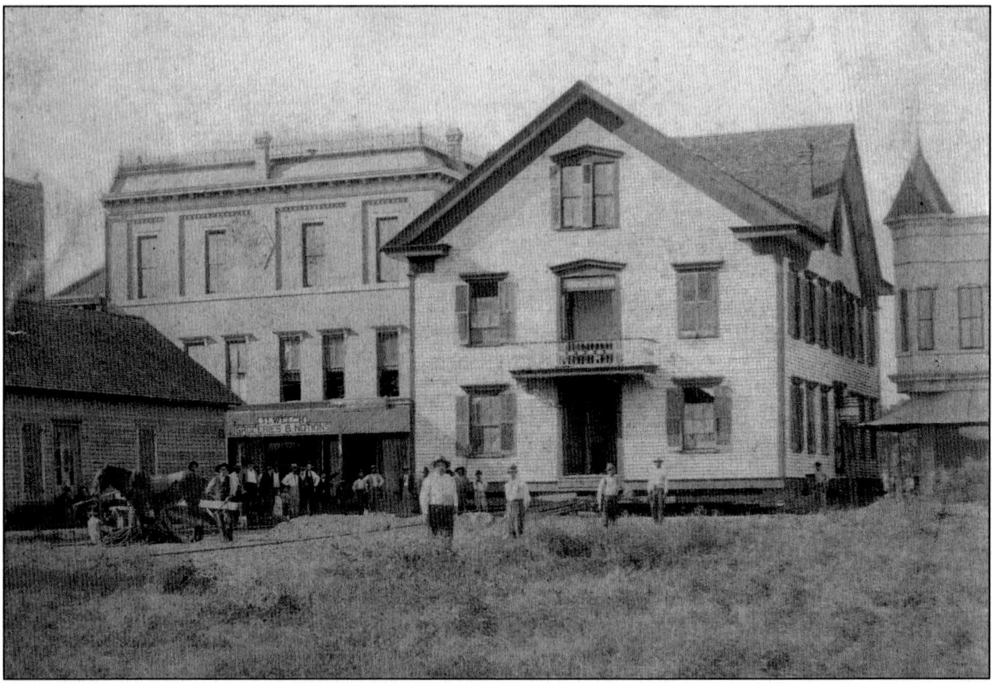

In 1891, Orange County sold the building to clear the site for a new courthouse. It was moved to become part of the Tremont Hotel and was demolished in 1956 for a parking lot. Taken at the corner of Magnolia Avenue and Pine Street, this photograph shows the courthouse during the moving process.

Two

1876–1895

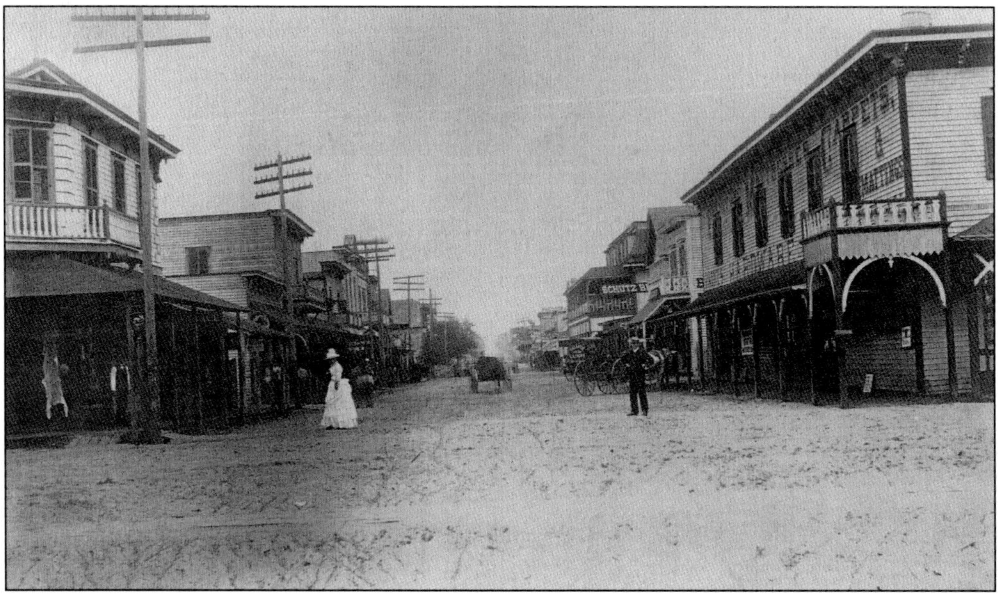

Between 1876 and 1895, Orlando experienced its first economic boom. The business district, part of which can be seen in this 1884 photograph of Orange Avenue, grew, and new settlers came from across the United States and abroad, seeking their fortunes in the warm Central Florida climate. Photographs from the 1880s and 1890s survive to illustrate these stories of tragedy and triumph.

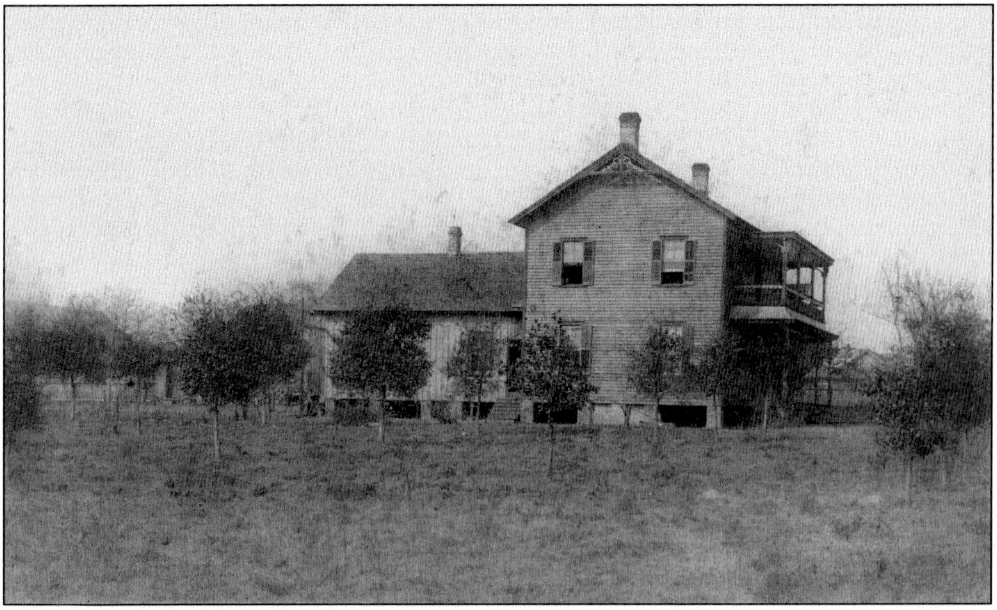

Seth French probably built the Lakeview House around 1877. He bought the property on East Central between Magnolia and Rosalind Avenues from Jacob Summerlin in 1875. French sold it to S.B. Harrington in 1881. Mahlon Gore lived in the hotel when he first came to Orlando in 1883. Sarah E. Shaw bought the Lakeview House in 1897 and, with her niece Carrie Shaw, built it into a select boardinghouse. Carrie Shaw married Eugene Sperry, and together they ran the Lakeview House until 1916, when they sold it to Claude Raulerson. It continued in business until 1924 as the Lakeview and remained at least one year longer as a boardinghouse. By 1955, it had been demolished; today, the University Club of Orlando occupies the site.

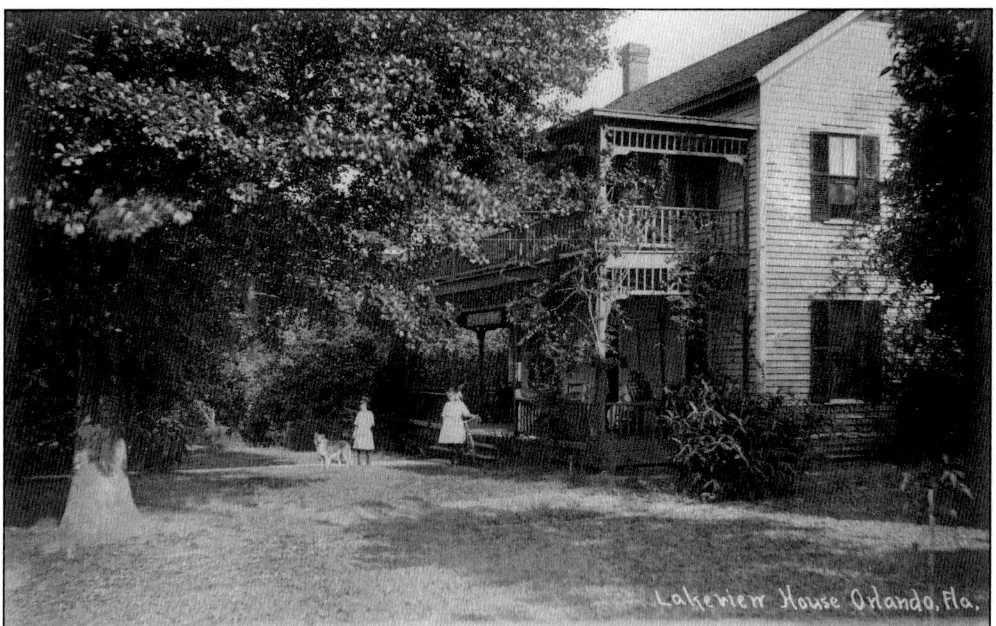

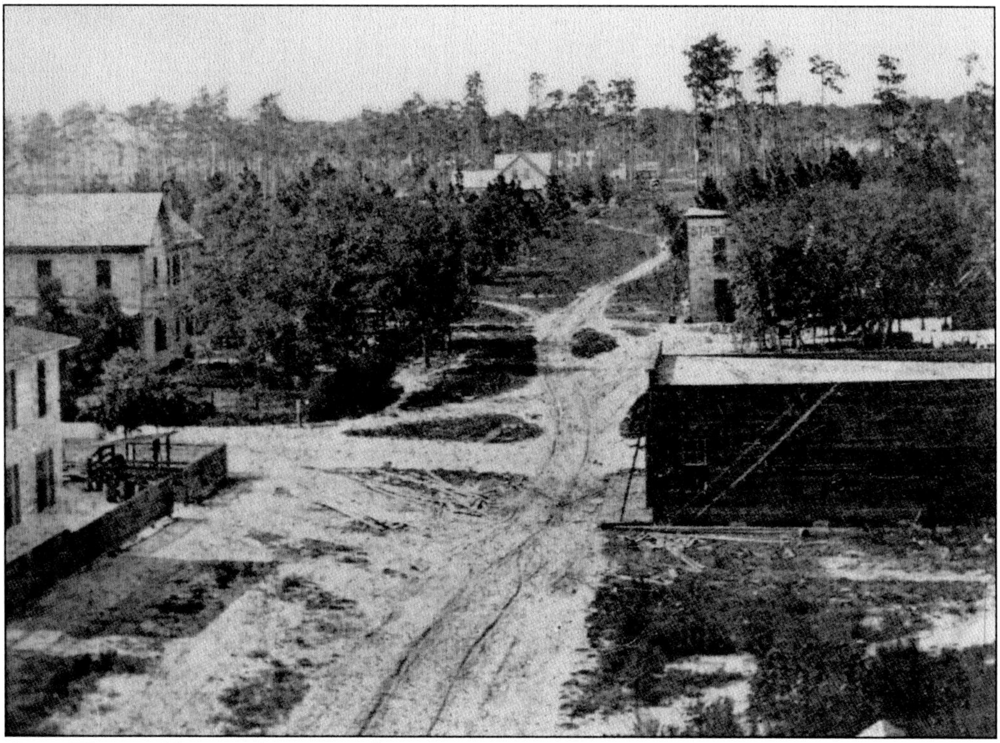

Capt. Thomas Shine, a director in the First National Bank, built his two-story frame house, seen in the background of this photograph, in 1879 at the corner of Orange Avenue and Jefferson Street. Shine and his wife, the former Martha Virginia Eppes, great-granddaughter of Thomas Jefferson, hosted many brilliant parties in the house, a showplace boasting Orlando's first indoor bathroom.

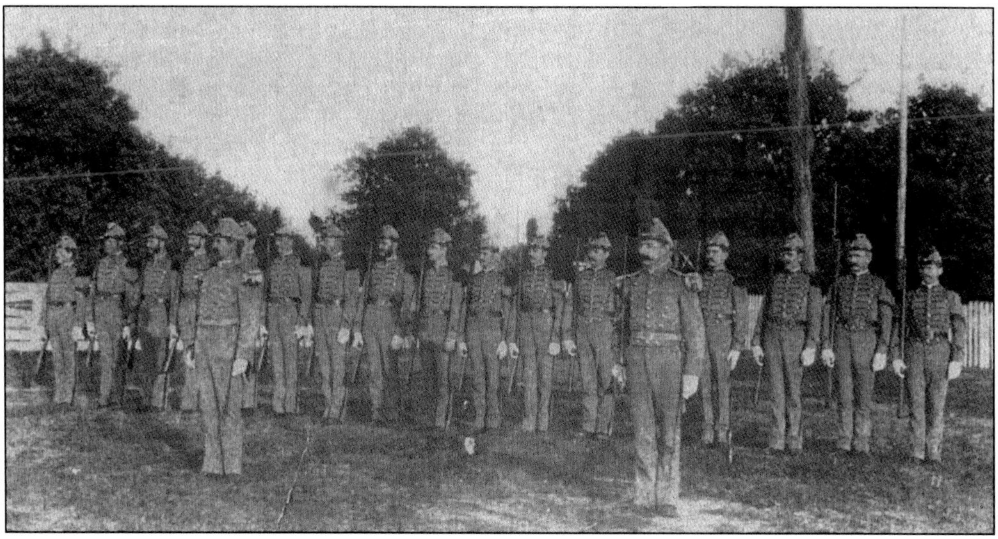

When Captain Shine, front row at left, died in 1889 after a long march with the Orlando Guards, his widow married Episcopal clergyman Henry Williston Greetham. The family lived in the house until 1914. Ida Hand bought it in 1919 and lived there until 1922. In 1923, the house was gone. Today, it is a parking lot.

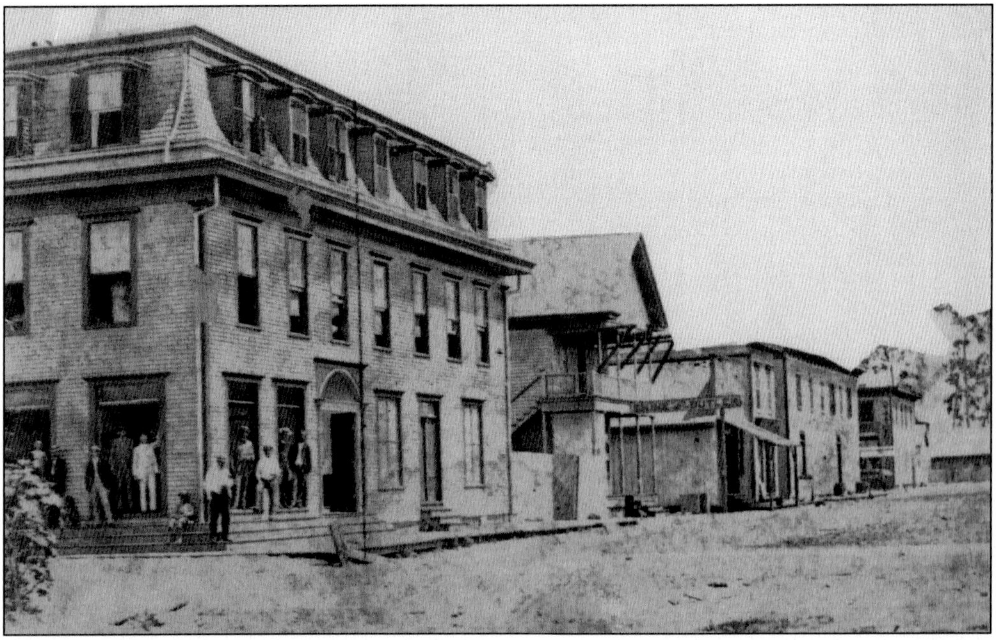

The Lucky House (later called the Charleston House) opened in 1879 at Orange Avenue and Pine Street. James L. Giles bought the hotel, seen at left in this c. 1880 photograph, from Samuel A. Luckie in 1891. Giles had it cut into two parts; one part joined the Tremont Hotel, while the other became the Duke Hall boardinghouse. The Plaza now occupies the Charleston House site.

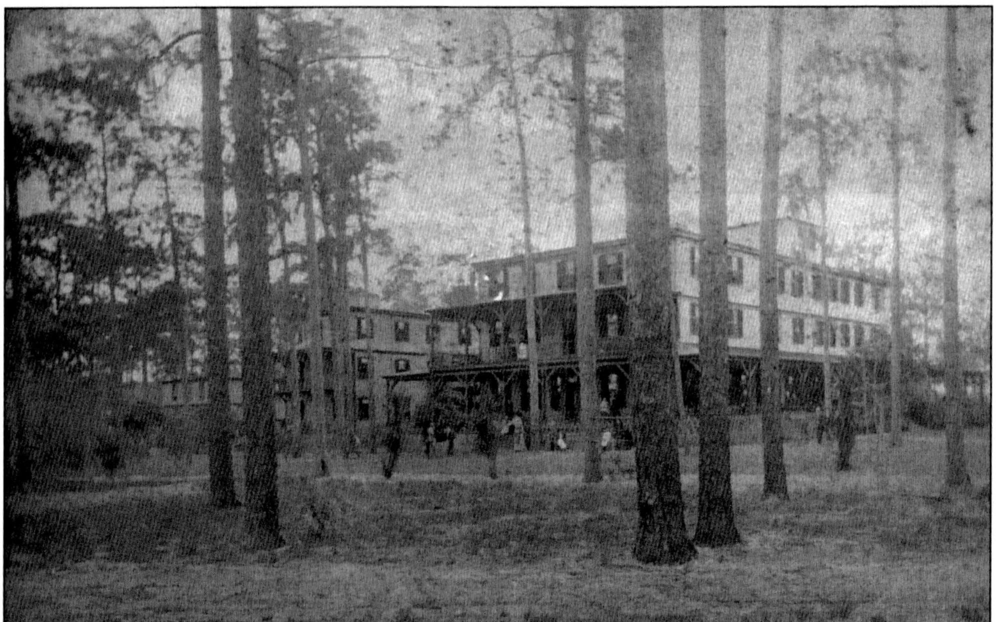

Seen here in what may be the only remaining photograph of the property, James Willcox's West End Hotel was built in 1880 in 40 acres of pinewoods on West Livingston Street. The popular inn, remembered for festive dances and brilliant winter balls, burned to the ground in 1887. Exposition Park and the fairgrounds later took its place. Today, the Bob Carr Performing Arts Centre occupies the approximate site of the hotel.

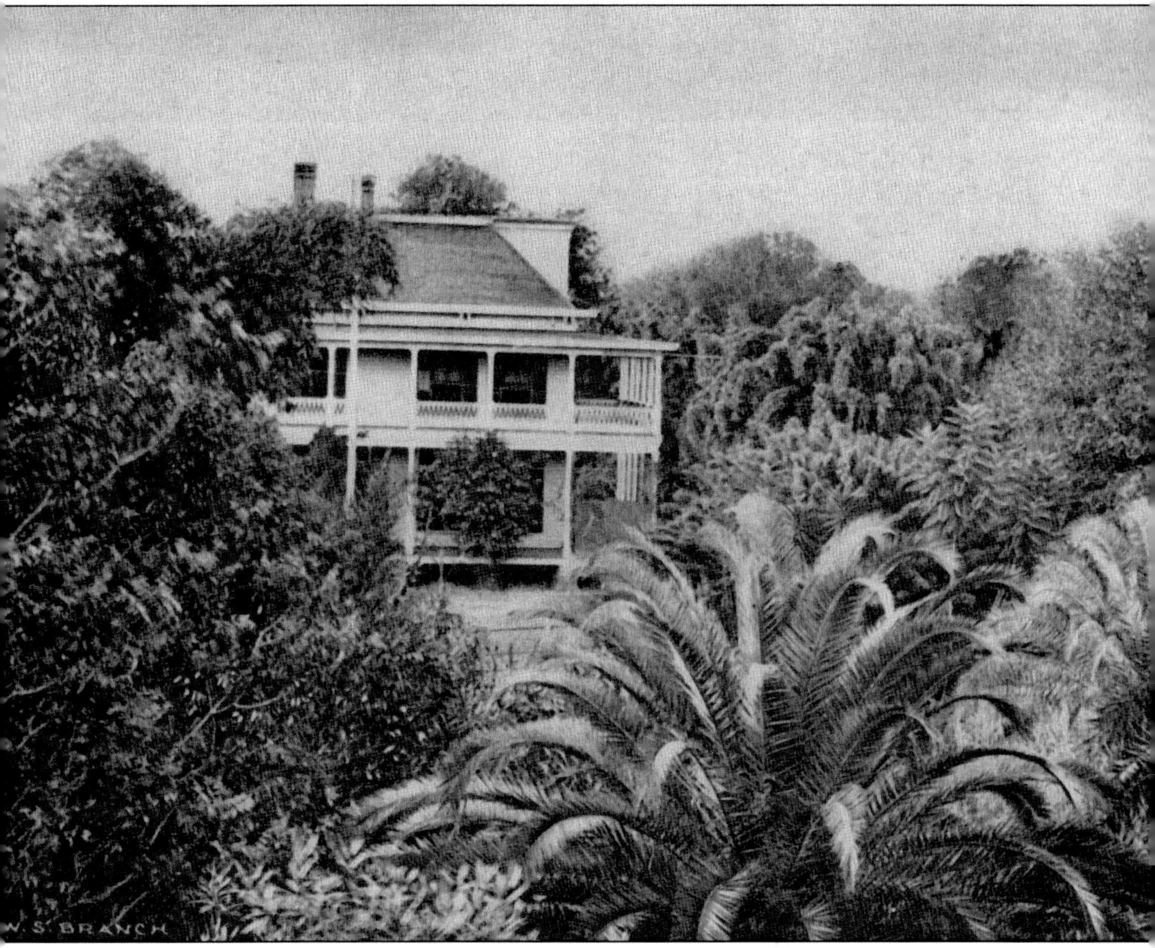

Horticulturalist Leo P. Wescott bought property in Orlando's Original Town in 1881, and contractor Eben Shaw built a large frame house for him. Wescott planted extensive gardens and orchards and later bought additional land for a greenhouse across Magnolia Avenue. In 1889, Martha Wescott bought Court Street north of Wall Street where it crossed the Wescotts' property, and in 1890, the Wescotts sold the house and grounds to Leslie Pell-Clarke. In 1900, the Pell-Clarkes donated the house to the Protestant Episcopal Church for a home for the bishop of the diocese. Bishop William Crane Gray and his wife, Fannie, were the first to live in the home, which became known as the Bishopstead after its donation to the church. Orange County bought the property from the Episcopal Church in 1925 and demolished the Bishopstead to build a new courthouse, completed in 1927. Today, the courthouse is the home of the Orange County Regional History Center.

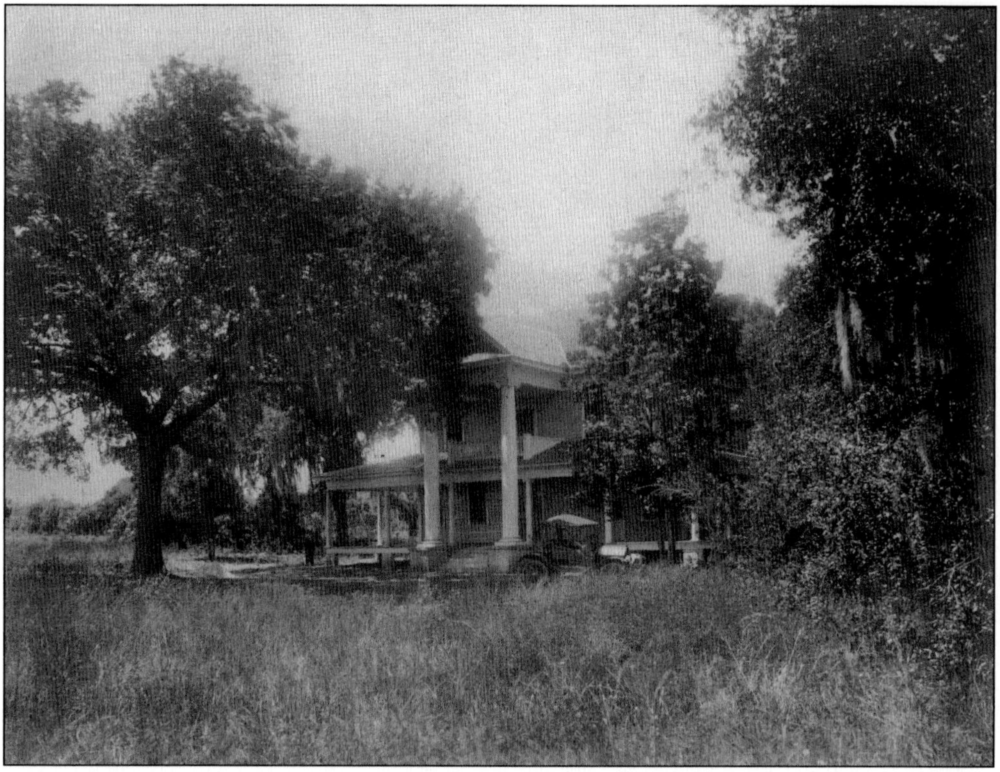

Valhalla, seen here around 1910, was built on Lake Rowena in the 1880s, possibly by Percy Keating, who bought land in the area from James Willcox in 1886. Lucius L. Payne, a county commissioner, bought the Keating land in 1912, purchased adjacent land, and in 1937, created a subdivision he called Valhalla.

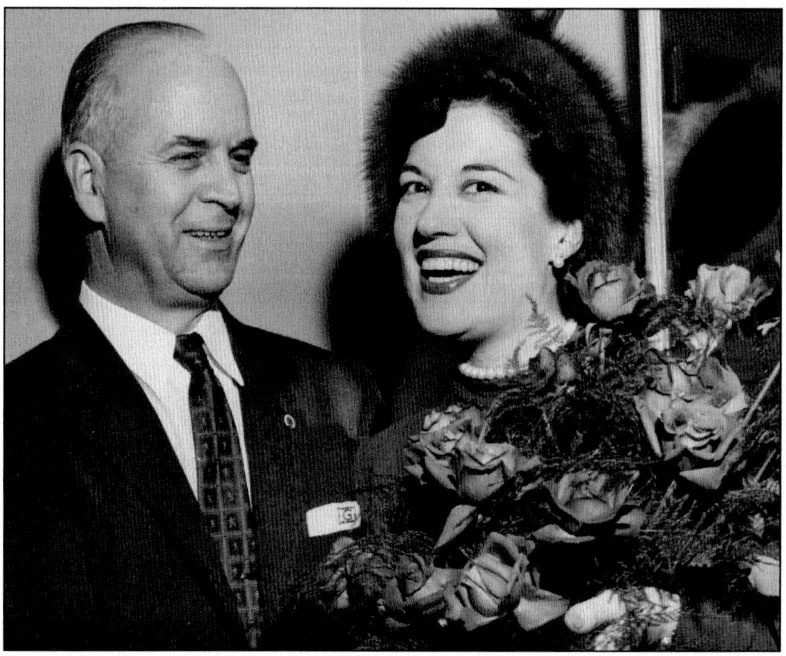

Clerk of courts C.M. Gay, seen here in 1956 with actress Toni Gilman, bought Valhalla from Aline Payne in 1944. The Gays lived there in the 1940s and had the old house demolished before the family created two Rowena Park subdivisions in the 1950s. A new house was built on the site of Valhalla in 1954.

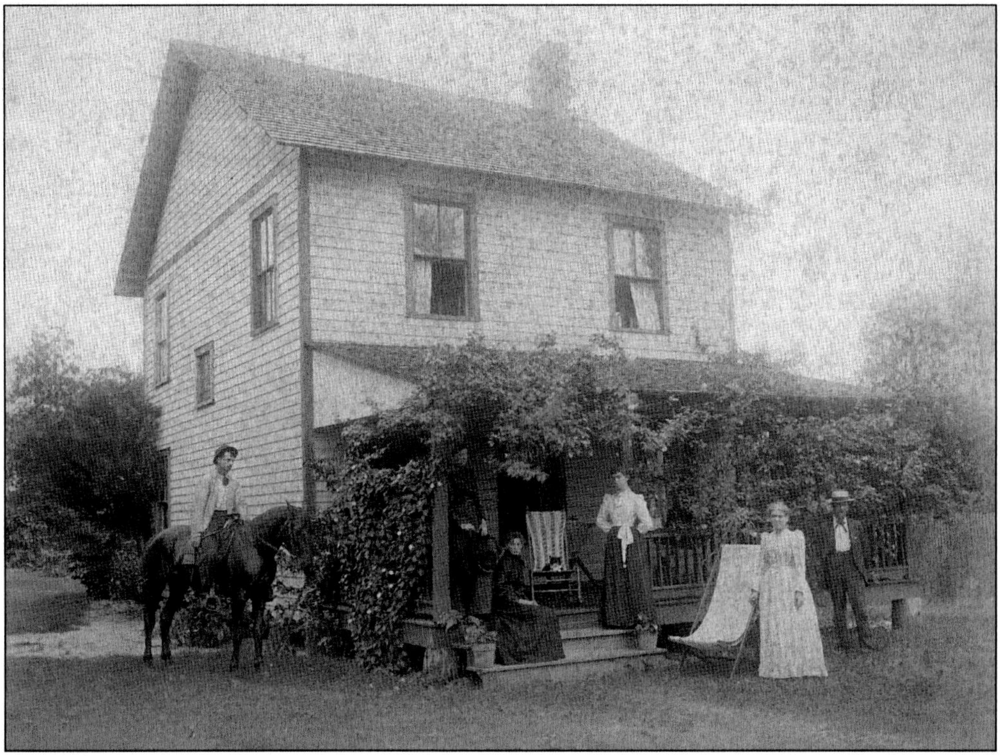

Charles G. Bennett, seen in the far right of the photograph, came to Central Florida in the 1880s with the English Colony, a group of settlers from Britain who hoped to establish themselves as citrus growers. Bennett bought 10 acres of land on East Central Boulevard and built a two-story frame house where he planned to grow and sell exotic plants.

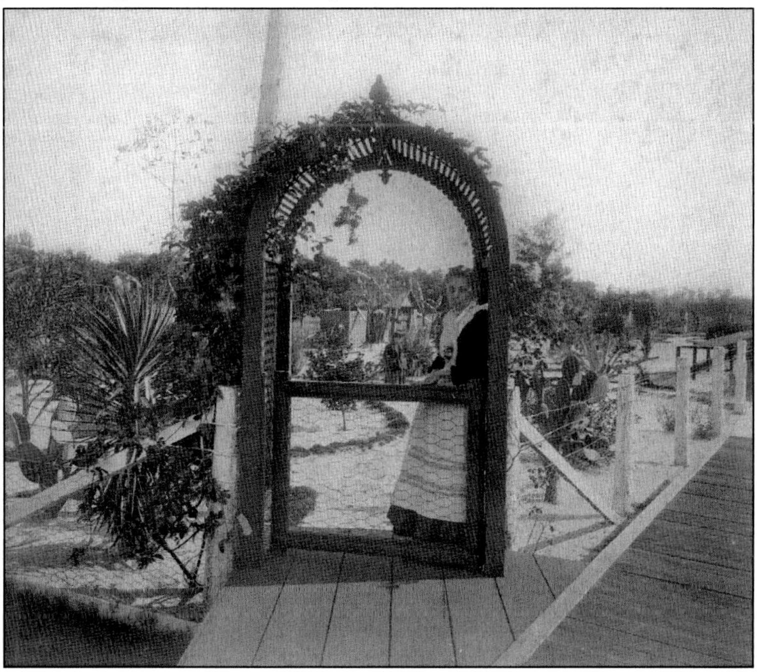

Bennett surrounded his home with the first landscaped garden in Orlando. Finding no market for rare plants, Bennett later returned to England. His son, also named Charles, stayed to become Orlando's first florist, but after the Great Freeze of 1895, he too returned to England. Abandoned, the gardens grew up in weeds, and the house later burned to the ground.

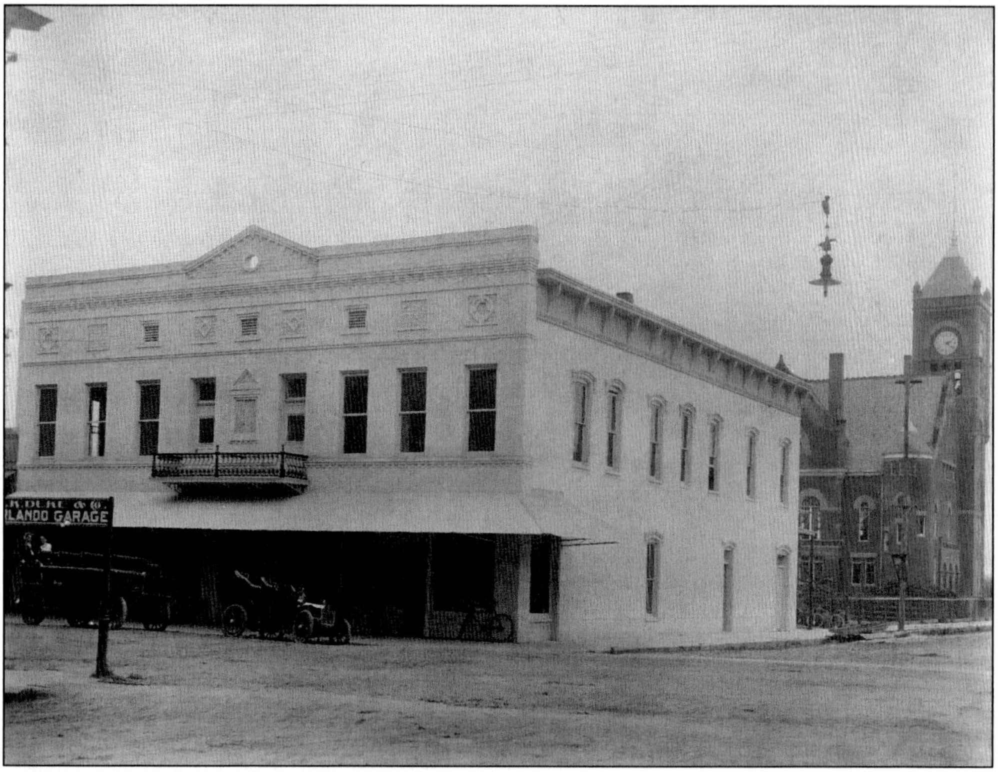

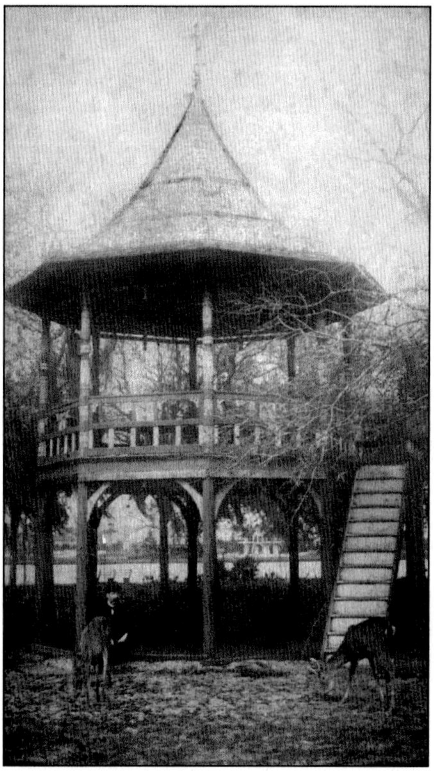

The Cheney Building at Orange Avenue and Central Boulevard was constructed in the late 1880s. John Cheney enlarged the building, possibly in 1906, explaining the date on the facade. Sold in 1919, the structure was demolished in 1922. The State Bank of Orlando, now One North Orange, has occupied the site since 1925. This c. 1910 photograph shows Orlando's first sightseeing bus at the far left.

Orlando realtor N.L. Mills opened a park in 1886 on the south side of Lake Eola at Central Boulevard and Osceola Street. He built a circular bandstand and cages for his menagerie of wild animals, which became a tourist attraction. Band concerts frequently offered entertainment. Mills gave up the park after the Great Freeze of 1894–1895. The bandstand was demolished in 1923, and high-rise apartments now occupy this site.

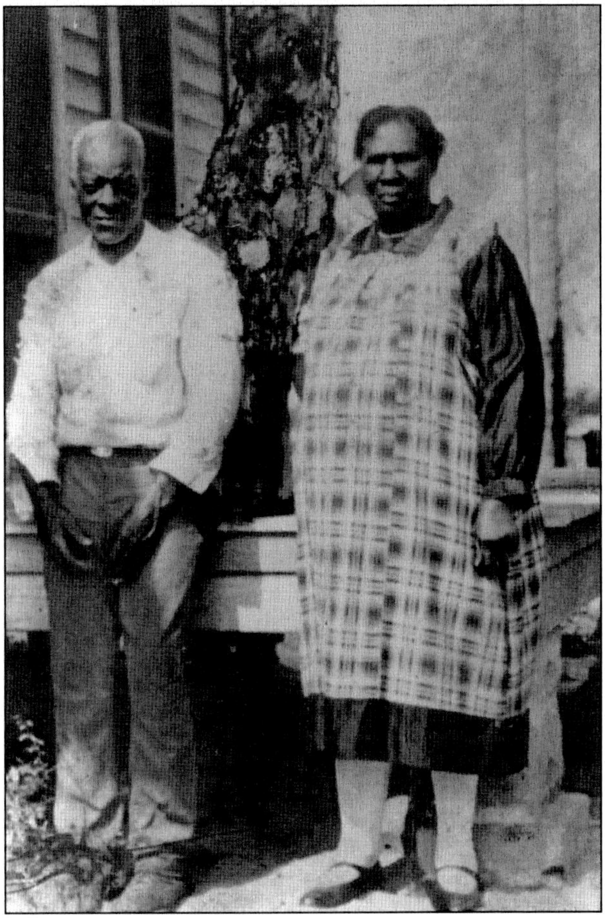

Orlando's growing prosperity in the 1880s attracted former slaves hoping for a fresh start in Florida. The African American settlement they established along Fern Creek, about a mile east of downtown Orlando, became known as Jonestown, named for pioneer residents Sam and Penny Jones. Twenty-one families lived in Jonestown in 1891.

Built in a low-lying area, Jonestown flooded frequently. The community of two churches, one school, one store, and 76 residences ceased to exist after a flood in 1939. The city took advantage of the devastation to relocate the families to a segregated African American neighborhood west of downtown. Public housing for whites replaced Jonestown on East South Street.

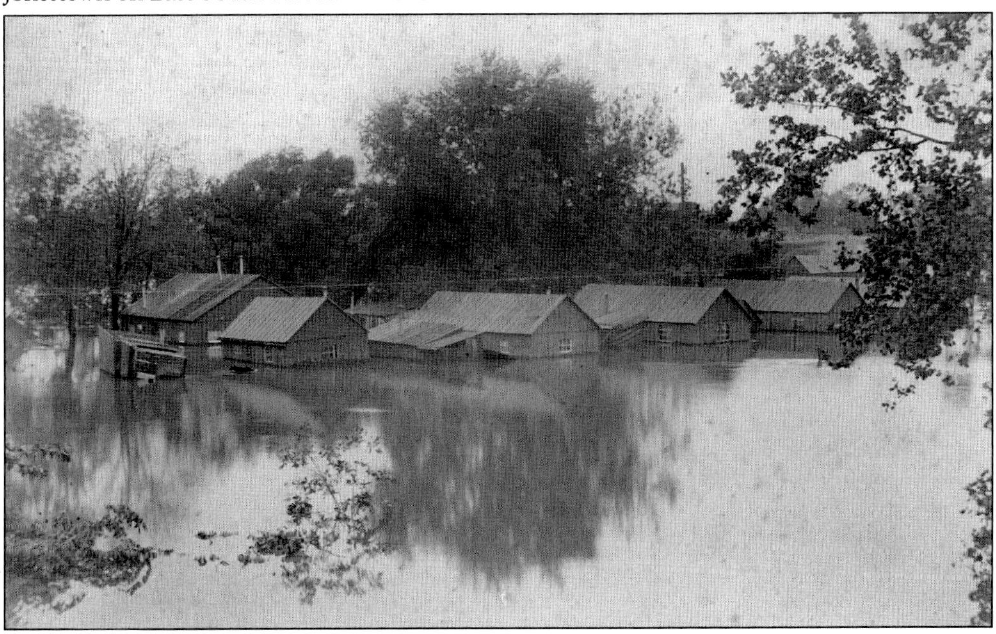

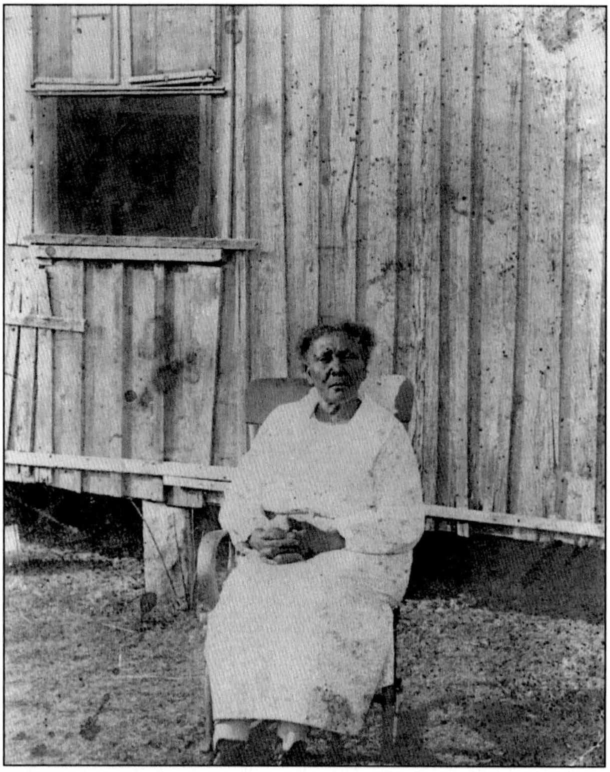

Most Jonestown residents worked as laborers, but Milo Cooper, former body servant for Jefferson Davis, operated a barbershop on East Pine Street, and Ellen Paine cooked for many years at the Duke Hall boardinghouse. Isaac Cleveland was a carpenter, and E.F. Wooden ran a grocery store. Though she was born into slavery, Doshia Green, pictured here, persevered and owned her own home in Jonestown.

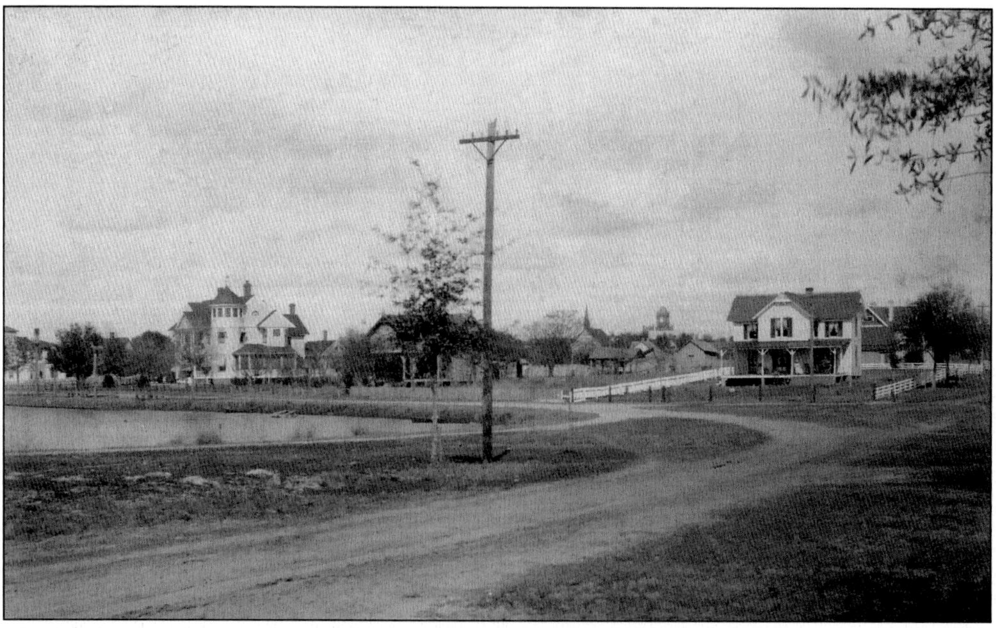

The house at Lucerne Circle and Delaney Drive, seen in the right of the photograph, predated the Lucerne Hotel, which burned to the ground in 1886, suggesting that Wilmon Whilldin built it before he sold the property in 1885. It had several owners and became the Lucerne Lodge Guest House in the 1950s. The property was sold in 1972 to the Expressway Authority for the East-West Expressway.

The first train arrived in Orlando on the South Florida Railroad in 1880, and a station opened the following year on West Church Street along the railroad tracks. The small wooden building with perpendicular boards replaced Joseph Bumby's feed and grain store as the passenger and freight office for the railroad, which ran between Sanford and Orlando. By 1886, the South Florida Railroad ran daily trains between Sanford and Tampa.

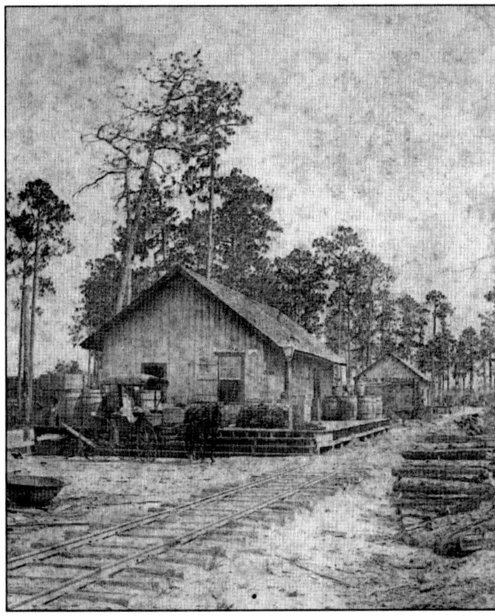

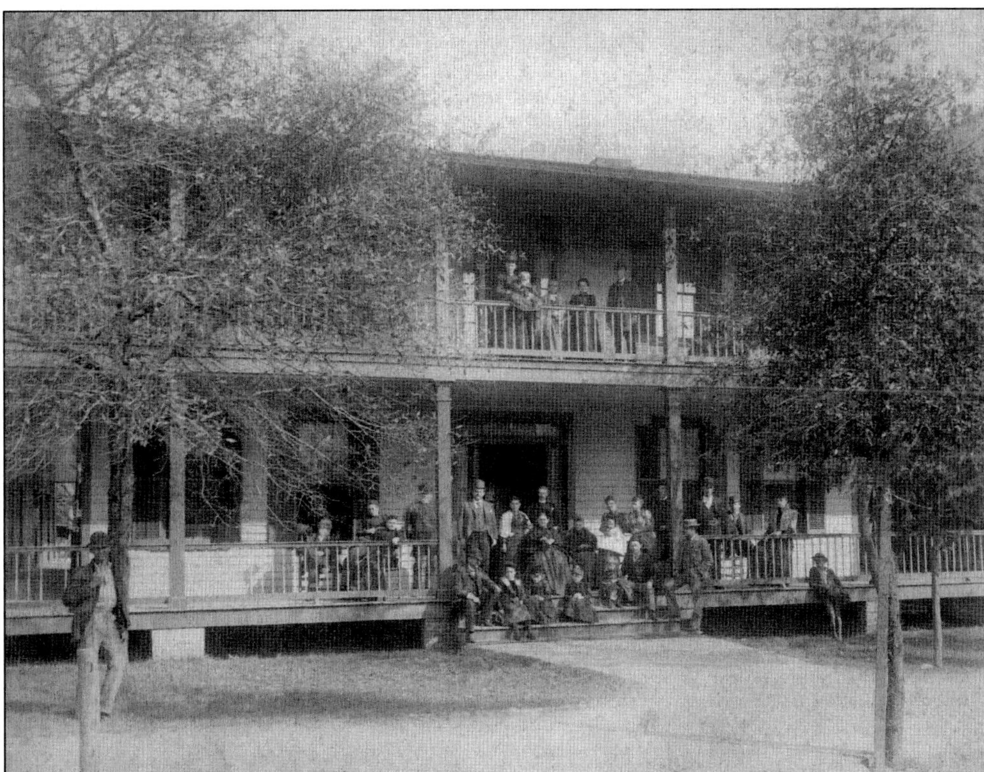

In 1881, Thomas "Big Tom" Shine built the Magnolia Hotel at the corner of Orange Avenue and Pine Street. The two-story frame hotel, with its wide porches on the first and second floors, became a social center and served as headquarters for several political conventions. Moved twice and buried behind larger buildings, the Magnolia Hotel became a furniture warehouse that is rumored to still be standing.

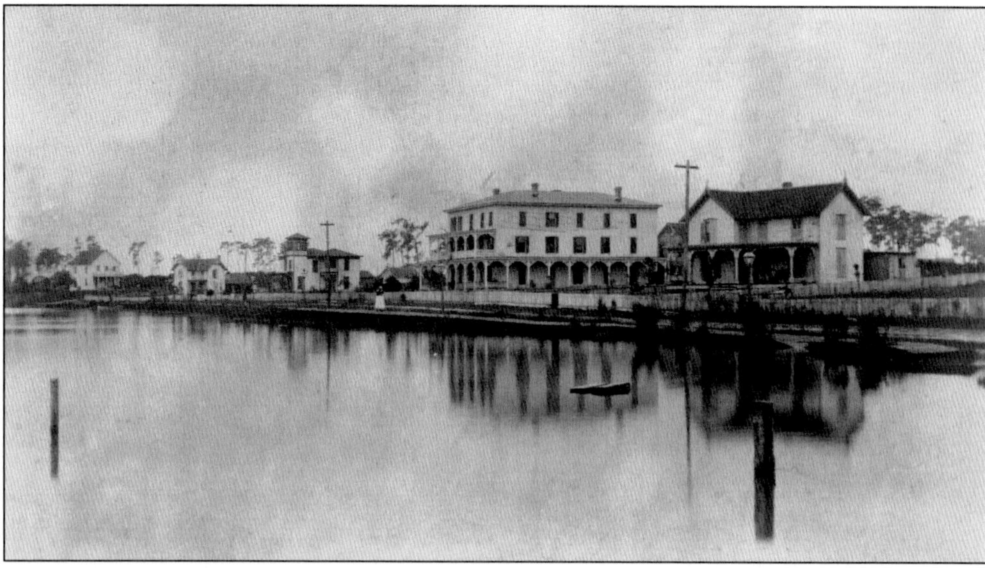

R.A. Starkey built the Lucerne Hotel, seen here second from right, on the north side of Lake Lucerne in 1881. Mr. and Mrs. A.G. Branham stayed in the hotel until their home, also on Lake Lucerne, was built. Ellen Branham described the large three-story hotel as a commodious yellow brick building. The Lucerne Hotel burned to the ground in 1886. The Dr. P. Phillips House occupies the site today.

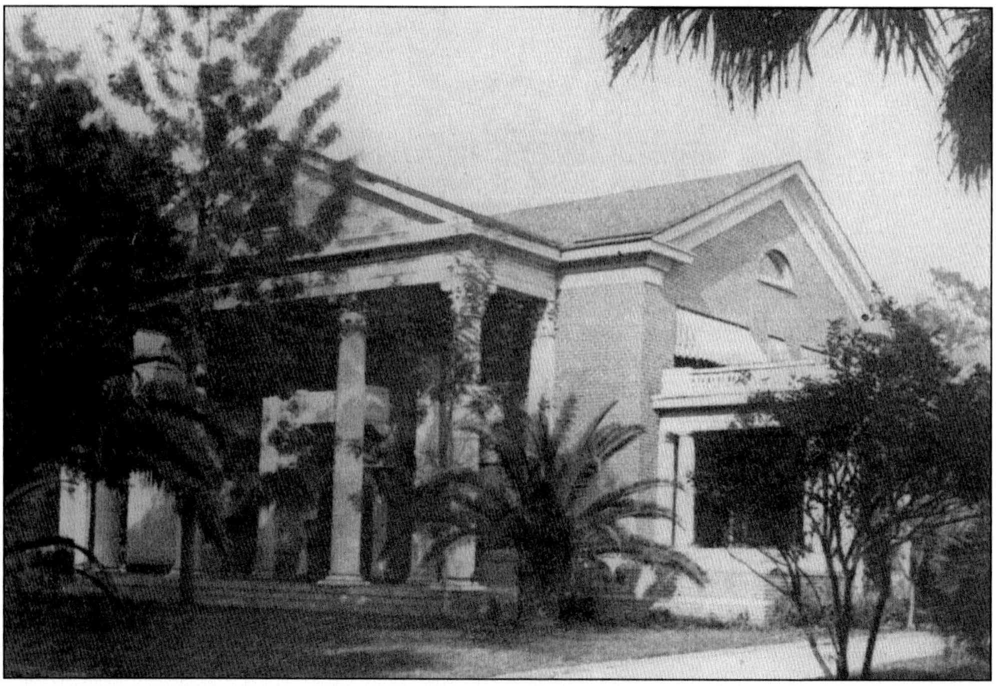

C.R. Webber built the house at Jefferson Street and North Orange Avenue in 1891, installing one of Orlando's first cesspool sewers. Braxton Beacham, who erected the Beacham Theatre in 1922, bought the house in 1900 and remodeled it into a residential showplace. It became a hotel in 1926 and a mortuary in 1928. The Beacham House was demolished in 1935 to clear the site for a 10-story building.

A hardware store owned by three Orlando pioneer families occupied the two-story brick building at the corner of Orange Avenue and Church Street from 1881 until 1924. Started in 1881 by Cassius A. Boone, shown here, who came to Orlando as a schoolteacher in 1870, it was reportedly the largest hardware and furniture store in Florida. Boone traded the business to Joseph Guernsey in 1895 in return for grove acreage.

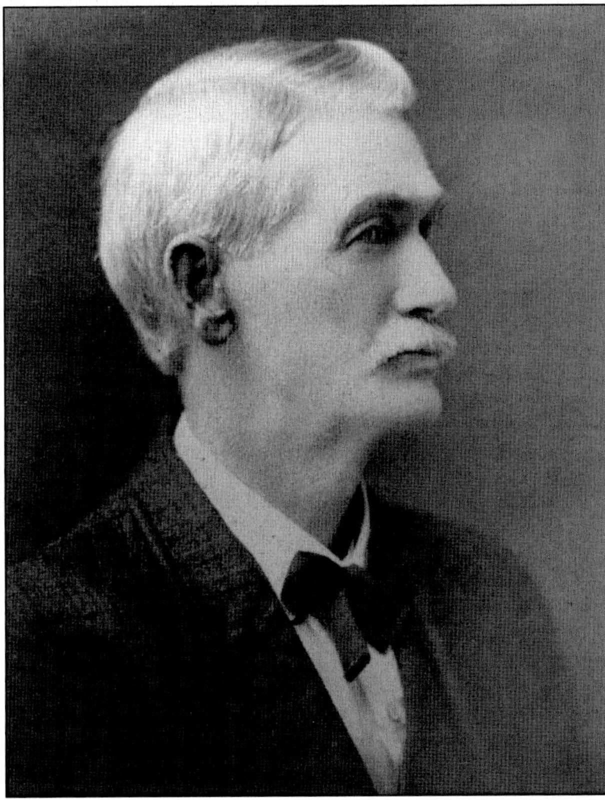

Joseph Guernsey operated the store, seen here in 1887, with his four sons until his death in 1922. His sons sold the store to the Joseph Bumby family in 1922, and in 1923, the Bumby family leased the property to the F.W. Woolworth Company. The Woolworth Company demolished the Guernsey Block in 1924 to construct a new store building.

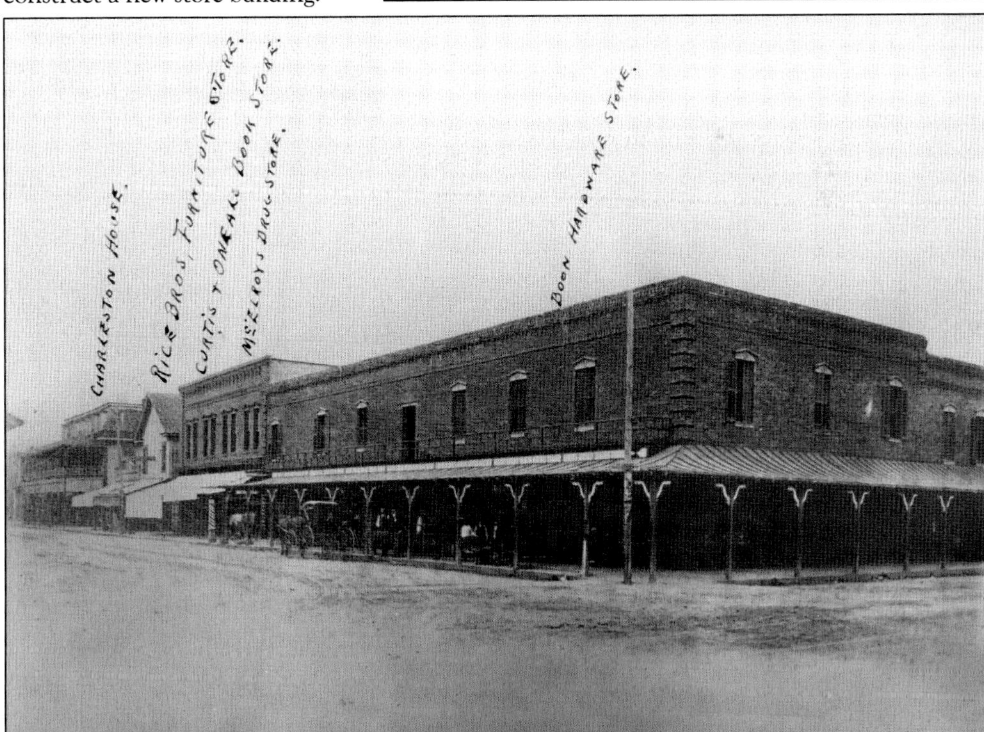

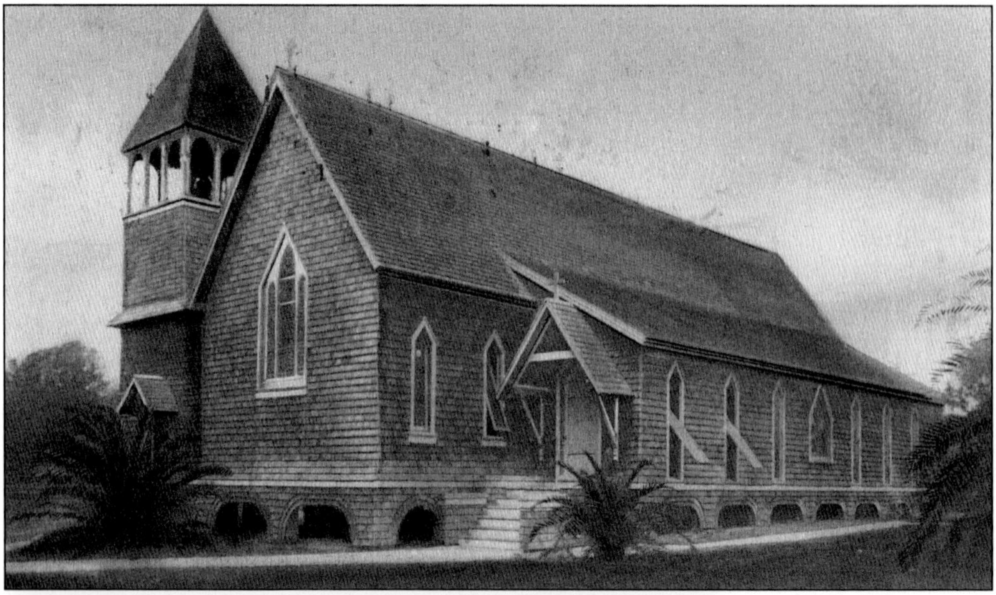

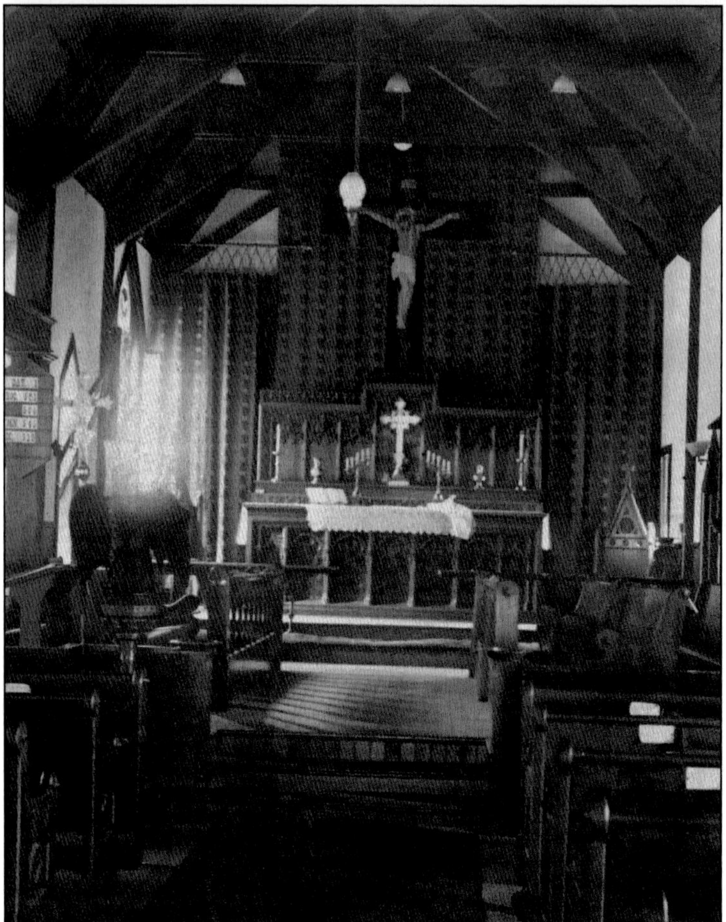

Francis Eppes, grandson of Thomas Jefferson, moved to Orlando in 1867 and conducted Orlando's first Episcopal service in his home. In 1882, St. Luke's Episcopal Church built a small church on the present site of the Cathedral Church of St. Luke. In 1902, St. Luke's was designated the Cathedral Church for South Florida, the sanctuary was enlarged, and the name was changed from St. Luke's Parish to St. Luke's Cathedral. In 1922, the old church was moved south to make space for the new cathedral to be built on the corner of Robinson Street and Magnolia Avenue. The old structure was used as a parish house after the cathedral opened.

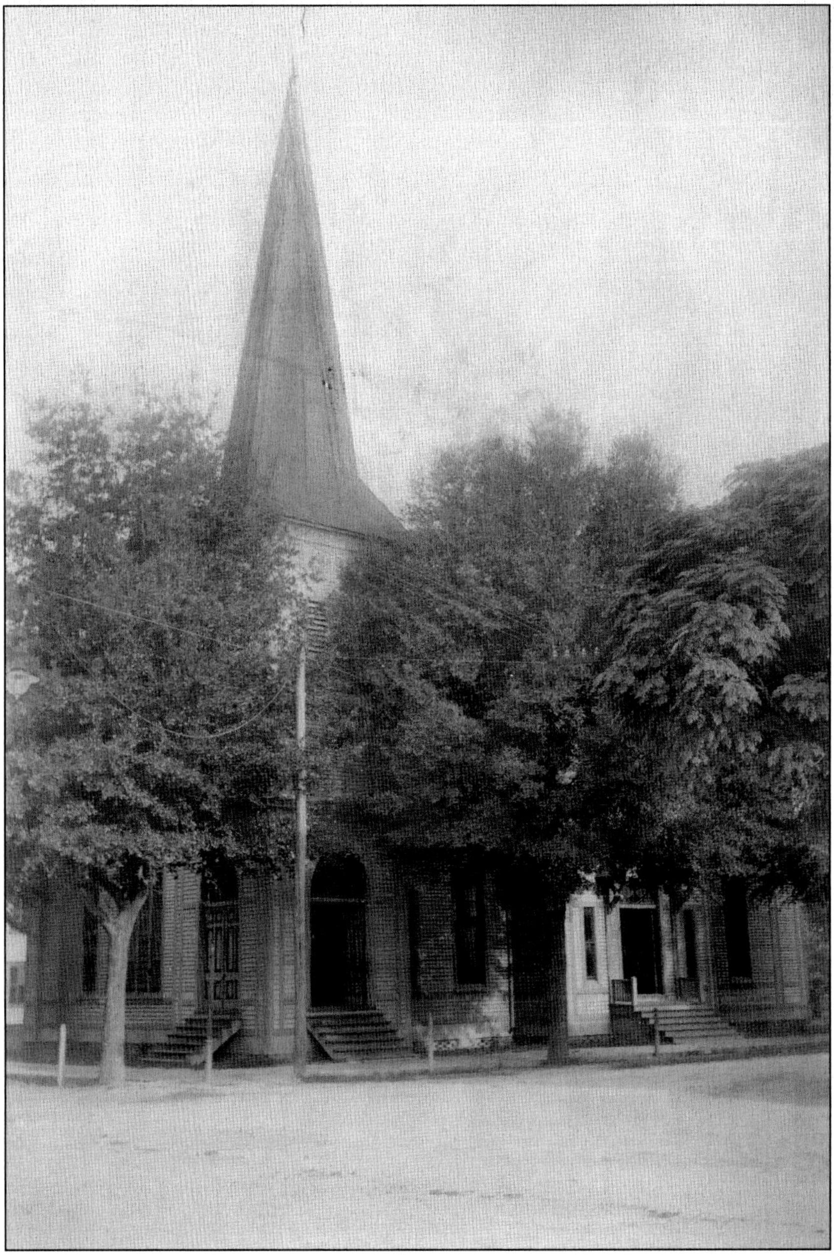

Eleven adults and their children formed the First Presbyterian Church of Orlando on March 18, 1876. Initially, the congregation met at the home of Benjamin and Eliza Gould, founding members of the church. They then met at the Union Free Church until Orlando's Presbyterian congregation constructed their first permanent church in 1883. The new structure was necessary to accommodate the church's 105-member congregation. The wooden church, whose steeple dominated the Orlando skyline, was located at the northeast corner of West Central Boulevard and the railroad. The building, measuring 40 feet by 60 feet, cost $4,300 to construct. The church burned to the ground in 1887, forcing the congregation to meet in the Orange County Courthouse and Opera House until a new church was built in 1889. Today, the site of the original church is a parking garage.

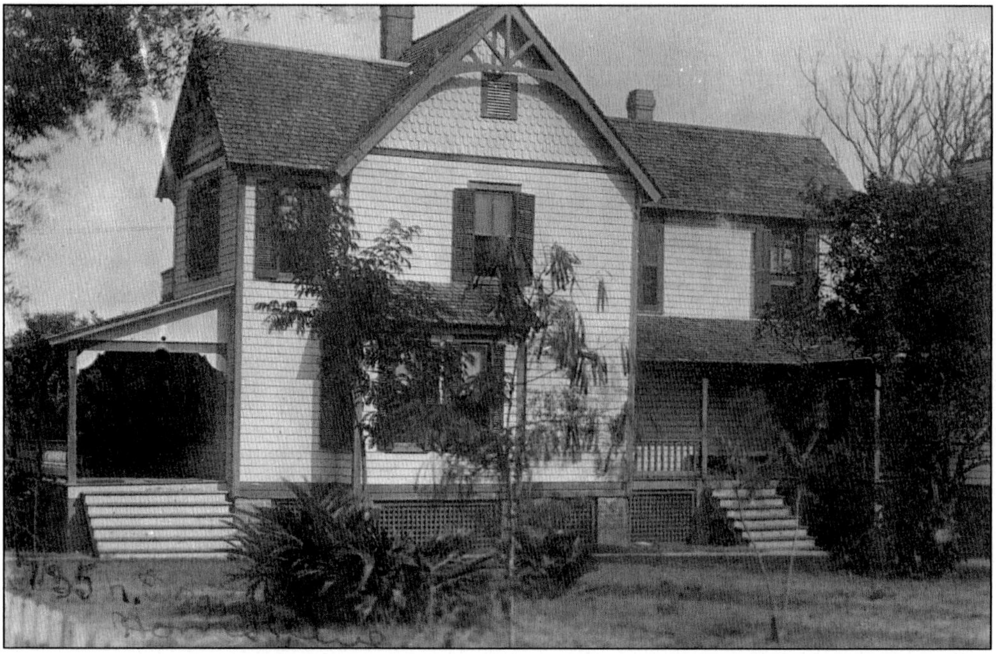

Frederick A. Lewter came to Orlando from North Carolina in 1884. He went into business and began to buy property. In 1885, he married, and in 1886, his wife, Linnie, bought three lots on North Orange Avenue from F.R. Webber. It is not known whether Webber or Lewter built this house, but the Lewters had 11 children, and they added to the house numerous times.

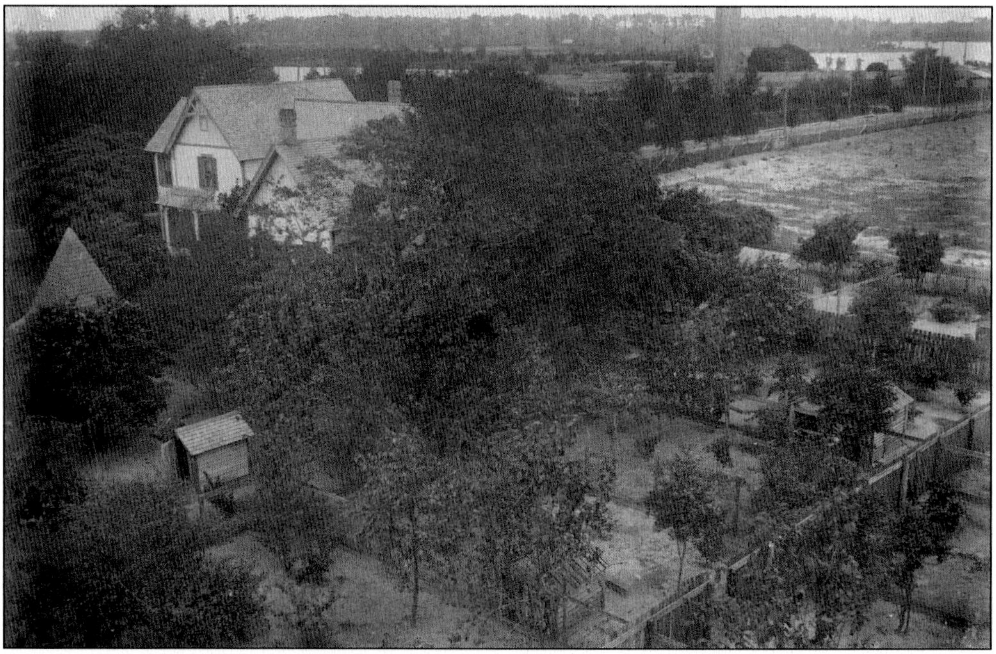

Lewter farmed and raised chickens; the coops are visible in this photograph. At one time, his place was known as the Standard Poultry Farm. He died in 1924. Linnie Lewter died in 1955 in the house that she had moved into as a bride. The Lewter House was demolished in 1959 to build the Florida National Bank. The property is now vacant and part of a future condominium project.

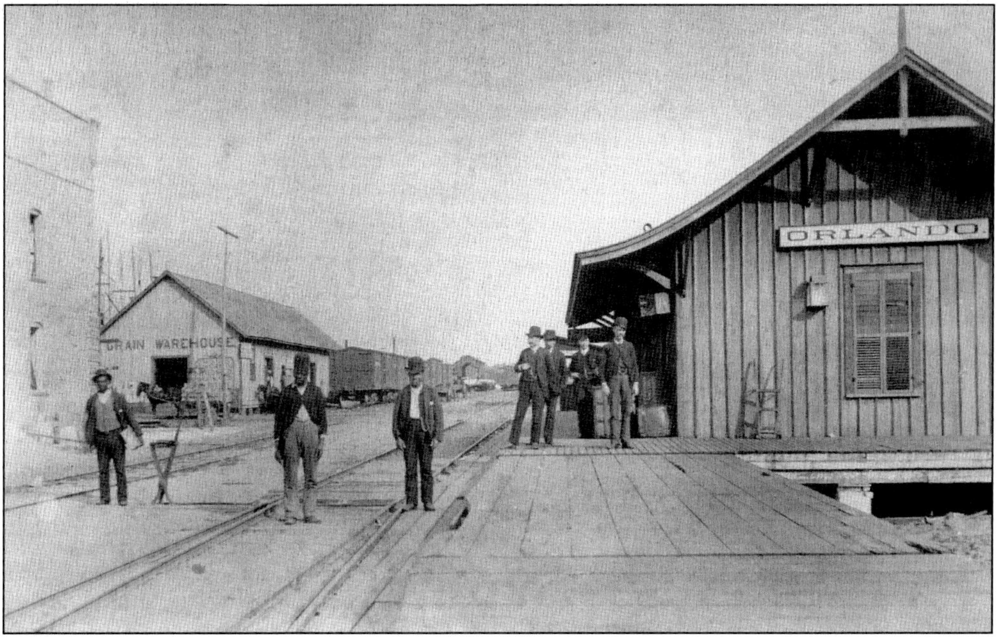

Orlando's second railroad depot, shown here in 1886, was built about 1883 on the opposite side of the railroad tracks from the 1881 depot. Around this time, the railroad was extended to Tampa. Before this, Orlando was Florida's southernmost destination via rail. The depot was torn down around 1890, and the current Church Street Station Depot was built in its place.

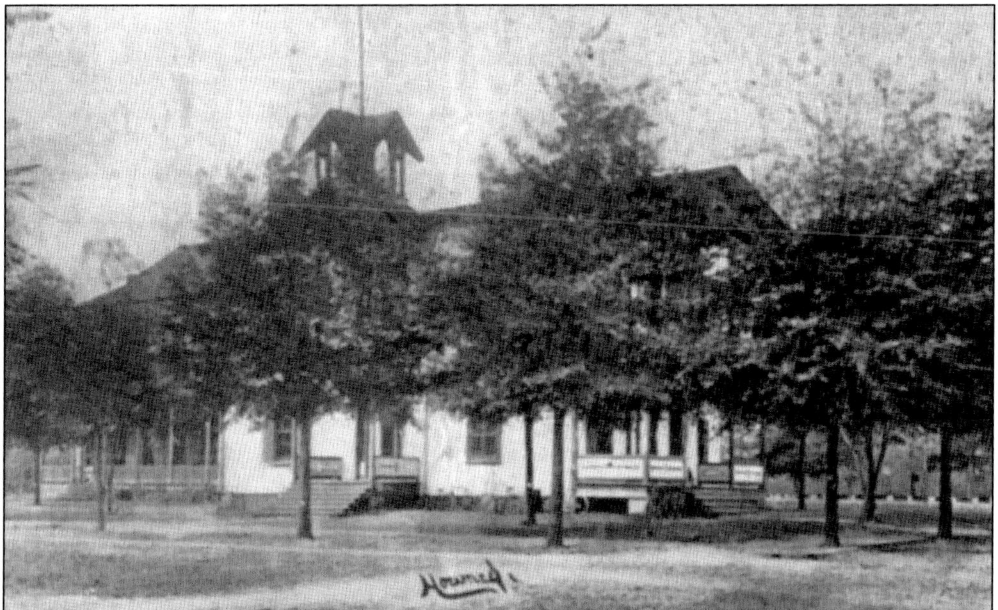

The Methodist Episcopal Church built the South Florida Institute on South Orange Avenue in 1884. It offered public school classes, as well as religious instruction, because Orlando's public school did not offer higher-level classes at that time. When the institute failed in 1886, the city acquired the building for an elementary and senior high school. The school burned in 1905. The Orlando City Hall now occupies the site.

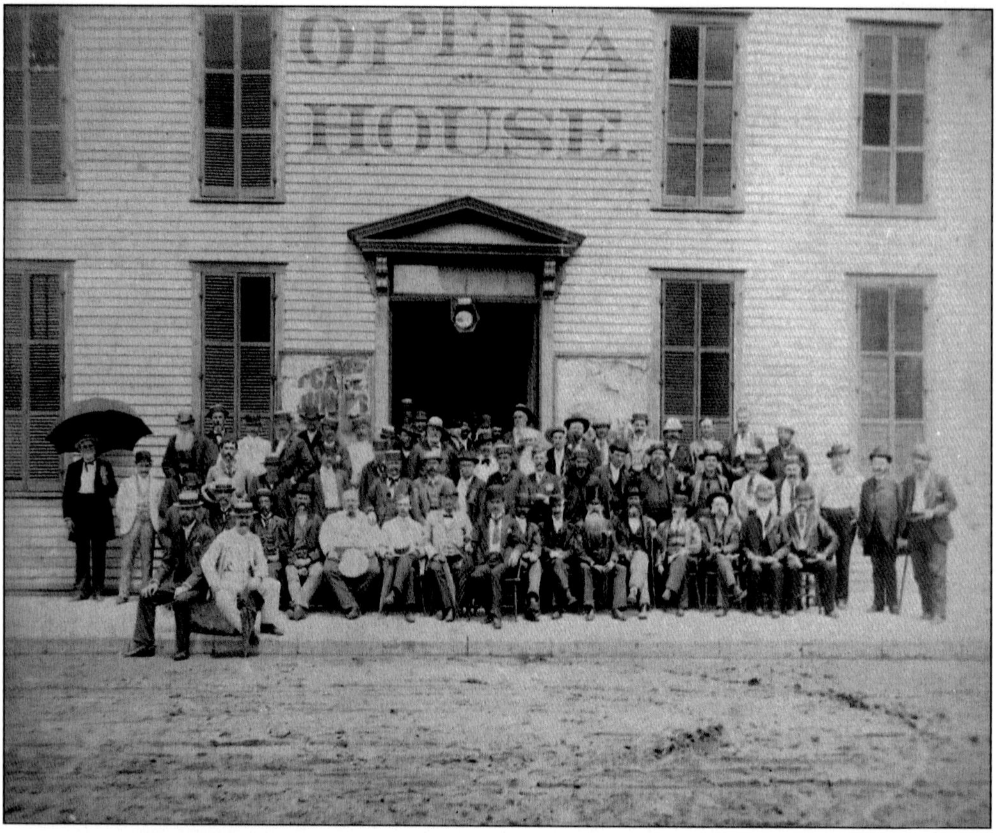

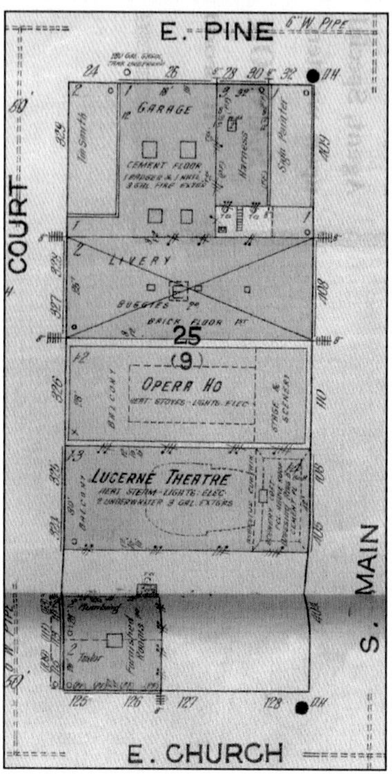

In 1884, Charles Weimer hired N.C. Stubblefield to build an opera house, seen in the undated photograph above, on Court Street midway between Pine and Church Streets. Constructed of wood with no lathe or plaster, the Opera House had double front doors opening on Court Street, and at the opposite end, its stage door opened on Main Street, now Magnolia Avenue. Wooden benches provided seats, and the light came from kerosene lamps with tin reflectors. Local productions alternated with traveling shows and minstrels. After a storm in 1889, owner W.R. O'Neal repaired the building and later refurbished it in 1897. In 1915, it became a garage and automobile repair shop, and in 1917, O'Neal demolished the building to erect a three-story garage to sell Haynes-Hupmobile automobiles.

Orange County built a new $10,700 jail at Orange Avenue and Washington Street in 1884. Prisoners exercised and several were hanged behind a high board fence surrounding the jail. Braxton Beacham bought the building in 1917 and moved it in 1919. The Beacham Theatre, now a nightclub, took its place.

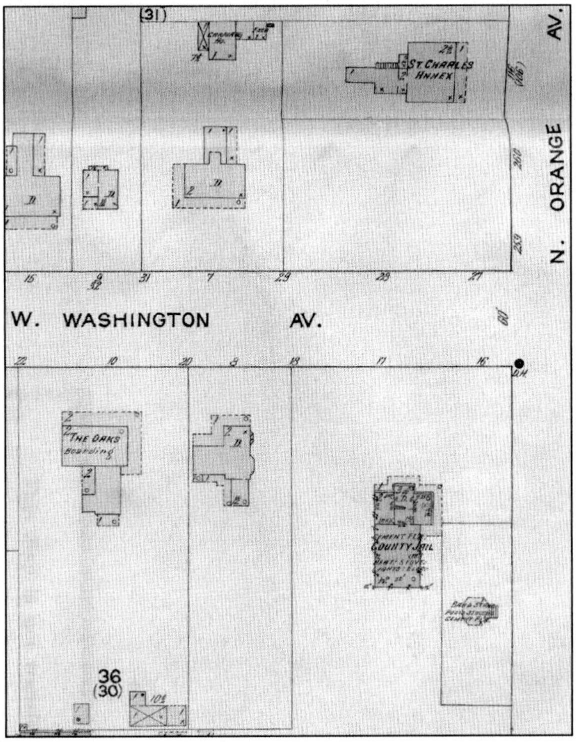

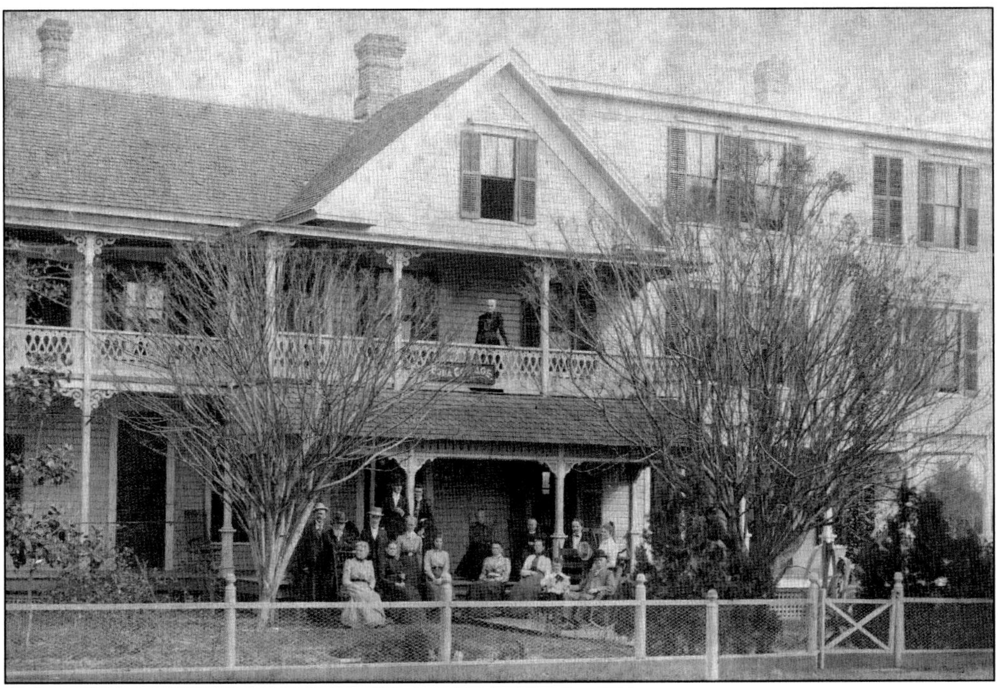

M.L. Knight built a large two-story house on Magnolia Avenue in 1884. In 1900, Hannah Paul bought the house and remodeled it into a 30-room hotel she called Eola Cottage. In 1923, the board of education bought it for Magnolia School, which later became the Orange County Vocational School. Today, a parking garage shares the site with a vacant commercial building.

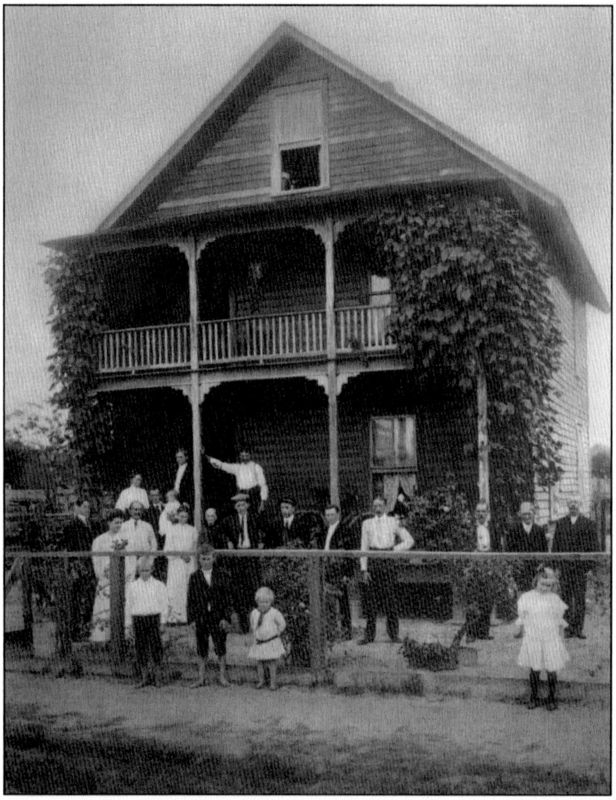

Frances Swearingen operated the Ferns Boarding House at 400 West Church Street from sometime before 1907 through 1923. In 1923, Frances sold the property to William Ingram, who then sold the property in 1933 to Mary T. Walker. The home was torn down, and a store was built in its place. Today, the site of the former Ferns Boarding House lies underneath the Amway Center.

Citrus grower Wilfred Story built the house on East Lucerne Circle at Ponce de Leon Place in 1884. In 1887, he sold it to tailor George Green, who constructed an addition. John Fuller bought the home in 1903, and his widow sold it in 1937. The Green House property became the site of an Art Deco–style apartment house in 1942. That building is now a commercial office complex.

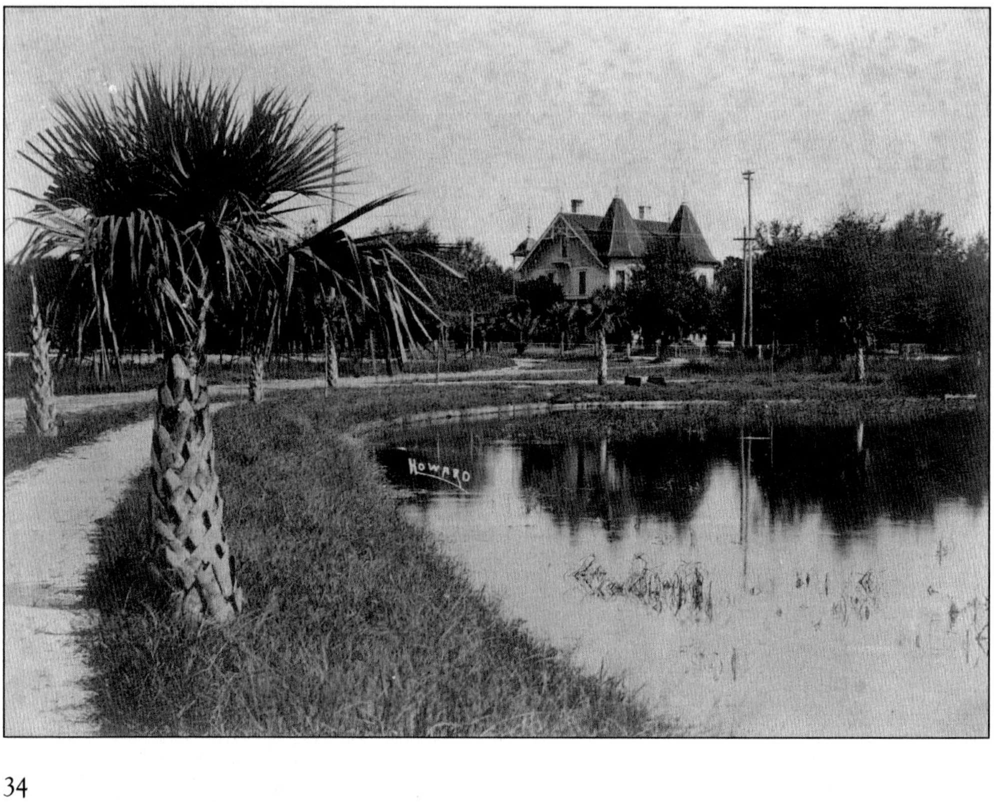

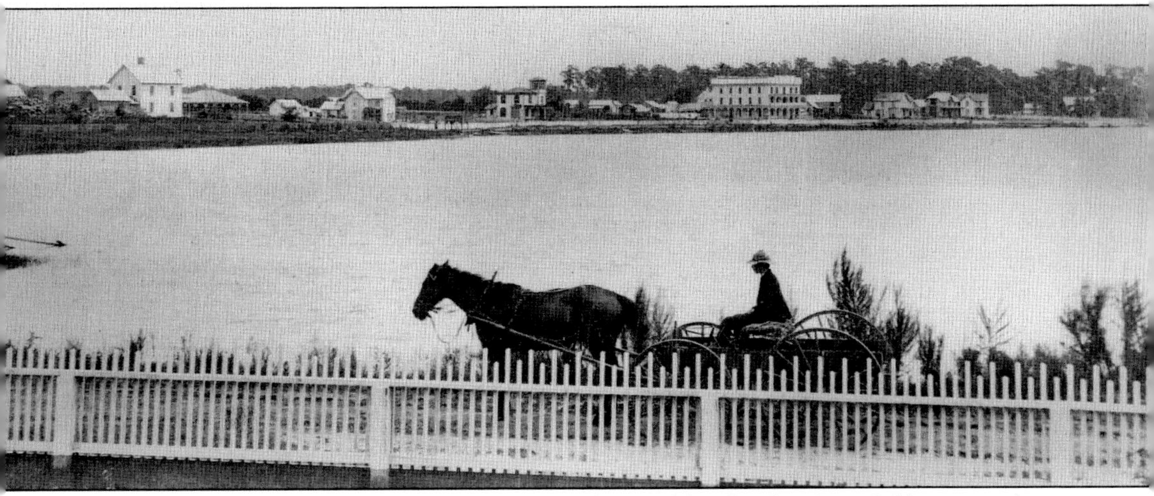

Dr. James Nixon Butt came to Orlando in 1884 and moved his family of six children into the house at the northeast corner of Lucerne Circle and South Main Street, third from left in this photograph. The home was built for him by W.H. Whidden. Doctor Butt practiced medicine in Orlando for many years. He built a brick block on West Church Street for his office and drugstore and later built another building on South Orange Avenue. Doctor Butt sold the house in 1894. It changed hands several times before Mary W. Knox, wife of James A. Knox, bought it in 1902. In 1911, Knox took out a building permit for improvements to the house, which he called the Windermere Boarding House. He sold it in 1913 to Lucie S. Bryant, who operated the boardinghouse until her death around 1924. The Butt House was demolished in 1935.

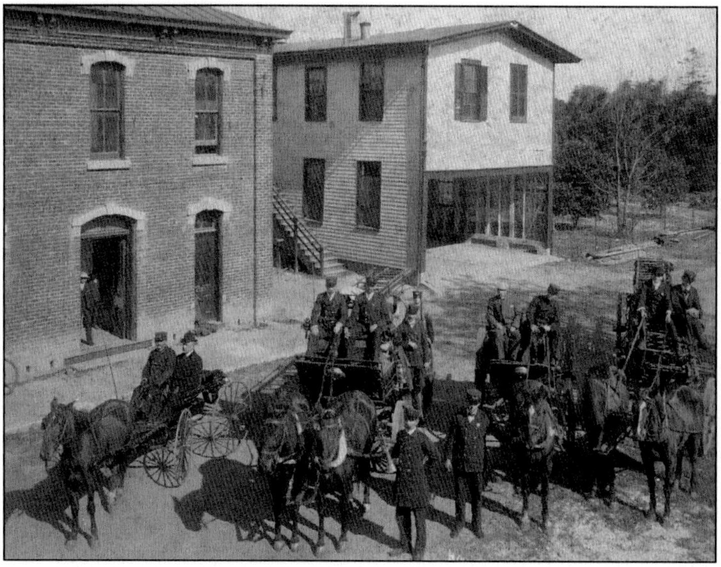

Orlando established a fire department in 1885, and the firemen requested a horse, harness, and hose wagon. A two-story frame building on Wall Street became the first fire station, seen in the right side of this photograph. The building served as the fire station until 1919, when a new fire station opened on North Magnolia Avenue. Today, it has been replaced by a nightclub.

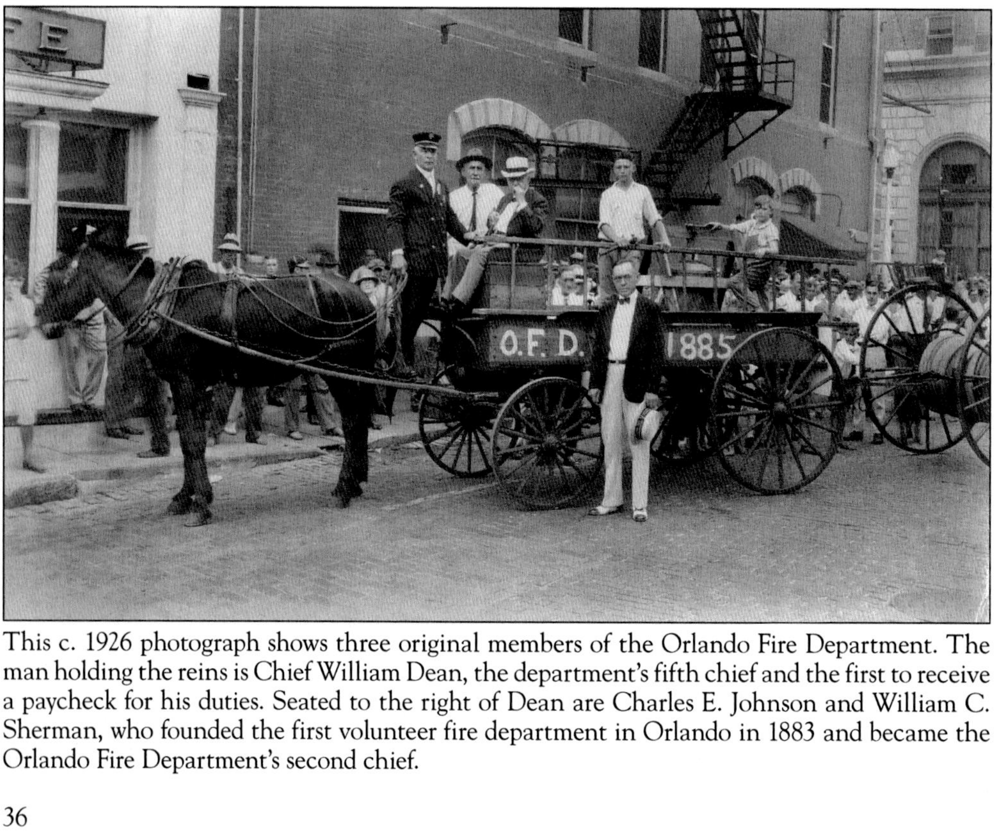

This c. 1926 photograph shows three original members of the Orlando Fire Department. The man holding the reins is Chief William Dean, the department's fifth chief and the first to receive a paycheck for his duties. Seated to the right of Dean are Charles E. Johnson and William C. Sherman, who founded the first volunteer fire department in Orlando in 1883 and became the Orlando Fire Department's second chief.

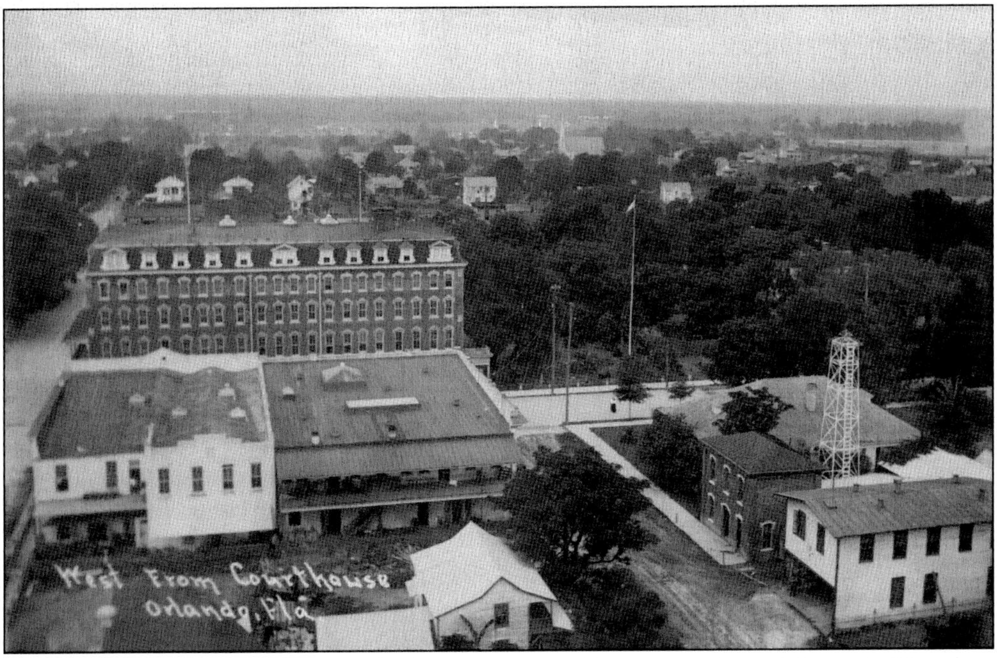

Orlando's new government met in the Orange County Courthouse from 1875 until 1885, when a city hall was built on Wall Street. The two-story brick building, visible in the lower right corner of the photograph, housed the city government until 1919. The fire bell rang from a tower behind city hall, and the city jail was just behind the fire tower. Nightclubs now line that block of Wall Street.

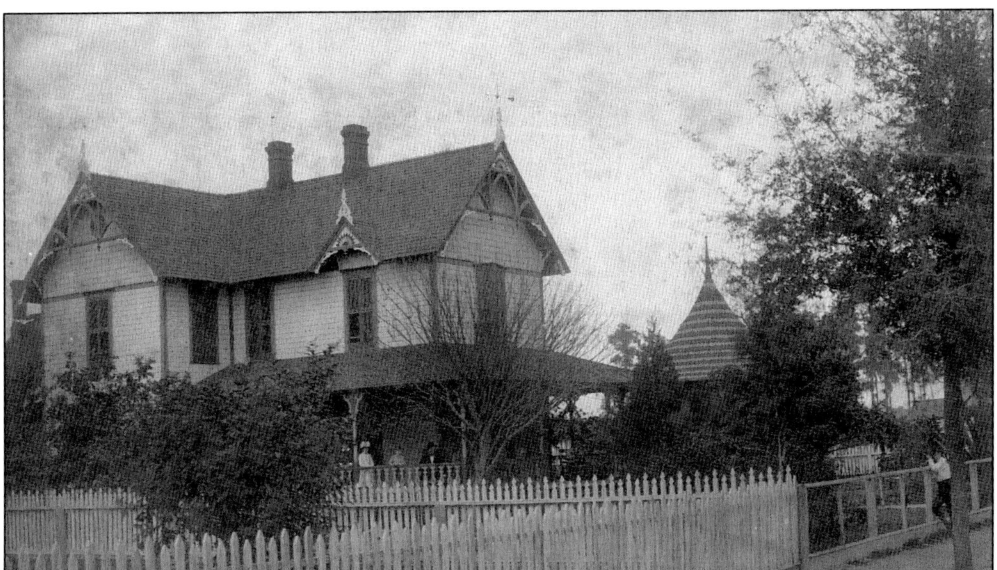

Capt. James B. Parramore bought a building lot at North Orange Avenue and Concord Street from James Willcox in 1883 and constructed his house, seen here around 1910, soon after. Mayor for six years, Parramore died in office in 1902. After his widow sold the house, it changed hands several times, and by 1925, it was a vacant lot. Today, Firestone Live nightclub operates on the site.

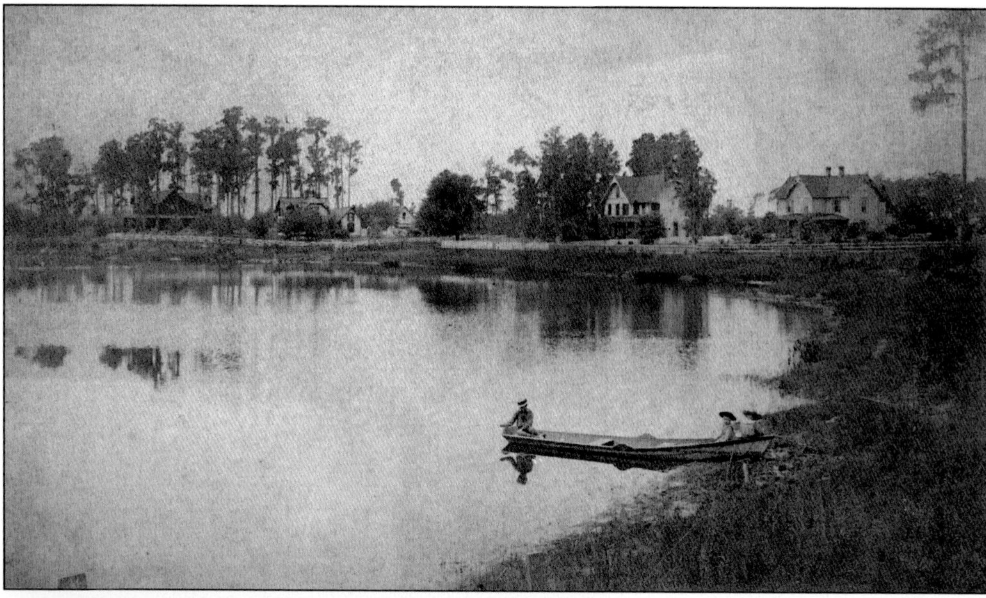

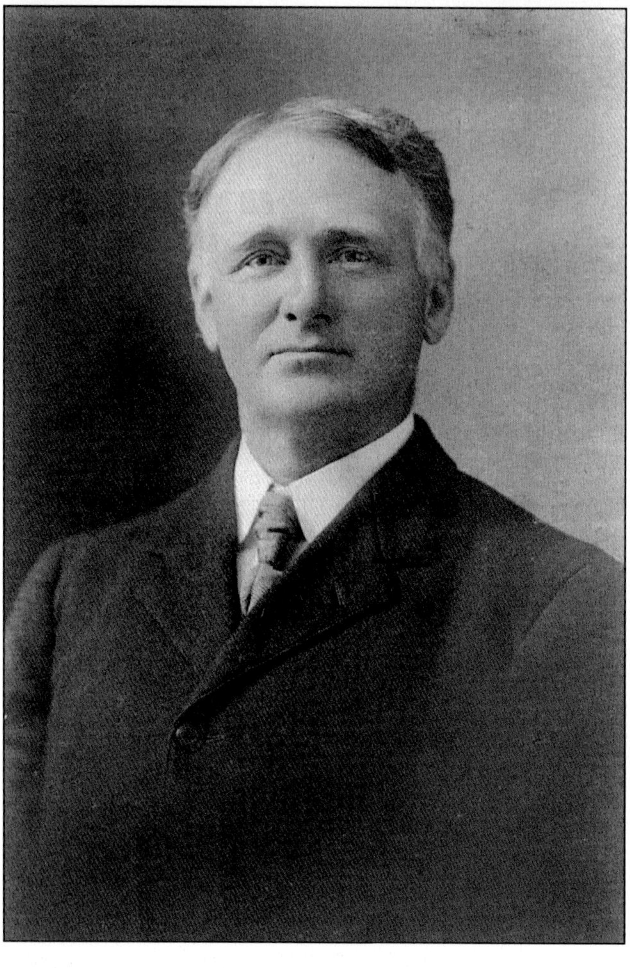

Five newly married couples built large Victorian houses on Lake Street and Euclid Avenue on Lake Cherokee in 1885 and 1886. The line of five houses became known as "Honeymoon Row." The Cheney/Odlin, Newell, and Weeks Houses have been lost, leaving the Poyntz/O'Neal and Gunby Houses still standing. Orlando recognized the Lake Cherokee Historic District in 1981, including the remaining houses in Honeymoon Row.

Lawyers John Moses Cheney, seen here, and Arthur Fuller Odlin built the Cheney/Odlin House in 1886 as a shared dwelling. The men received their law degrees from Boston University in 1885 and became partners. Cheney was a judge and civic leader in Orlando, and Odlin was attorney general and, later, a judge in Puerto Rico. They sold the house around 1900, and it was destroyed in 1915.

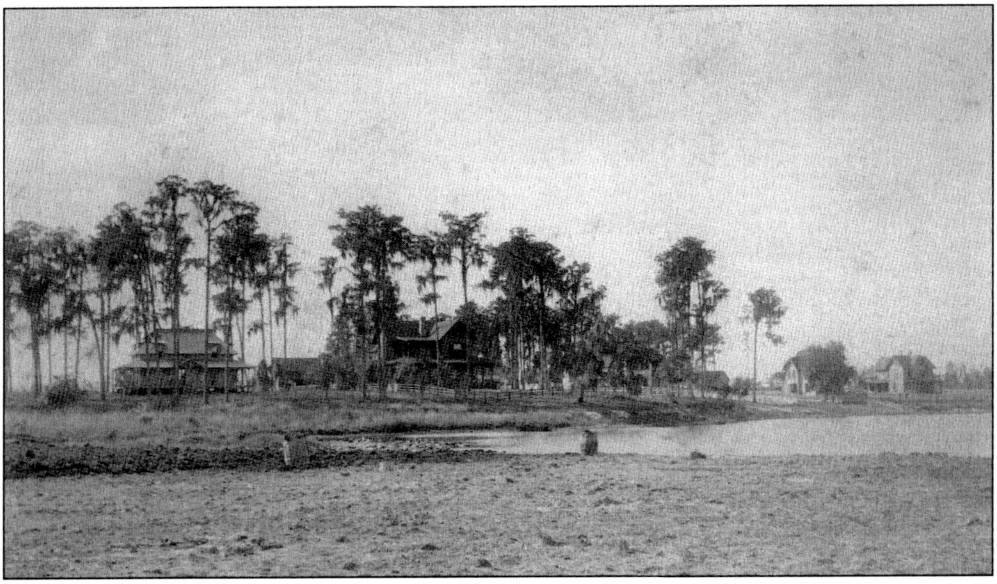

John Wingate Weeks built his house, seen here second from left, on Honeymoon Row in 1885; he and his wife lived here for three years before moving to Boston. A former naval officer and politician of note, John Weeks served as secretary of war under Pres. Warren Harding. The Weeks House was demolished in 1944.

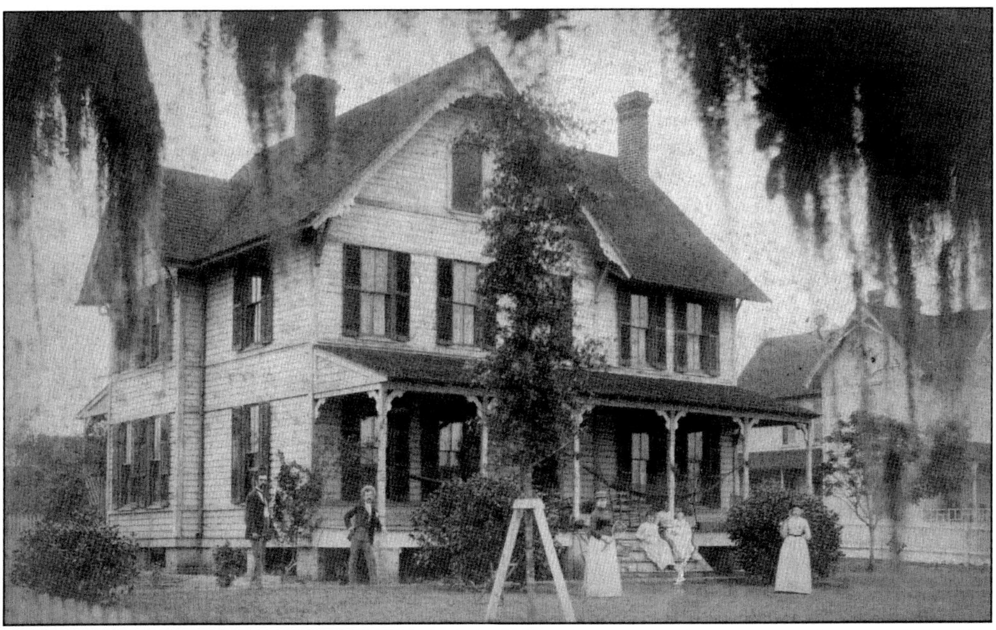

Prominent Orlando attorney George Newell built his house on Honeymoon Row in 1885. His wife, Susan, was a charter member of the Rosalind Club. Despite George's death in 1890, the family lived in the house from 1885 until 1970. In 1975, the house became the first residence in Orlando placed in the National Register of Historic Places. This recognition could not save the house, as it was demolished in 1975.

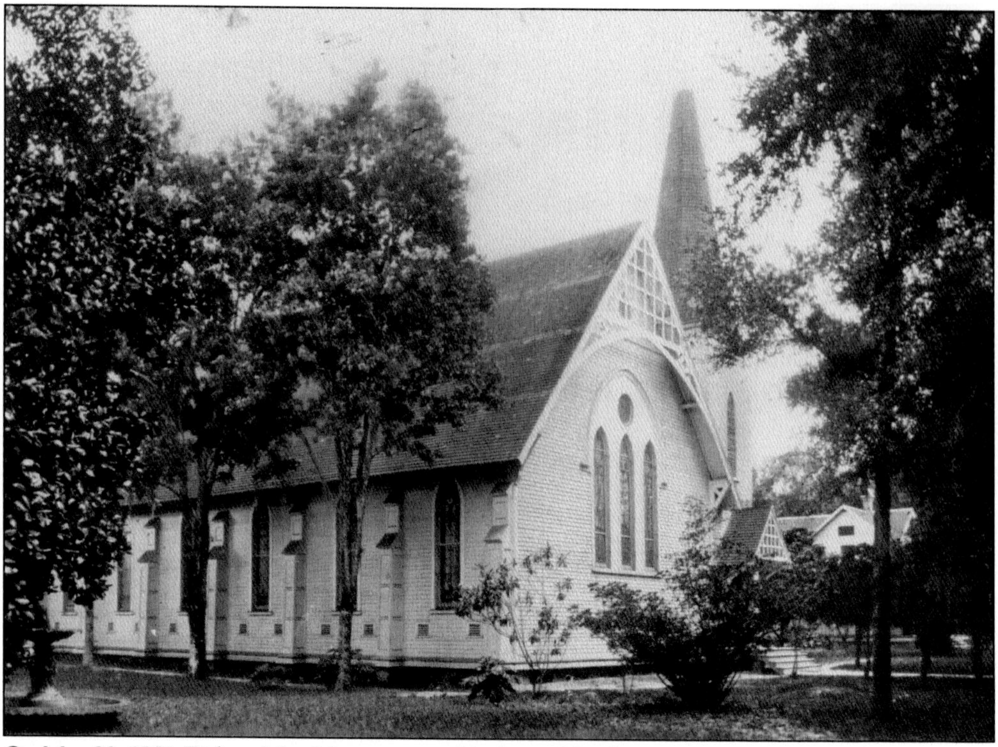

On May 20, 1881, Bishop John Moore, second bishop of St. Augustine, purchased land on Orange Avenue and Robinson Street for the first Catholic church in Orlando at a cost of $1,050. The church celebrates its founding as 1885 with the arrival of Fr. Felix P. Swembergh; however, the cornerstone for the church bears the date January 23, 1887. St. James Church was completed in June 1891.

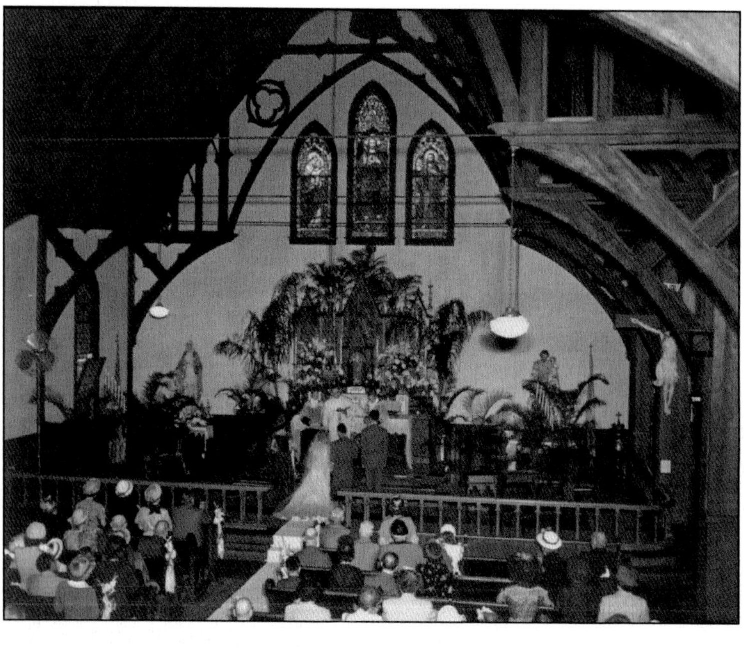

The St. James Church measured 40 feet by 70 feet and was designed by Kurz and Allison's Art Studio of Chicago. The building featured seating for 240 worshippers and boasted a bell tower at the front entrance. Helen Gentile and Andy Serros were married in St. James on February 7, 1950, one year before the church's demolition. The new St. James Cathedral was dedicated on the site in 1952.

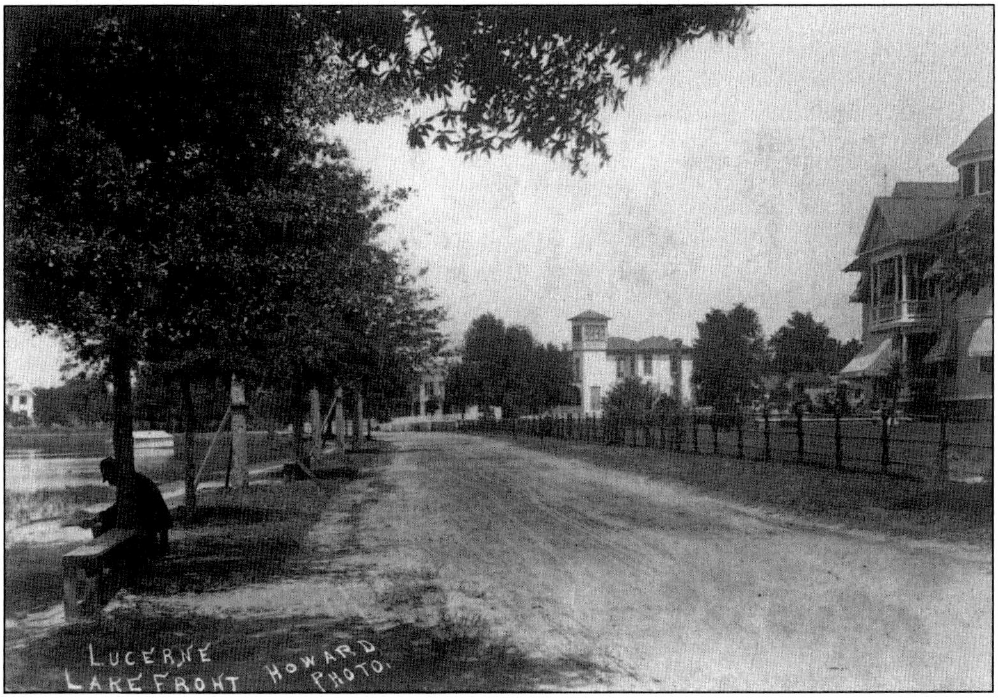

James A. Knox, an attorney who served as county treasurer and chairman of the board of public instruction, bought property on Lake Lucerne from developer Wilmon Whilldin in 1885. He built a house that featured a distinctive square tower and lived there until his death in 1931. His heirs sold the house to the First National Bank and Trust in 1932 to pay off a $10,000 mortgage. In 1936, Melville Smith bought the Knox House from the bank and lived there until 1971, when he sold it to the Orlando-Orange County Expressway Authority to make way for the East-West Expressway.

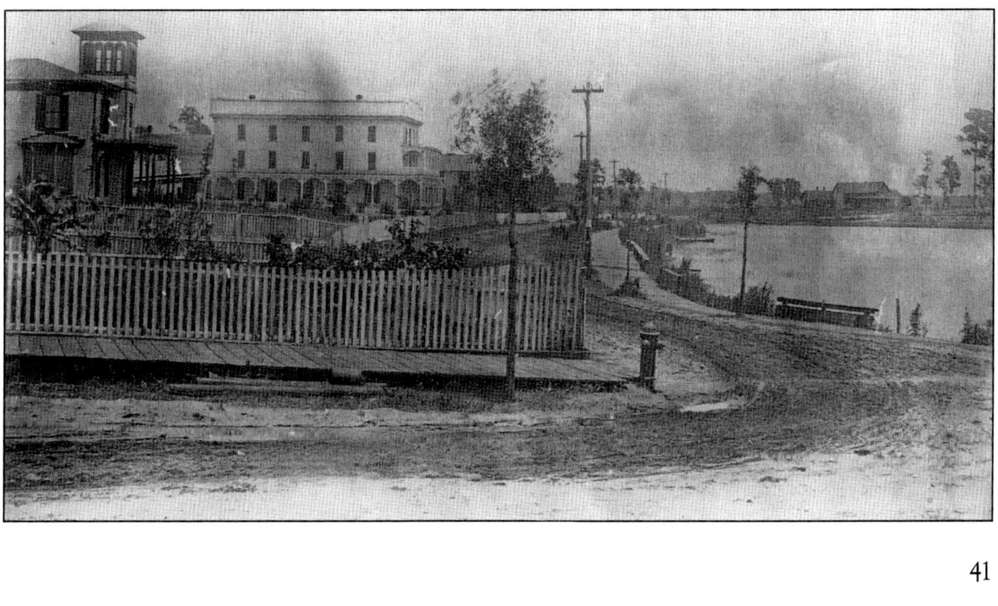

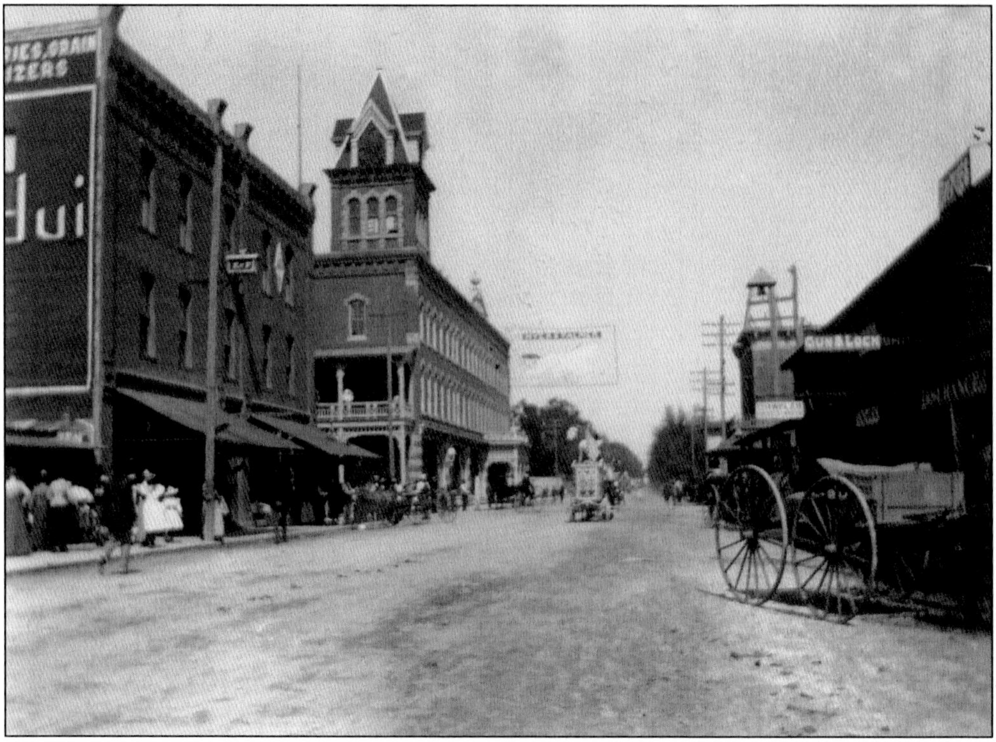

Harry Kedney built the San Juan de Ulloa Hotel, seen in the background at left. Orlando's first permanent hotel, it was constructed on the corner of Orange Avenue and Central Boulevard in 1885 at a cost of roughly $150,000. The largest building in Orlando at the time, it was three stories high and topped with a dome. Much to the surprise of many, the hotel stood for almost a century without an underground foundation.

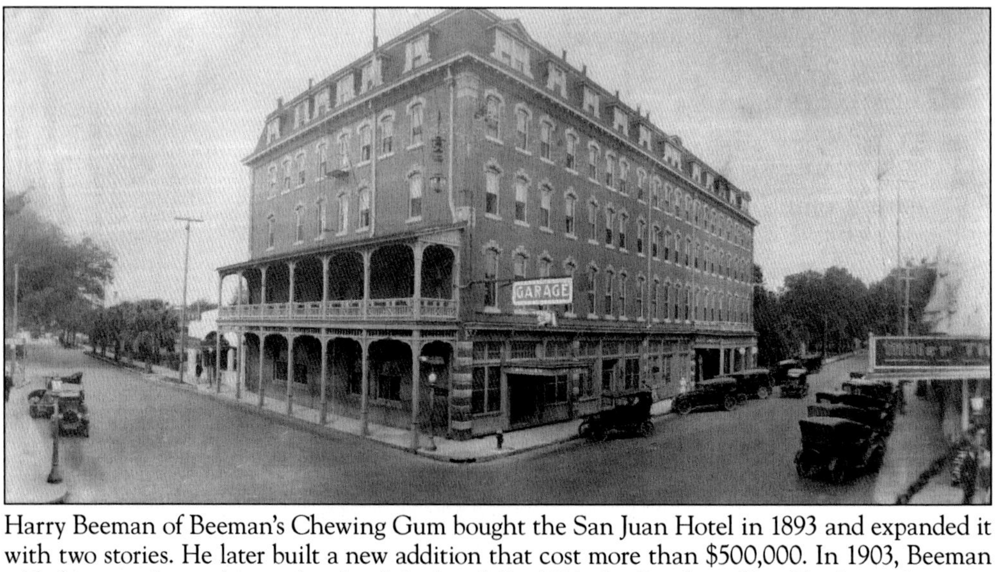

Harry Beeman of Beeman's Chewing Gum bought the San Juan Hotel in 1893 and expanded it with two stories. He later built a new addition that cost more than $500,000. In 1903, Beeman added a veranda on the north side of the hotel. By 1914, the San Juan Hotel had sample rooms for salesmen, a laundry room, café, and 12 private baths.

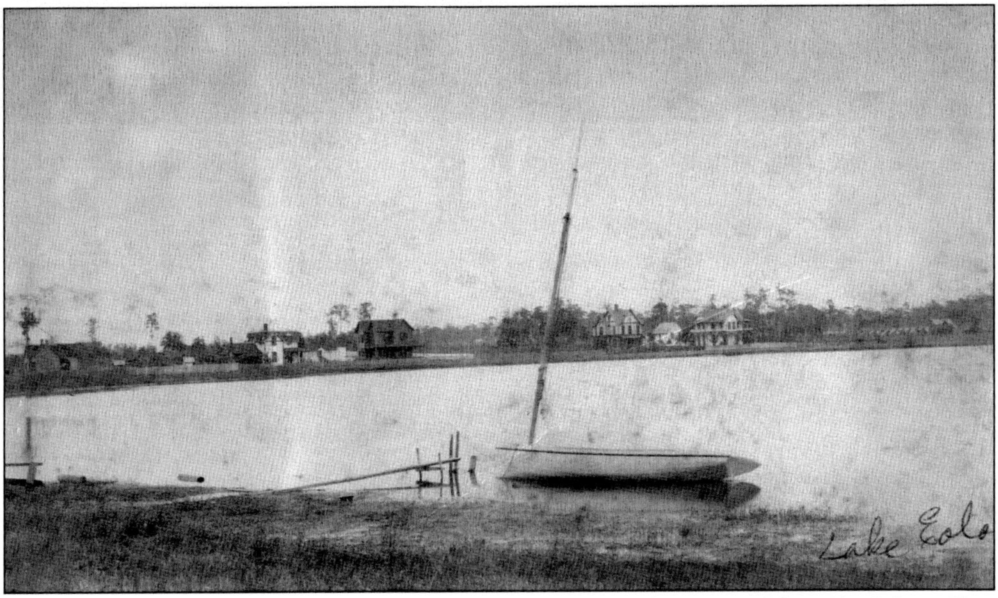

George Papot bought property in 1885 and built a house, seen here second from the left, on East Robinson and Broadway Avenues on Lake Eola. The Papots lived in the house until 1891. The house changed hands several times before Joseph Lawton bought it in 1908. The Lawton family owned the house until 1956, when they sold to National Standard Insurance Company. Today, high-rise offices occupy the site.

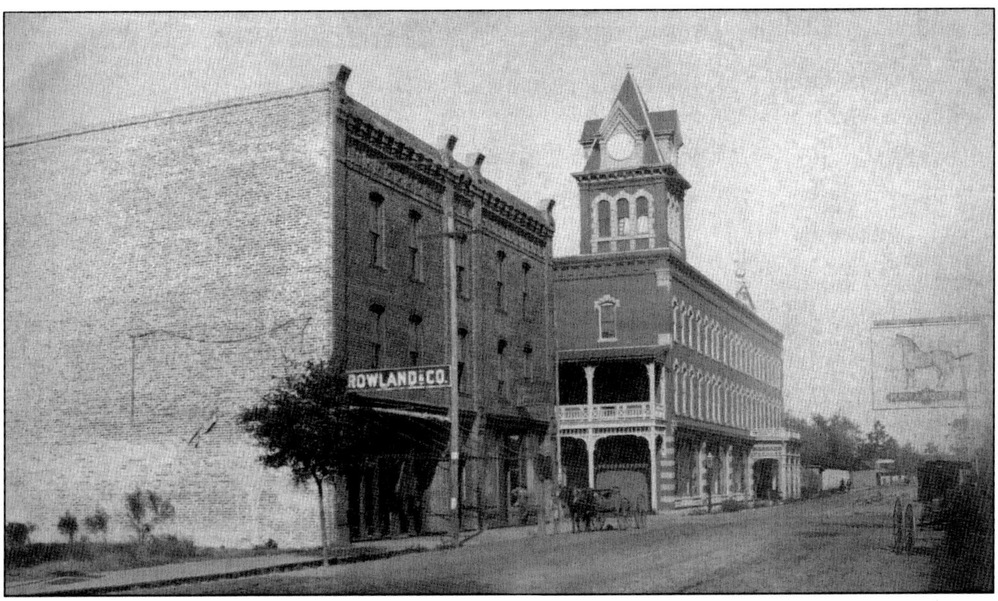

William Rowland and his sons opened a grocery store in 1886 in the newly constructed Browne Building, seen here in front of the San Juan Hotel on South Orange Avenue at Central Boulevard. In 1903, H.H. Dickson and S.E. Ives bought the Browne Building for their Dickson-Ives grocery Store. In 1920, they demolished the old building and erected a new store, now known as Two South Orange.

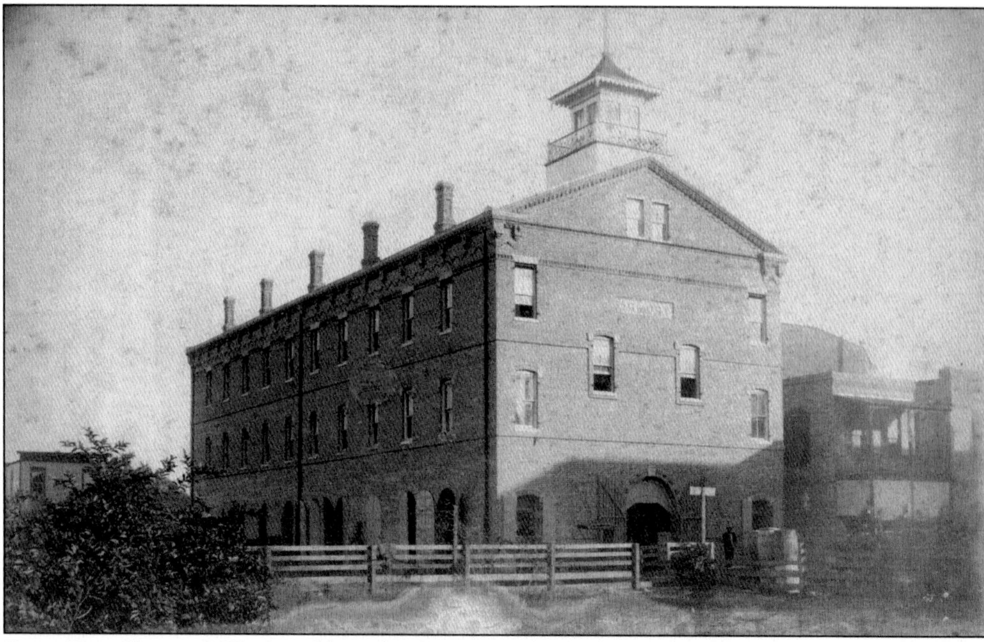

Capt. Tom Shine, C.W. Arnold, and L.O. Garrett built the Armory, Orlando's first large brick building, in 1886. Three stories high, 50 feet wide, and 150 feet deep, the Armory extended through the block between Court Street and Magnolia Avenue, with entrances on both streets. The city market sold fresh produce on the first floor, and attorneys maintained offices on the second. The third-floor auditorium provided meeting and entertainment space and a headquarters for the Orlando Guards, later renamed the Shine Guards in honor of Capt. Tom Shine. This photograph of the Leap Year Dance, held on December 29, 1904, was taken in the Armory's auditorium. Weather signal flags flew from the flagpole to warn of storms and freezes. A.E. Slausen demolished the old structure in 1932, salvaging the brick for new construction.

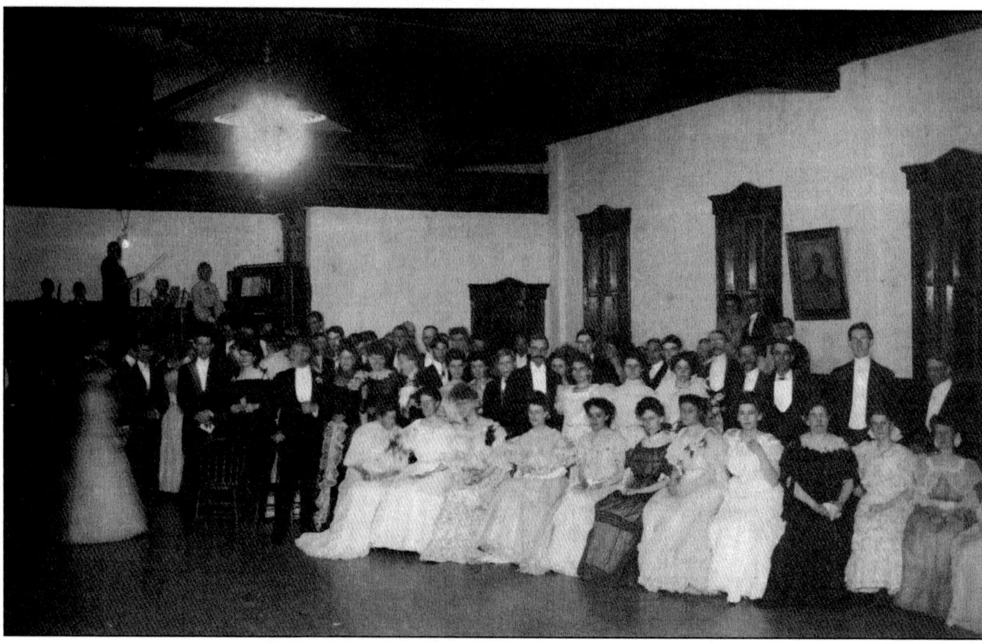

Established in 1886, the Mt. Olive Colored Methodist Episcopal Church occupied a building on East South Street in the Jonestown African American community. The church remained there until 1948, though most of the neighborhood had dispersed to the west side of Orlando. In 1949, the congregation moved to a new meeting place on Woods Street.

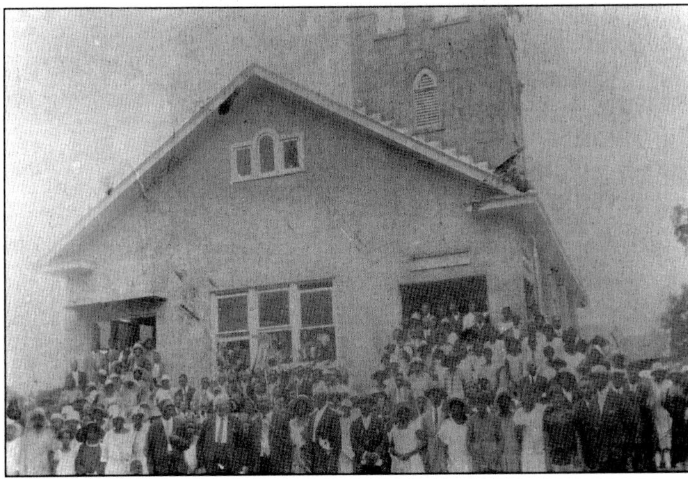

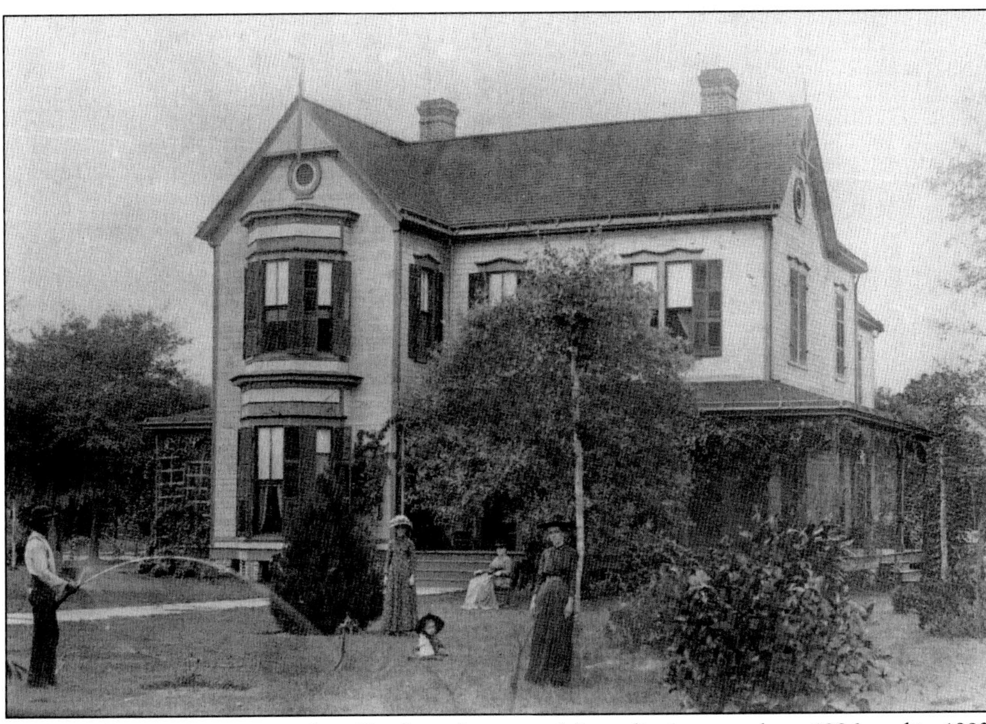

Nathaniel "Nat" Poyntz completed his large house on Magnolia Avenue about 1886, and in 1893, he sold the home to James D. Beggs. By 1900, the property had come into the hands of Alexander H. Darrow, who converted the house to a 16-room hotel called the Darrow Hotel. Renamed the Wyoming Hotel in 1905, the Nat Poyntz House was demolished in 1959. Today, the Orange County Courthouse occupies the site.

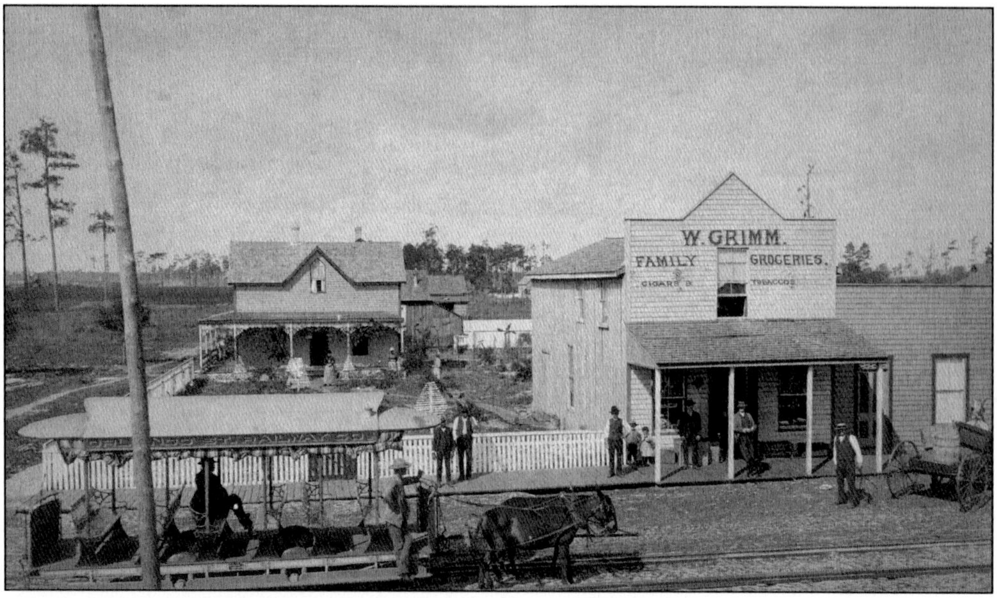

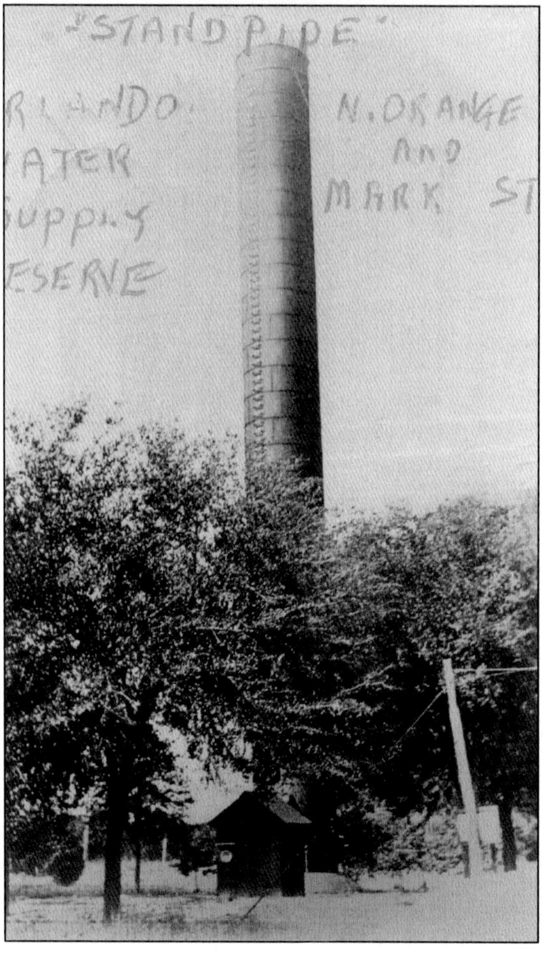

The Washington Grimm family came to Orlando about 1880, and Grimm built a two-story grocery store on North Orange Avenue around 1887. The store is listed in the 1887 *Orange County Gazetteer* at the northwest corner of Orange and Livingston Street. The family lived in rooms above the store before moving into a house on West Livingston. Grimm's son sold the property in 1893, and today, it is a vacant lot.

The Orlando Water Company, precursor to the Orlando Utilities Commission, erected the 110-foot-high standpipe at North Orange Avenue and Marks Street in 1887. Twelve feet in diameter, it held water from a pumping station on Lake Highland to create pressure in water mains for fighting fires. It was demolished in 1920, and commercial buildings now occupy the site.

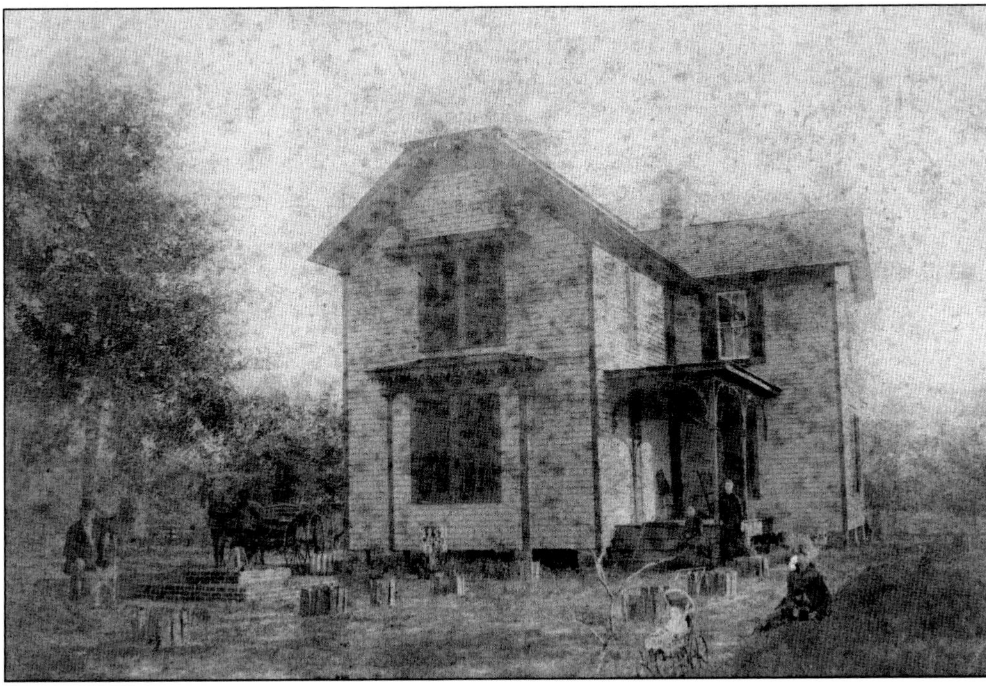

John T. Beeks, Orange County superintendent of public instruction from 1878 until 1894, bought land south of Lake Lucerne in 1883. His two-story frame house, seen here in 1885, may have been the first residence on Irene Street, which was renamed Gore Street in 1910 to honor former mayor Mahlon Gore, also an early resident. The Beeks House gave way to the Harry L. Beeman mansion in 1911.

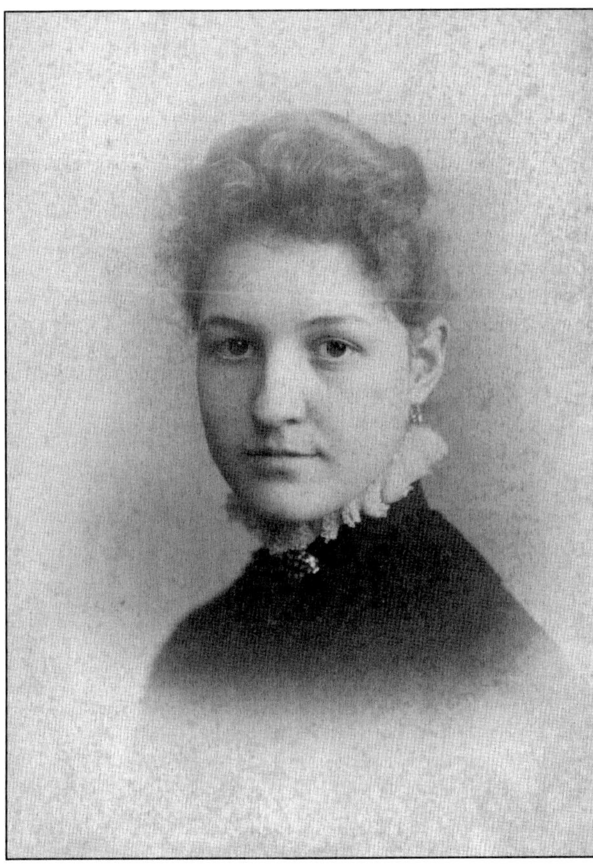

The Beeks family became known for their many pleasant gatherings. Their popular daughter Nellie, pictured here around 1890, made the house a lively social center. Nellie eventually married Clarence S. Van Houten, who resided northwest of Orlando. She continued to be active in the Orlando community, serving as secretary of the local Daughters of the Confederacy in 1898.

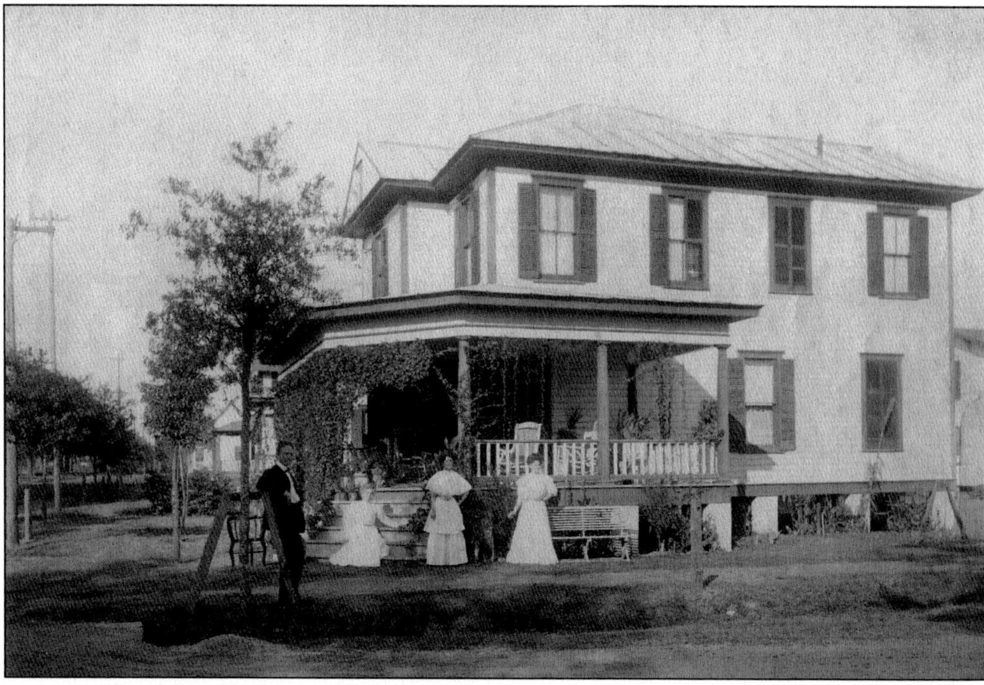

Benjamin Gould probably built the Gard House at the corner of Garland Avenue and West Central Boulevard about 1887. The Gard family lived in the house from 1907 until about 1924, but they likely never owned it. In 1919, Hyman Lieberman bought the home from George Macy. Lieberman replaced the house with a gas station in 1924. A high-rise office building went up on the site in 1982.

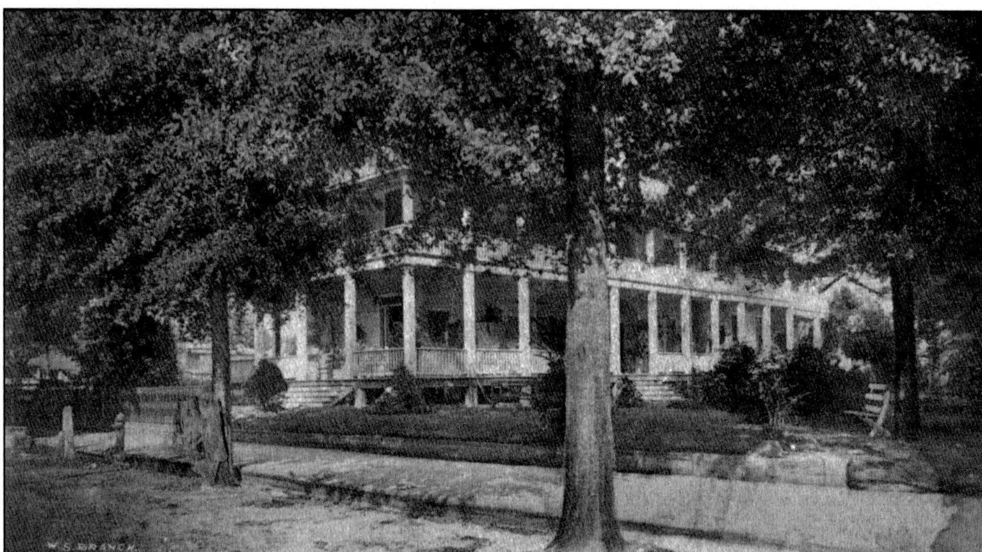

The Windsor Hotel advertised its quiet location on Central Boulevard in 1887. In 1894, proprietor Belle Myers bought property on West Pine Street, and the hotel relocated. According to city directories, it continued in operation as the Windsor Hotel through 1924 and then was listed as "furnished rooms" until 1930. By 1955, the structure was gone, and a modern office building now occupies the site.

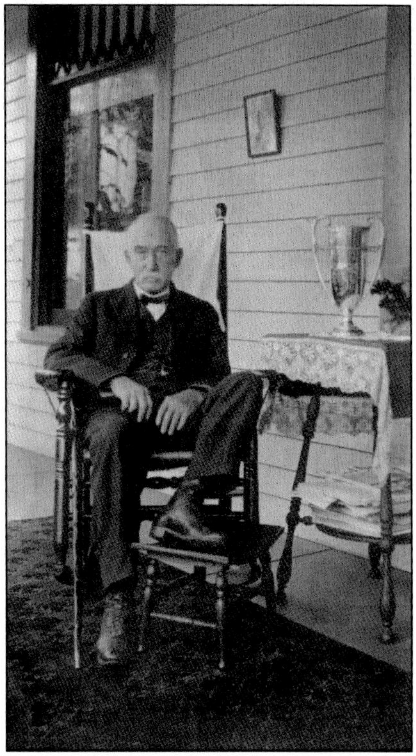

Mahlon Gore, pictured right, built Oakhurst, one of the first residences on Irene Street (now Gore Street) in 1887. The publisher of the *Orange County Recorder*, Gore served three terms as mayor of Orlando. In 1913, he sold the house to Isadore Ives, wife of Sidney Ives Sr., coproprietor of the Dickson-Ives Department Store. Ives enlarged the house and added screens to the porch. His widow lived there until she sold the house in 1944. In 1956, the Bahia Temple bought the property, and the house was probably demolished between 1944 and 1956. In 1992, the site became part of the medical complex surrounding the Orlando Regional Medical Center.

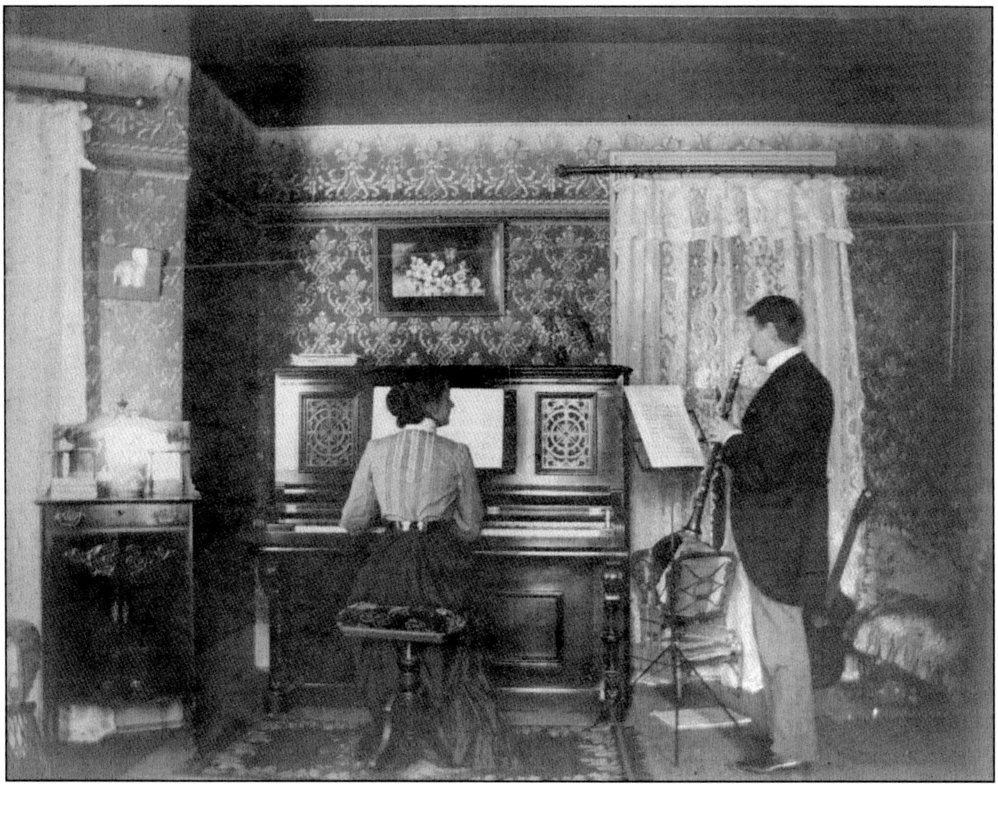

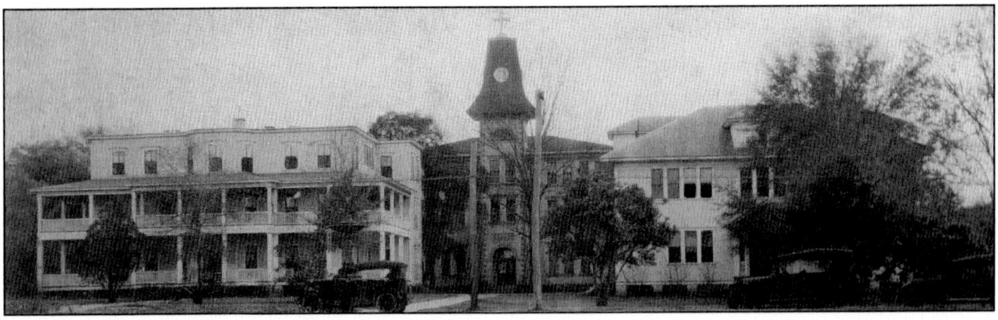

The Cathedral School opened in 1900 in the former W.R. O'Neal house, built about 1887 at the corner of East Central Boulevard and Liberty Street. The Episcopal Church bought the house in 1897 as a home for the bishop. After the Pell-Clarkes donated their home to the church, the O'Neal house became the first building of the Pell-Clarke School for Girls, renamed the Cathedral School for Girls in 1906. By 1910, the school occupied four buildings, including Cluett Hall, a three-story brick structure with a tower. The Cathedral School closed in 1968, and in 1970, the site was cleared for a multistory office building.

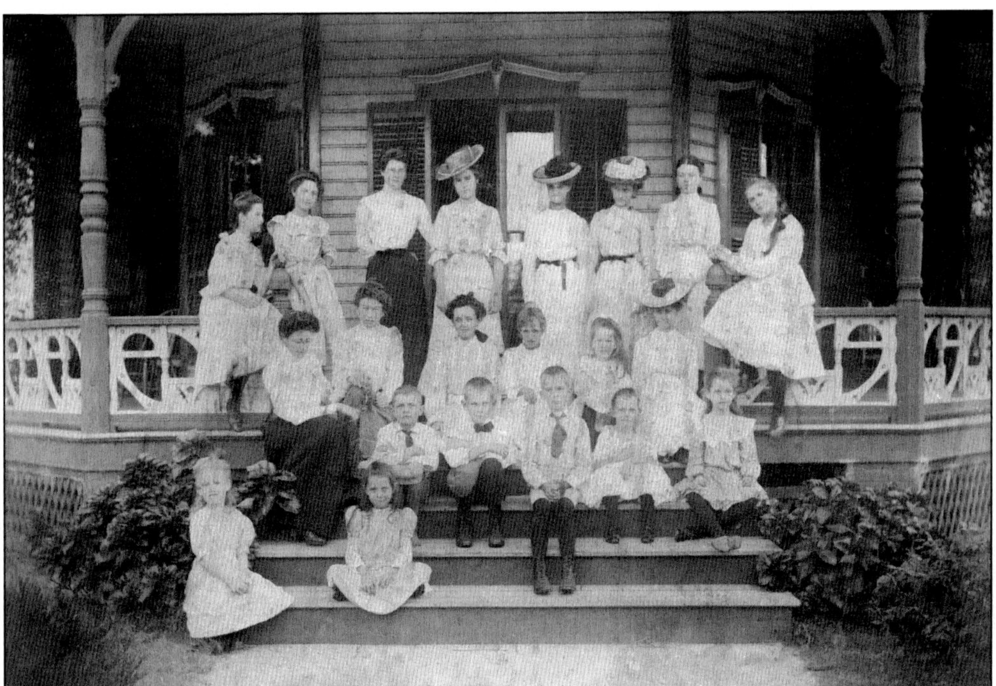

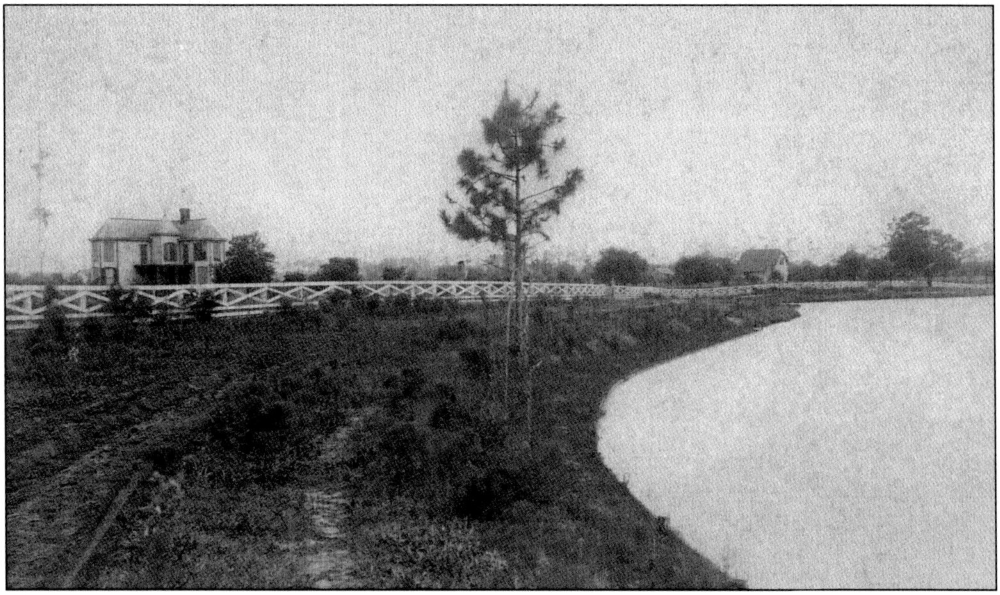

Alfred Birnbaum lived on Lake Lucerne in 1887, possibly in the house seen at left in this photograph, which A. Branham bought on Lucerne Circle in 1901. The Branham House was turned to face Agnes Court by 1925, and by 1970, it was gone. Today, the site is occupied by the Cathedral Cloisters Home for the Aged.

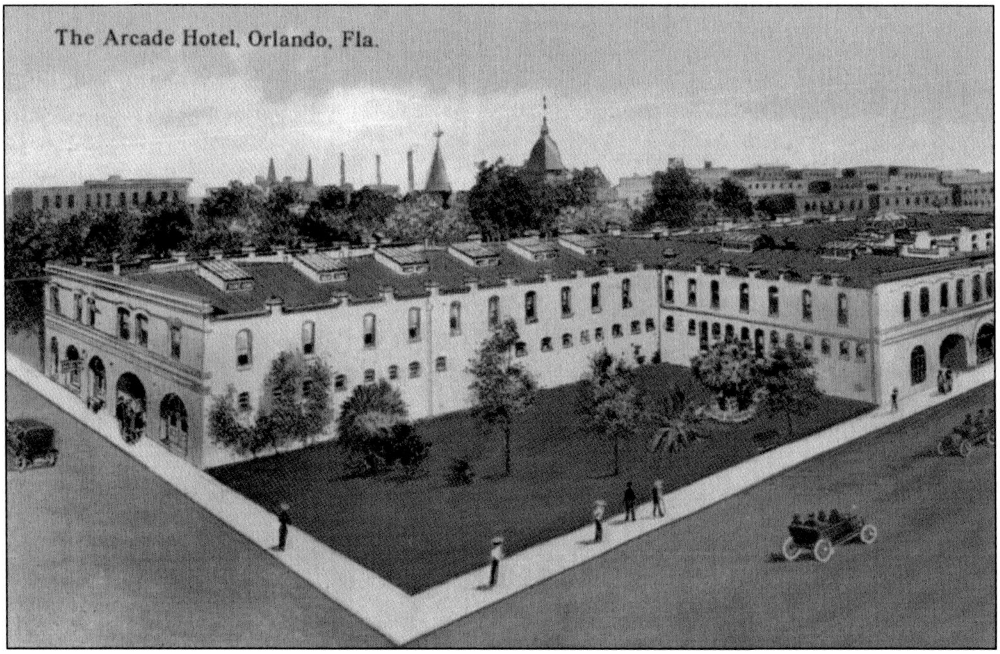

George W. Burden, who came to Orlando from New York in 1882, built the Arcade Hotel at the northwest corner of Orange Avenue and Robinson Street in 1888. The hotel burned to the ground in 1903, taking two houses with it. The property is now a parking lot for the St. James Catholic Church.

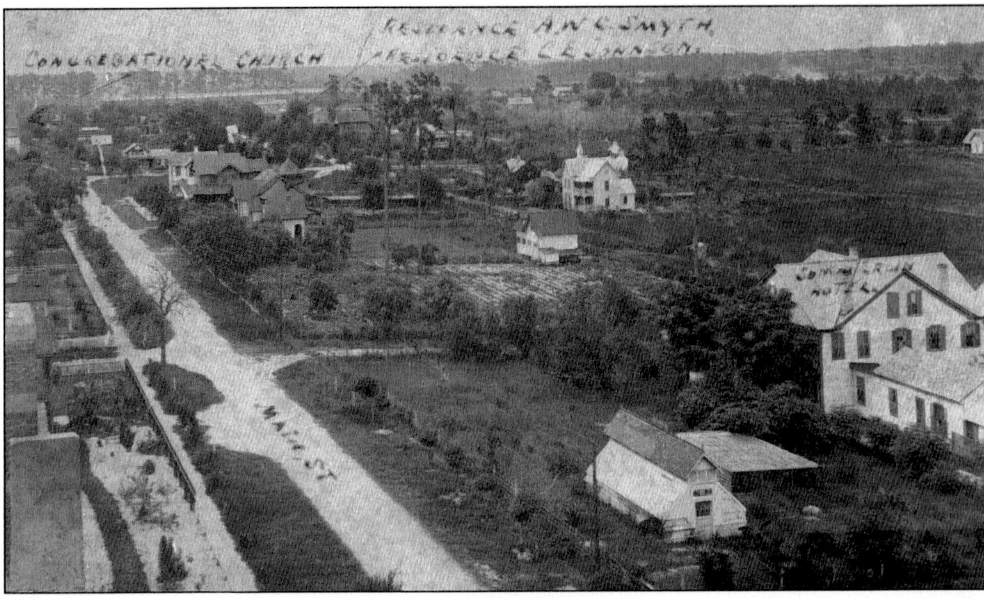

The Congregationalists built a church in 1888 at Robinson Street and Magnolia Avenue. The congregation declined, and in 1902, the few remaining members voted to merge with the Presbyterian Church. The building moved to Magnolia Avenue and Church Street and became a Sunday school for the Presbyterian Church. It was demolished in 1965.

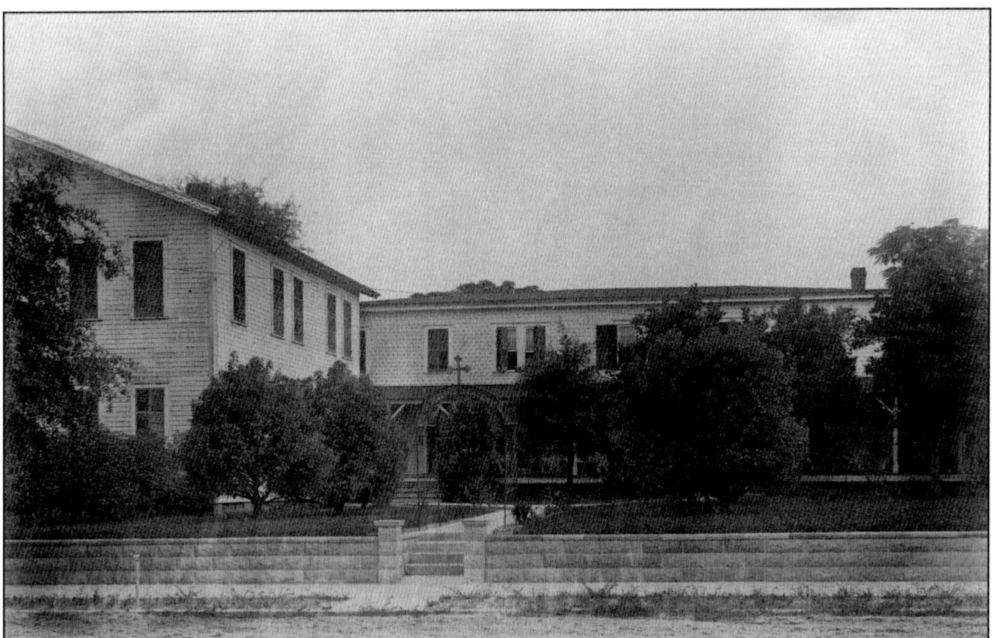

The Catholic Church built St. Joseph Academy, a large frame school and a convent at the corner of Magnolia Avenue and Robinson Street in 1889. The school relocated in 1929, and in 1938, the federal government bought the property and demolished the school to build a post office and federal building. Today, the downtown post office occupies the site.

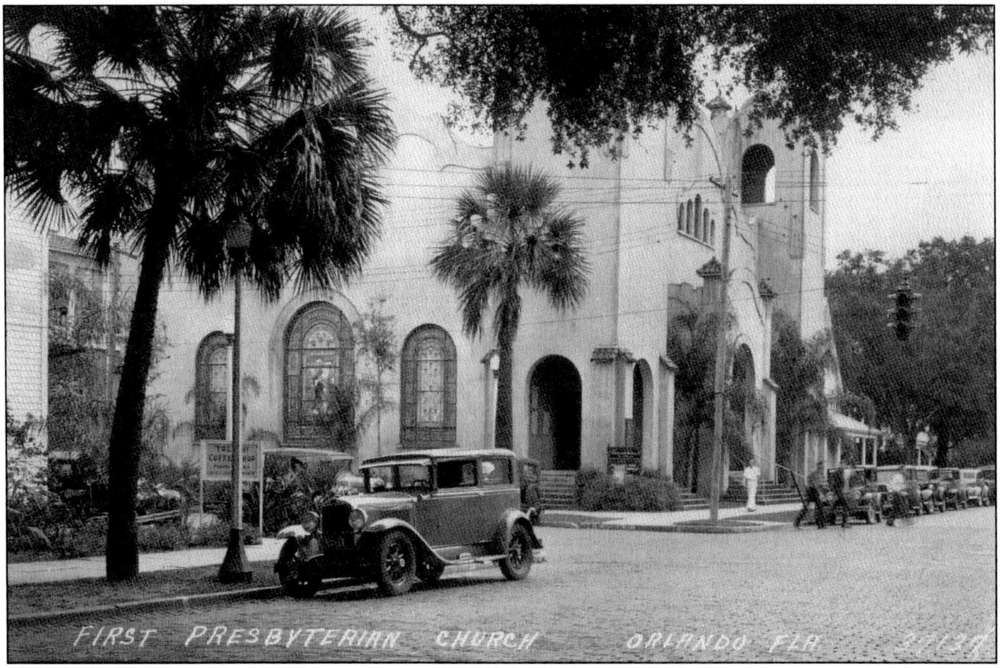

The Presbyterian church, built in 1889 on the southeast corner of Magnolia Avenue and Church Street, replaced the earlier church that burned in 1887. The congregation enlarged the building in 1912 and added stucco and stained-glass windows in 1914. A new structure replaced it in 1955, and the old church was demolished in 1958.

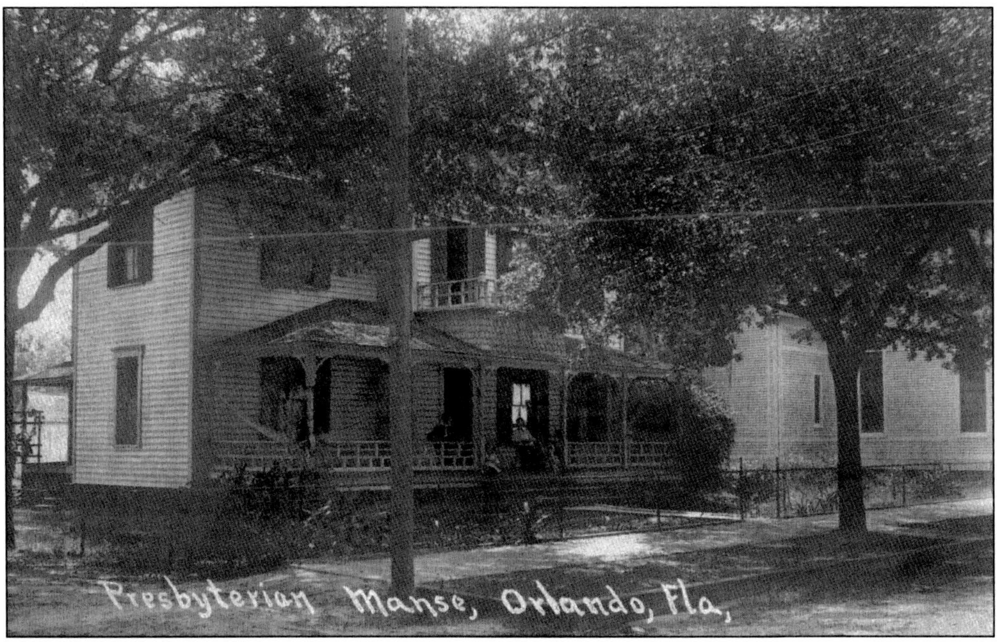

In 1907, Presbyterian minister Rev. Coleman Groves lived beside the church at 106 East Church Street at the corner of Church and Palmetto Streets. The Presbyterian Manse may have existed when the Presbyterian congregation purchased the property in 1887. The house was gone by 1925, but the property remains part of the Presbyterian complex.

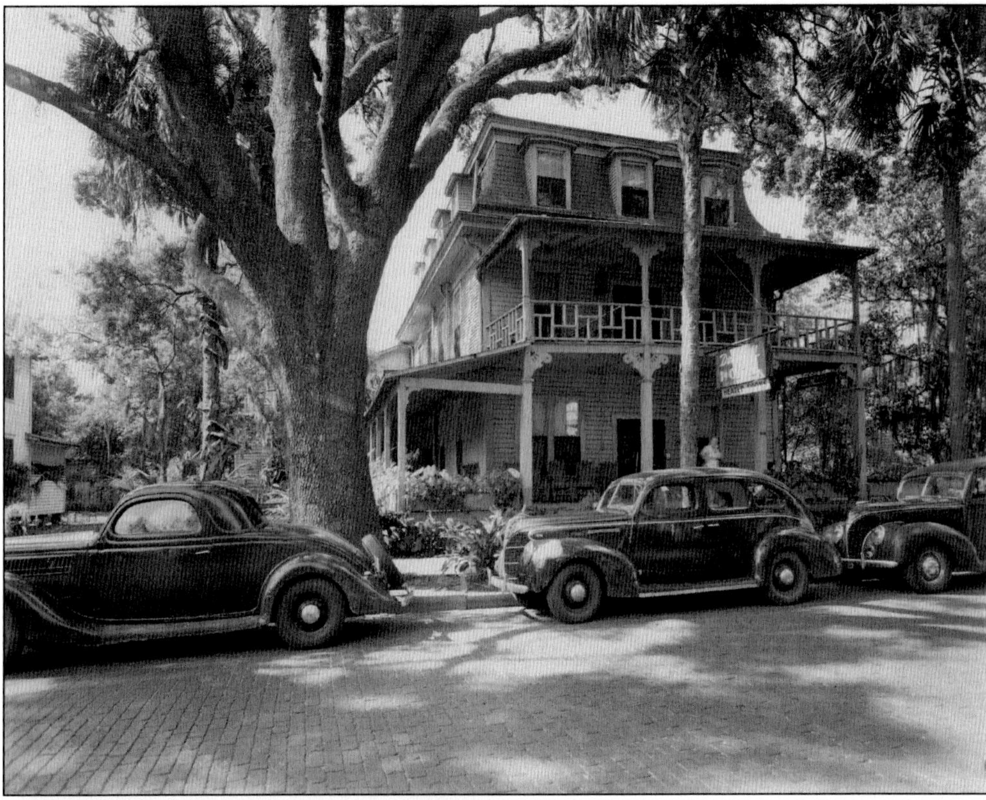

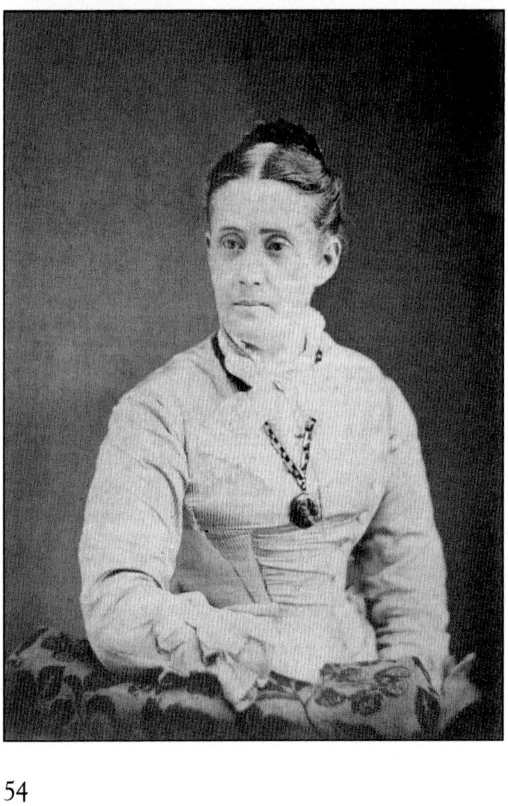

Samuel A. Luckie built the Lucky House on Orange Avenue in 1879 and later changed its name to the Charleston House. In 1891, James L. Giles bought the hotel, had it cut in half with crosscut saws, and sold half to Capt. J.W. Wilmott to become part of the Tremont Hotel. The other half went to judge A.R. MacCallum, who moved it to Pine Street for use as a rooming house.

James K. Duke, who had come to Orlando in 1879, bought the rooming house from Judge MacCallum in the 1890s and named it Duke Hall. Duke's wife, Mary, pictured at left, ran the popular boardinghouse known for its good Southern cooking until 1913. Her daughter Hallie Fernandez continued the establishment until 1940. In 1946, the First Baptist Church bought and demolished the building.

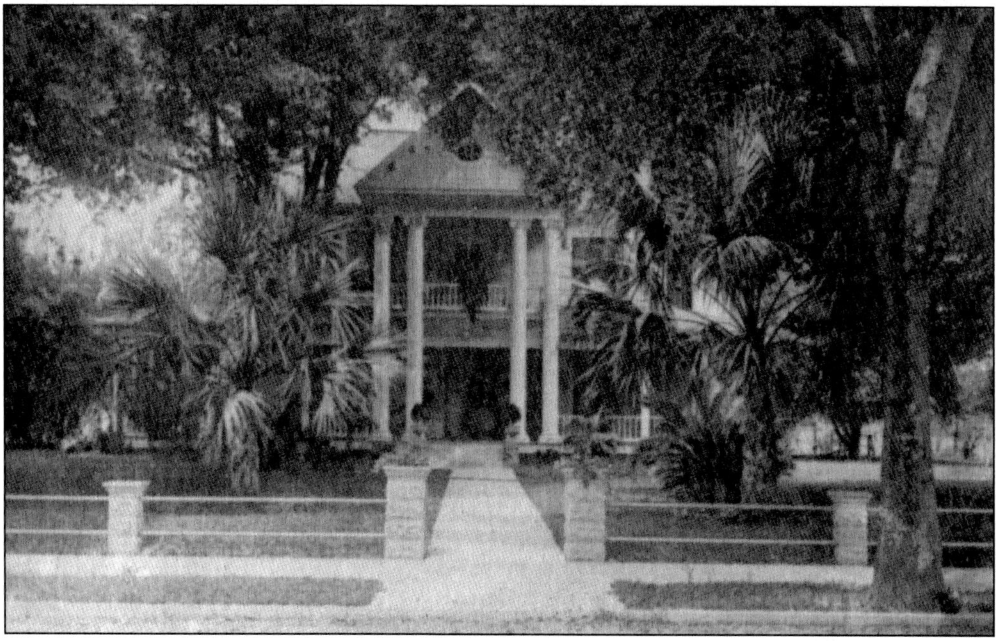

Former Orlando mayor and Florida state representative Willis Palmer married Martha Bayne McAlaster in 1891 and built a house on North Orange Avenue at Amelia Street. The home took so long to build, they called it Atlasta, for "at last it's done." This photograph appeared on cards handed out at their open house. His widow sold the house in 1918, and by 1925, it had been demolished.

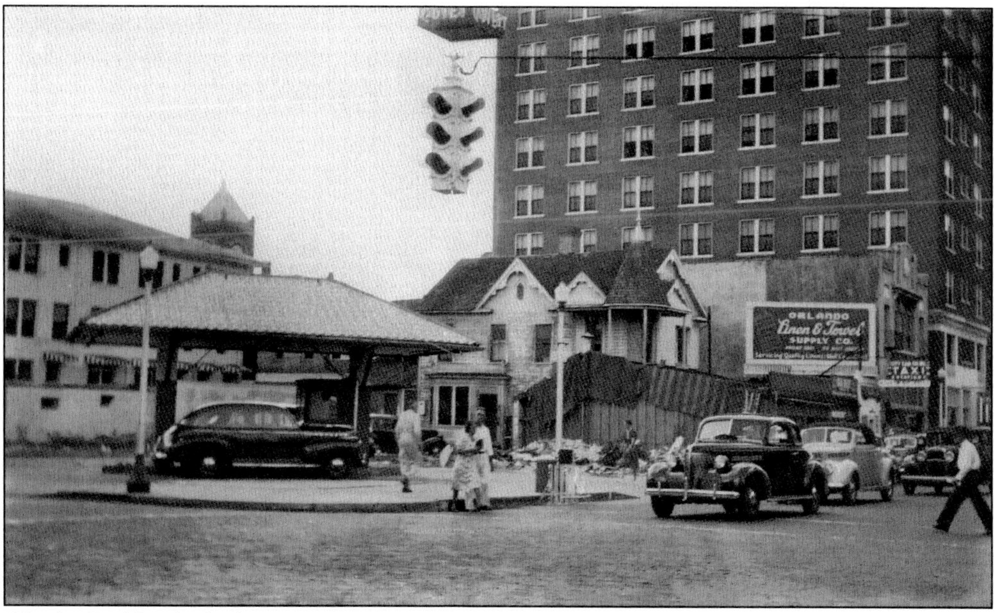

Charles Webber built the Harris House on North Orange Avenue in the 1890s. Dr. Robert Harris and his wife, Frances, lived there from 1901 until 1908, when Anna Hilpert bought the property. In the 1920s, Anna sold her front yard for commercial buildings, such as the gas station seen in this 1930s photograph of the house. She lived in the house until the Rutland Block replaced the house in 1942.

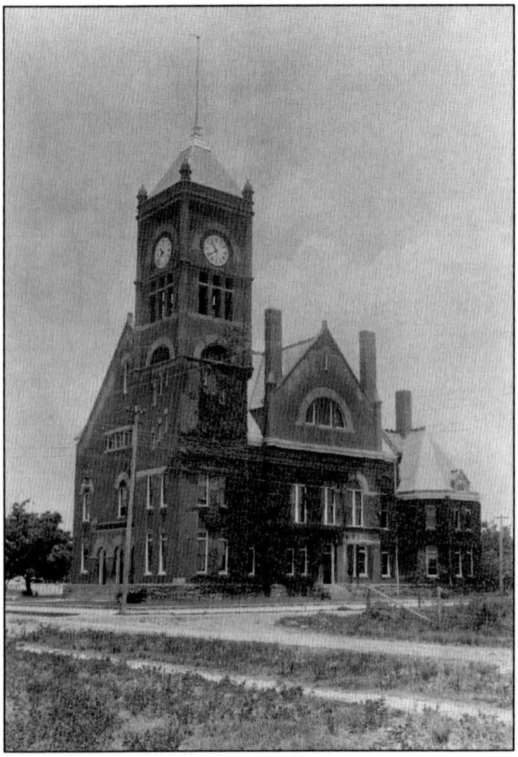

Orange County laid the cornerstone for its first brick courthouse on January 15, 1892. Heated with open fireplaces, the two-story building featured marble floors in the hall and foyer and many leaded stained-glass windows. On the southeast corner, an 80-foot clock tower housed a $3,000 clock installed in 1895 and a 1,500-pound bell tuned to G. The city's most famous landmark, the Red Brick Courthouse, was condemned in 1957 and demolished early in 1958. The Courthouse Annex, a new seven-story building, took its place in the Courthouse Square. Today, Heritage Square occupies the site where the 1892 Orange County Courthouse once stood.

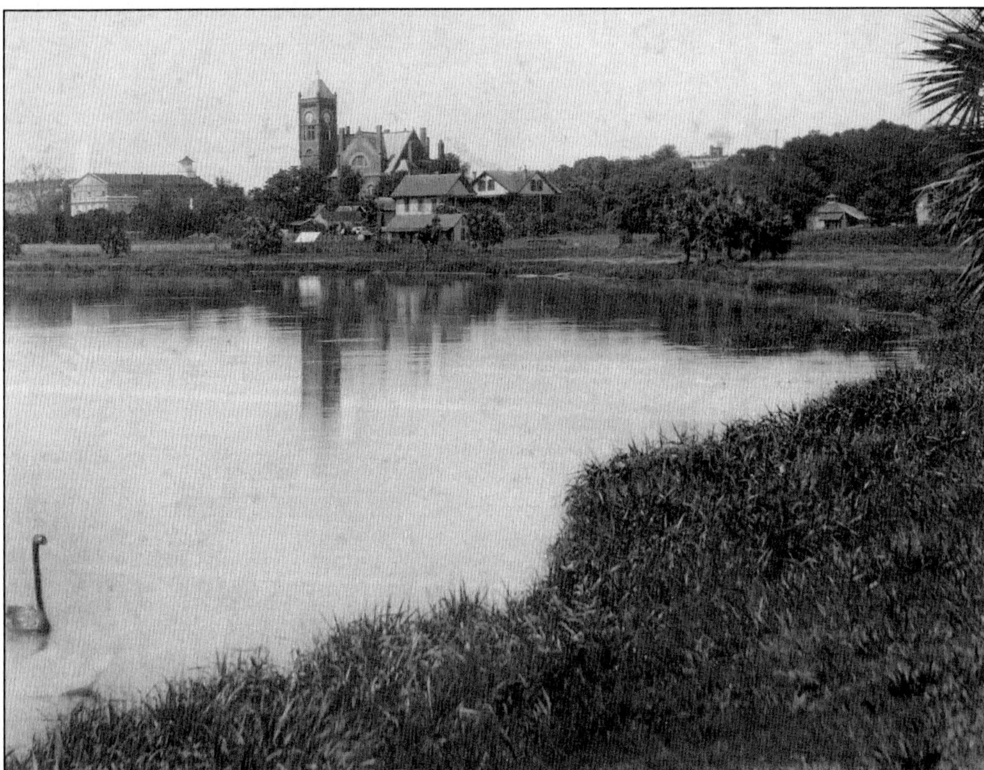

In 1893, the State Bank of Orlando and Trust Company moved into the new brick building constructed by James Giles on South Orange Avenue at Pine Street. After Col. T.J. Watkins bought the building, it became known as the Watkins Block. In 1908, the J.G. McCrory Company leased space there for a store. The McCrory Company bought the block in 1942 and demolished it to build a modern store.

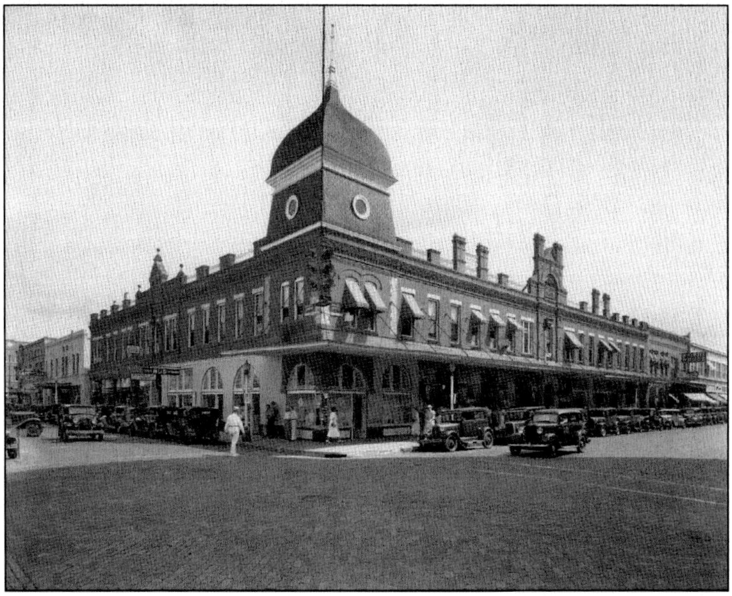

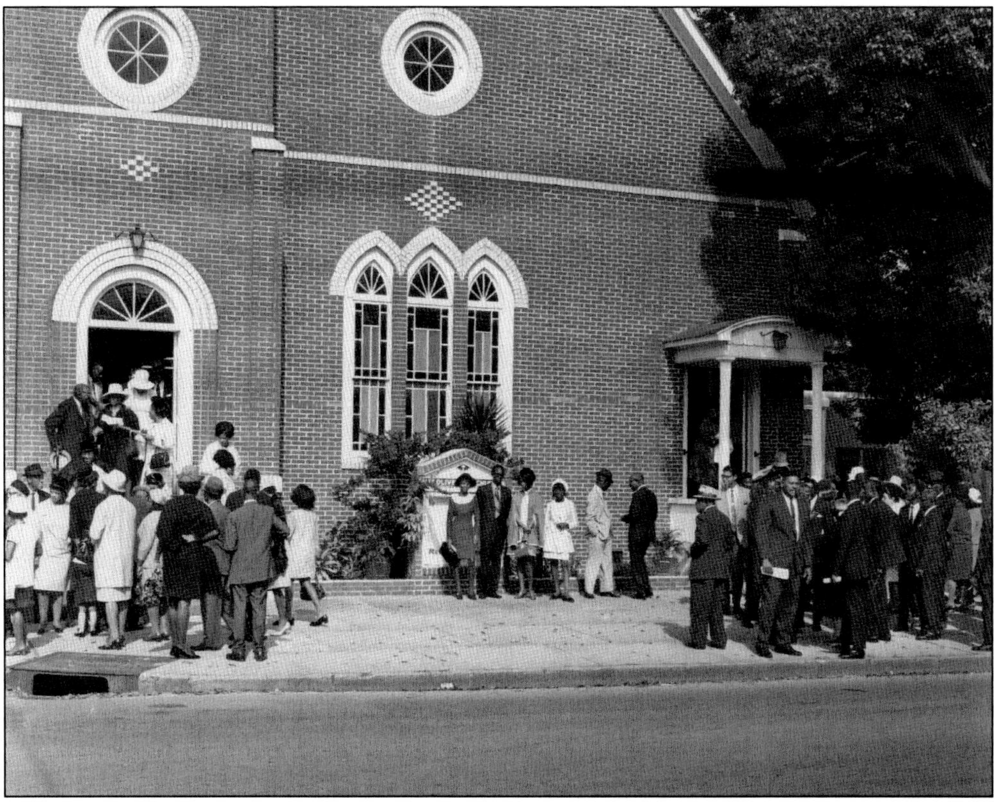

The Mt. Olive African Methodist Episcopal congregation bought property on West Washington Street in 1894 and built a brick church. After integration, business and government expanded into the African American neighborhoods, and in 1977, the Mt. Olive Church was condemned to provide parking for a new state building. The congregation pleaded with the city and fought the condemnation, but finally gave up the church they had built 83 years earlier.

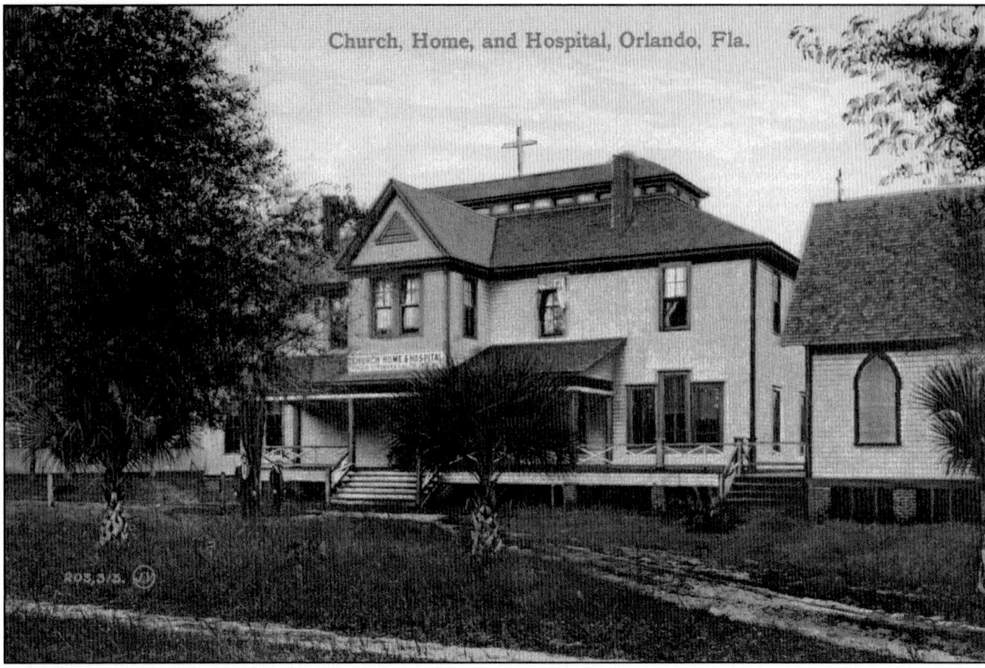

In 1892, a widow built seven cottages on Anderson Street. Unable to rent them, she donated them to become the Cottage Hospital, a home for dependent women. The Cottage Hospital, renamed the Church and Home Hospital in 1895 and St. Luke's Hospital in 1915, closed in 1918. Most of the buildings were demolished by 1925, and the rest fell to East-West Expressway construction in 1971.

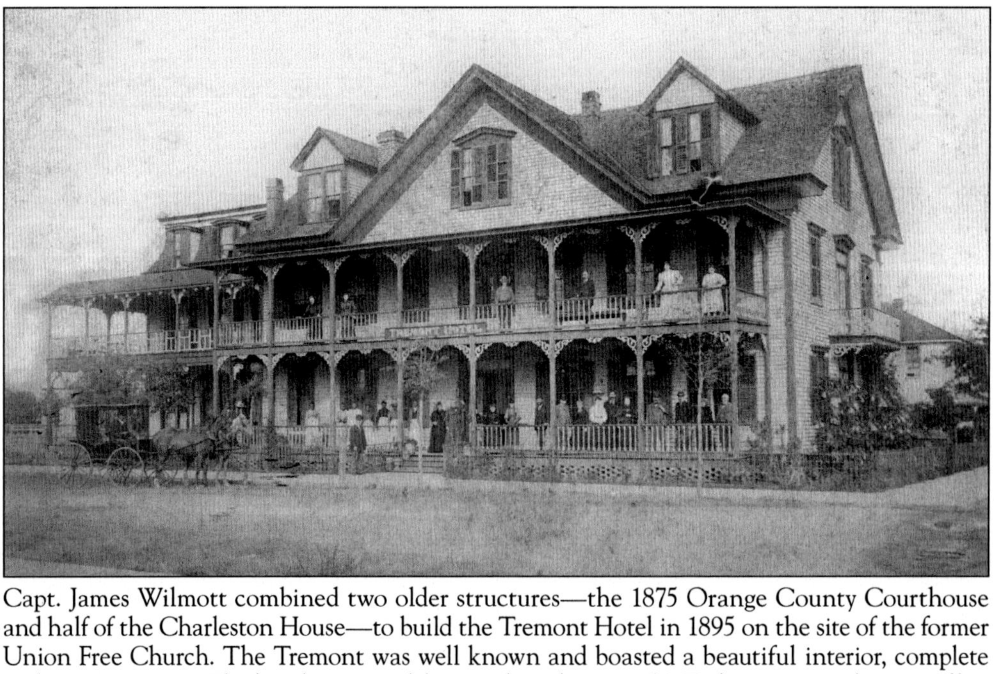

Capt. James Wilmott combined two older structures—the 1875 Orange County Courthouse and half of the Charleston House—to build the Tremont Hotel in 1895 on the site of the former Union Free Church. The Tremont was well known and boasted a beautiful interior, complete with a music room. The hotel was razed for a parking lot in 1956. Today, it is a multistory office building with an attached parking garage.

Three

1896–1920

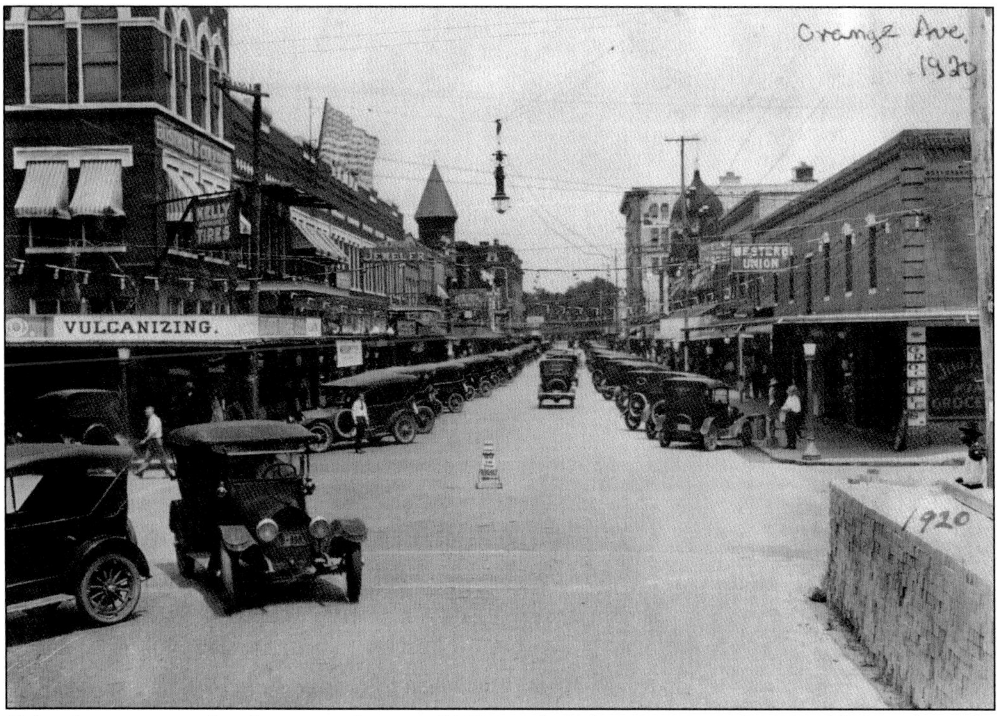

Orlando overcame the disastrous freezes of 1894 and 1895 and prospered as World War I brought new industry to town. The government constructed new facilities, and businesses moved away from wood construction to more permanent brick buildings. Institutions remained mainly downtown, but new houses moved further from the business section. In many cases, older, once-pretentious houses close to the city center were torn down and replaced by business blocks.

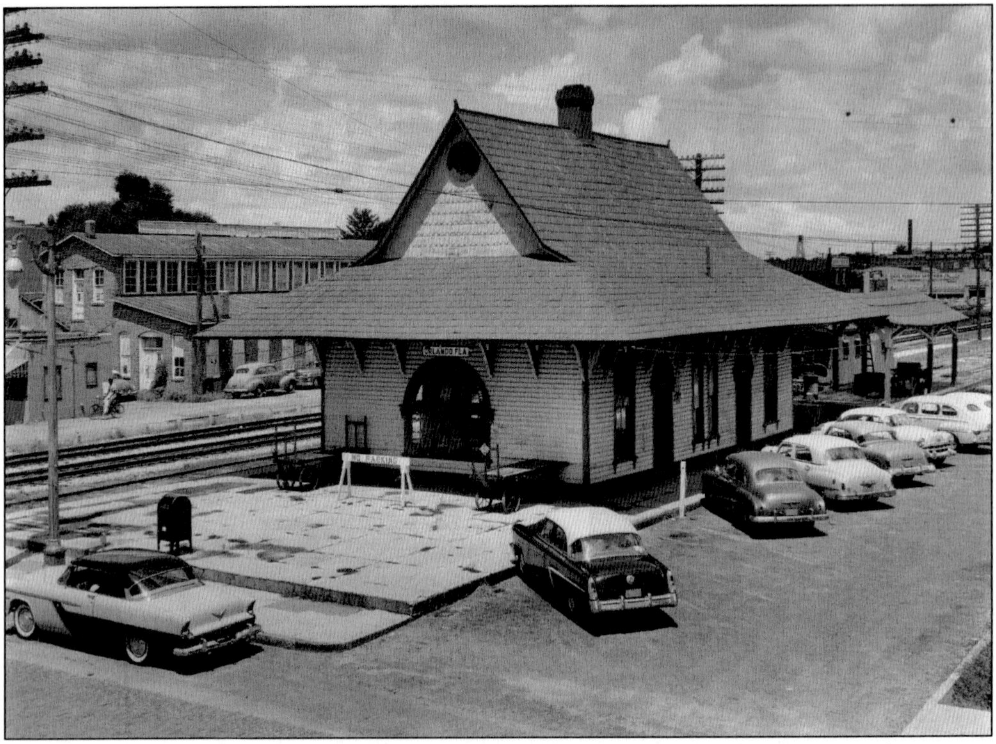

Construction of the Tavares, Orlando, and Atlantic Railway was completed in 1884; however, a permanent passenger depot did not exist until 1896. Prior to the completion of the permanent structure on the north side of Central Boulevard and the railroad tracks, the passenger depot operated out of an old boxcar on the south side of Central Boulevard. Over the years, the railroad changed hands several times and was known as the Florida Central and Peninsular Railroad Company, Seaboard Air Line Railway, and finally, after a merger with the Atlantic Coast Line in 1967, as the Seaboard Coast Line Railroad. The depot was razed in 1955 to make room for a parking lot, and the railroad suspended passenger service in Orlando.

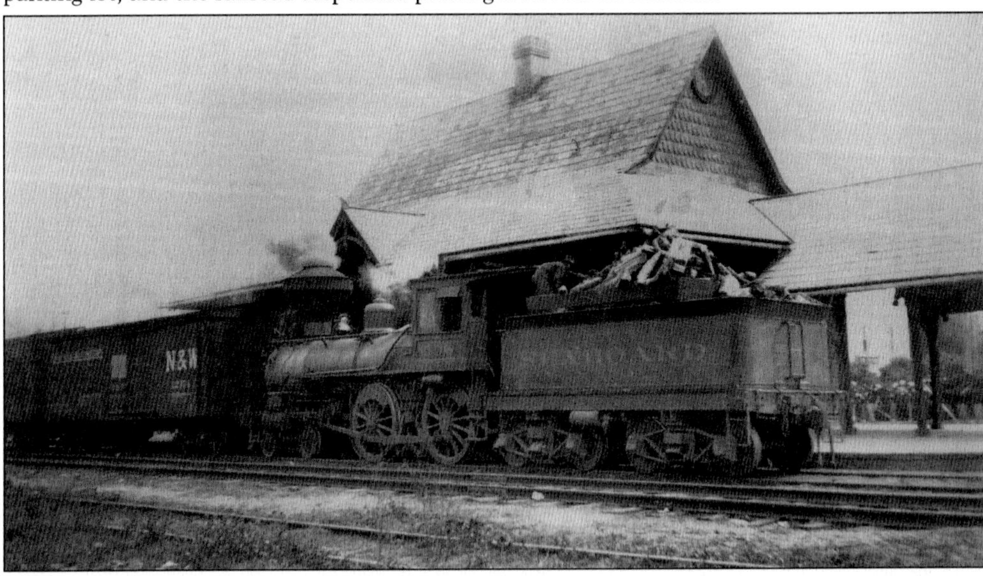

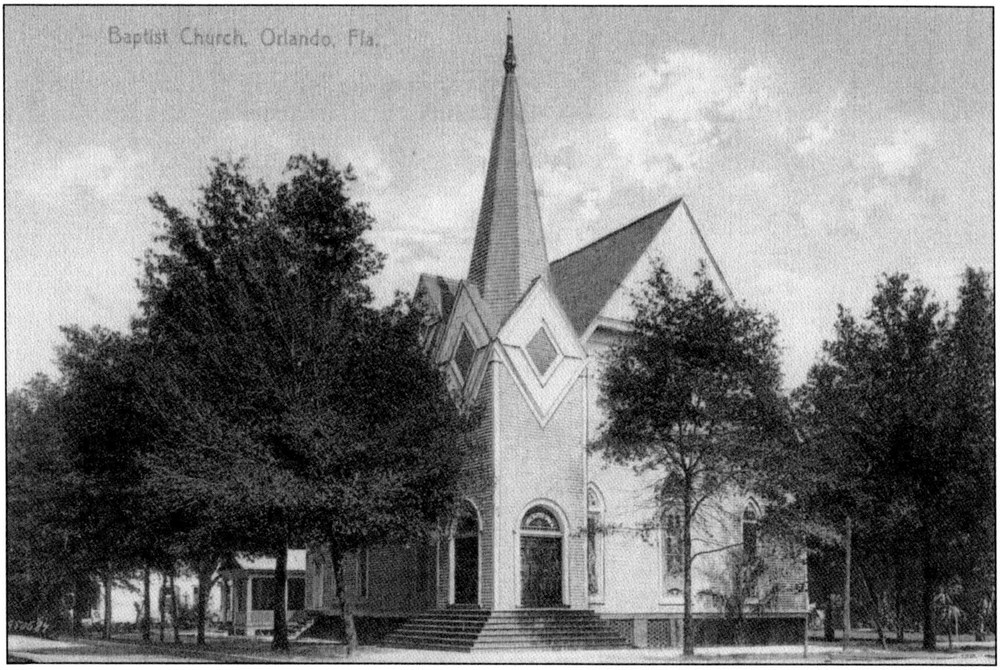

Orlando's First Baptist congregation dedicated its new church in 1897 at the southeast corner of Pine Street and Magnolia Avenue. It replaced a structure completed in 1882 at Garland Avenue and West Pine Street, which the church sold in 1893. A new brick building was dedicated in 1915 on the site of the 1897 church.

Though W.C. Nutt reportedly built the house on Boone Street in 1895, it more likely dates to 1897 when his wife, Elizabeth C. Nutt, bought the property. Elizabeth sold it to Mattie A. Rush in 1904, and Rush sold it to E.S. Keyes in 1919. In 1977, Helen Keyes sold the house to the city for a parking lot. Today, the block-long street is lined with parking garages.

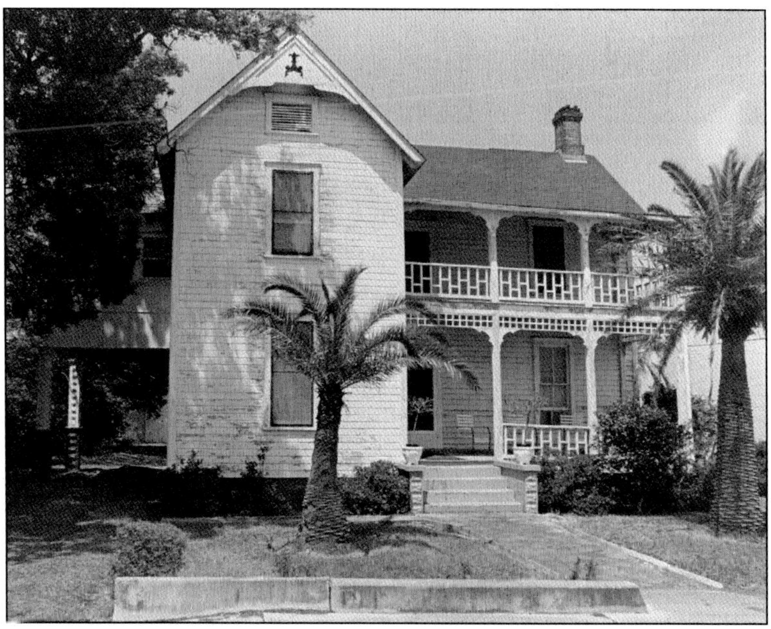

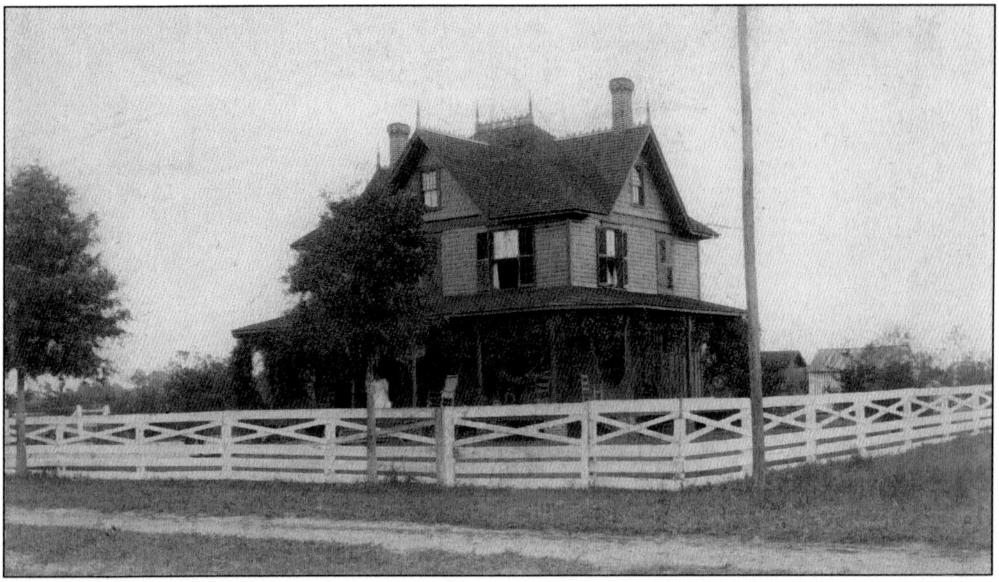

Samuel R. Hudson came to Orlando from Kansas City in 1891 and bought the *Orange County Reporter* from Mahlon Gore. He purchased property on East Washington Street (called Nall Street at the time) in 1897. The Hudson family lived there until 1957, when the last resident, Hattie Hudson, died. It is unknown if Hattie was Samuel's daughter or possibly his sister. She apparently willed the house to the Orlando Art Association, who sold it to Fry Leasing in 1959. Despite the sale, the art association maintained a gallery in the home until 1960. The Barr & Associates commercial building was constructed on the Hudson House site in 1961.

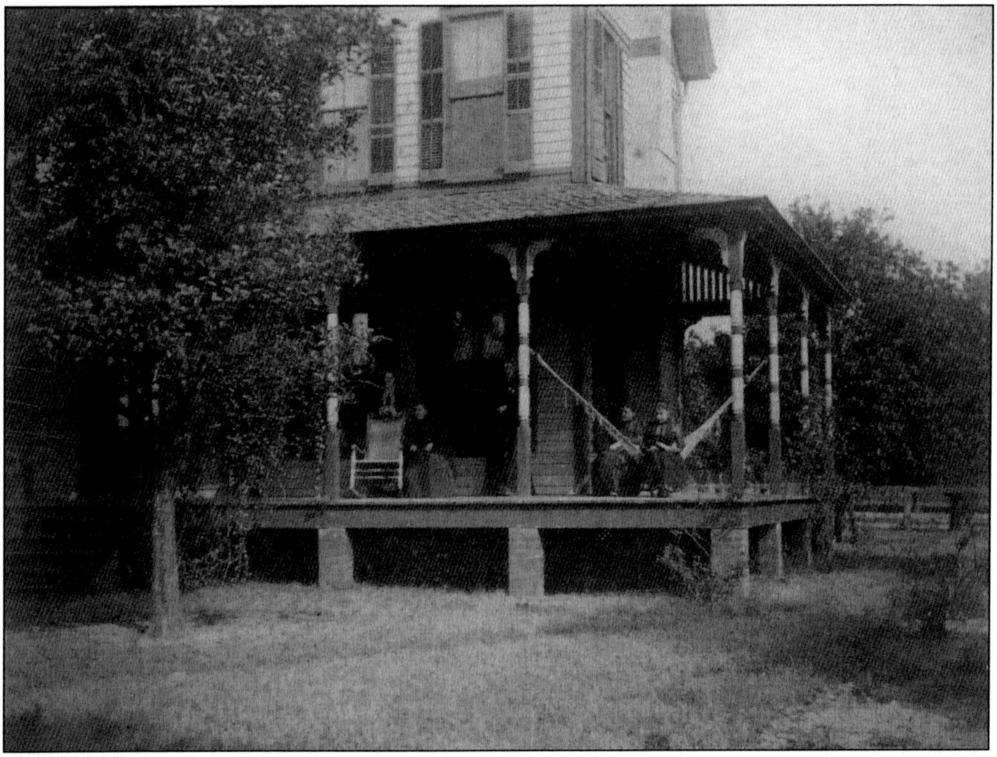

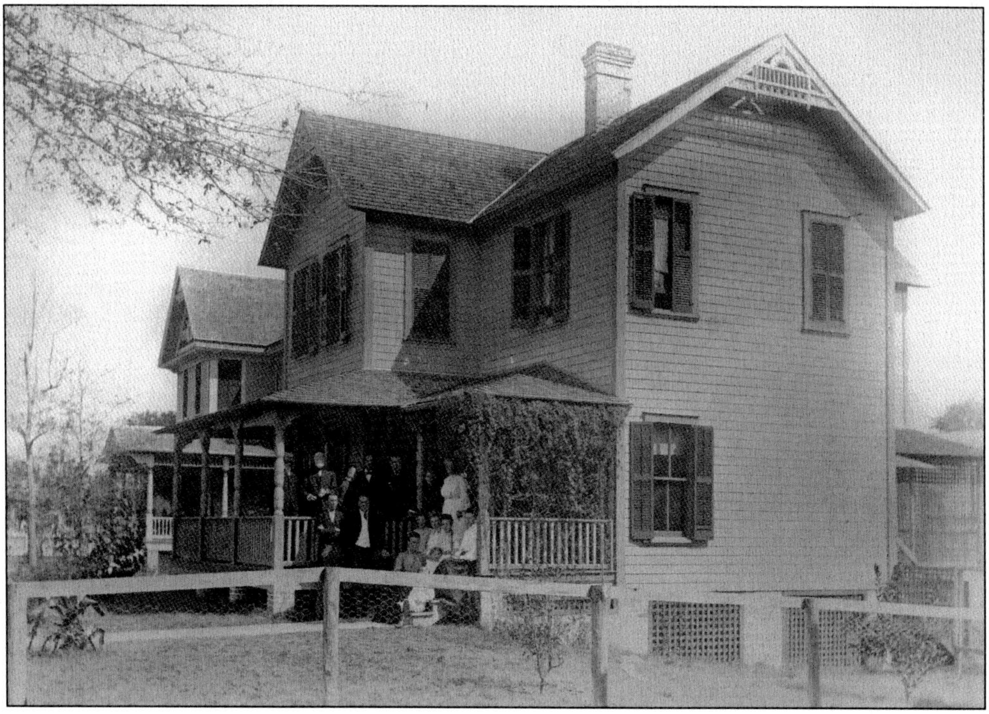

Dr. Eugene C. French built the house at 203 North Magnolia Avenue about 1898, when he moved to Orlando from Connecticut. He practiced medicine, bought a citrus grove, and became part owner of the Howard Book Store. Eugene, his wife Mary, and their children Bernice (pictured at right) and Kenneth lived in the house until 1928, when C.E. Johnson, president of South Florida Foundry and Machine Works, moved in. Mary French and her four children sold the house in 1939 to settle Doctor French's estate. Johnson moved out in 1941, and sometime after 1948, the house was demolished. A modern office building replaced it in 1951.

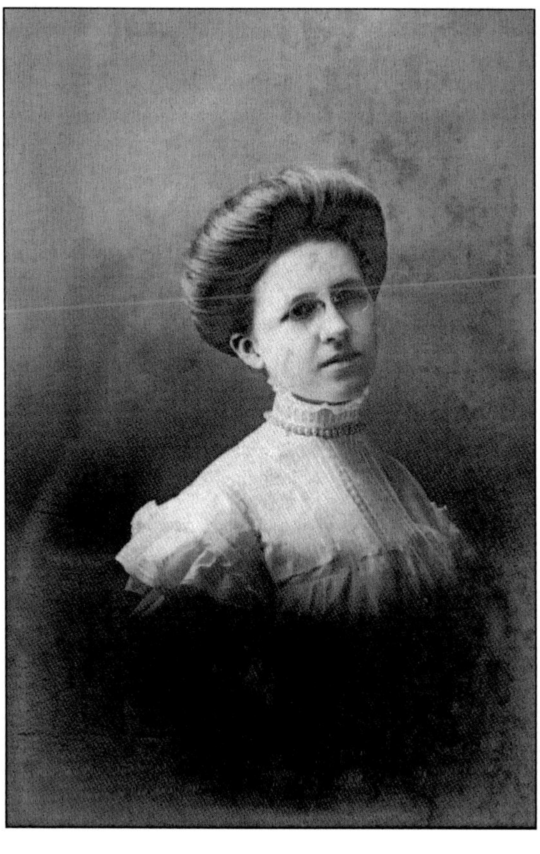

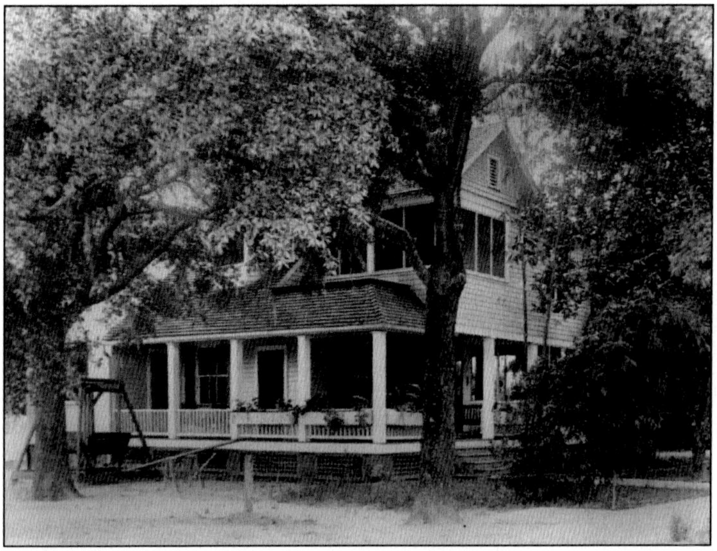

Capt. Benjamin Robinson, later elected mayor of Orlando, moved into the city when his first wife died in 1892. He married Marian Curtis in 1900 and moved into a house at 310 South Lake Street. In 1943, his widow sold the property to the Central Church of the Nazarene. The property became part of the Orlando Central Towers retirement community in 2008.

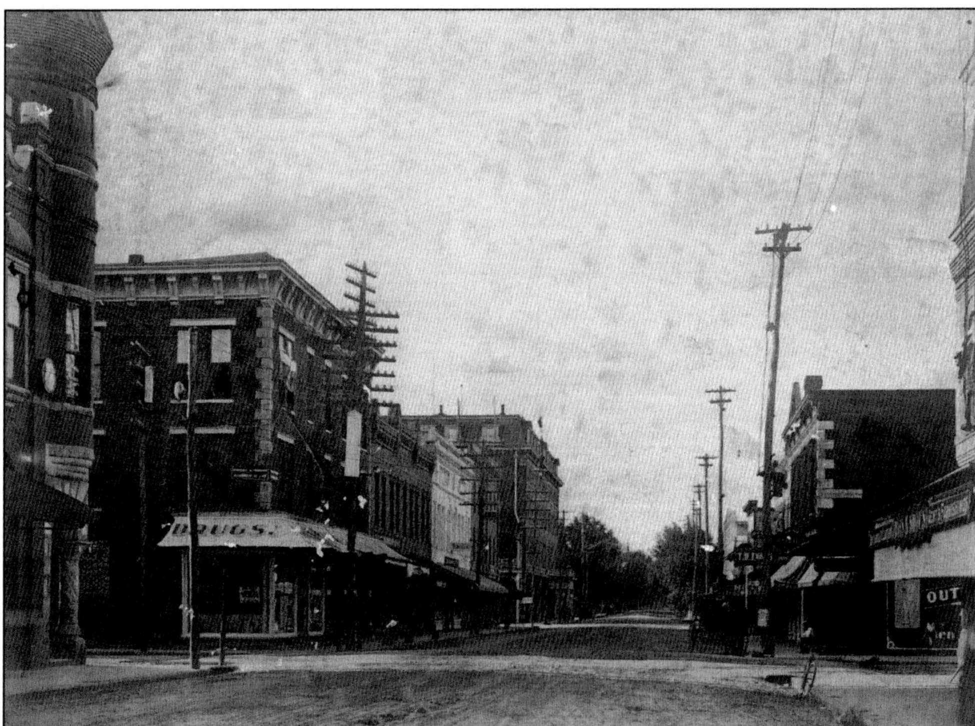

Dr. B. Abernethy established the Abernethy Drug Company in 1899 in the three-story brick building, visible in the left of the photograph with the word "drugs" on its awning. The drugstore at the corner of Orange Avenue and Pine Street became V.W. Estes and Company in 1912. The Estes Building housed a number of businesses over the years before it burned to the ground in 2005.

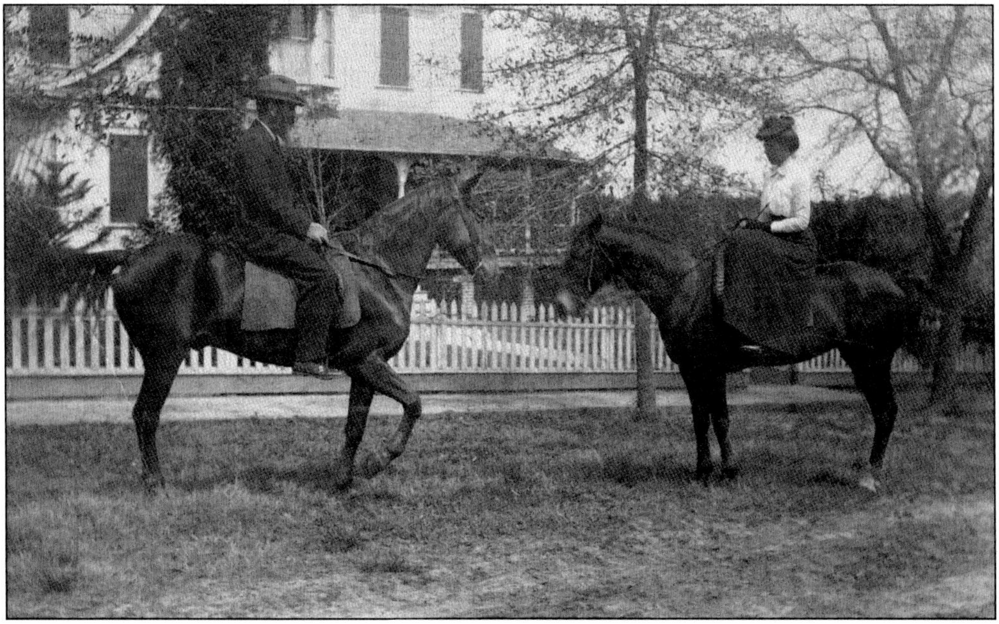

Algernon Haden, seen here with his wife, Clara Georgiana Haden, joined the English Colony in Orlando in the 1880s, but rather than oranges, he cultivated pineapples, which produced more quickly than citrus trees. After his pineapples froze, he planted oranges. He also owned an artificial palm company and the Orlando Telephone Company for a time.

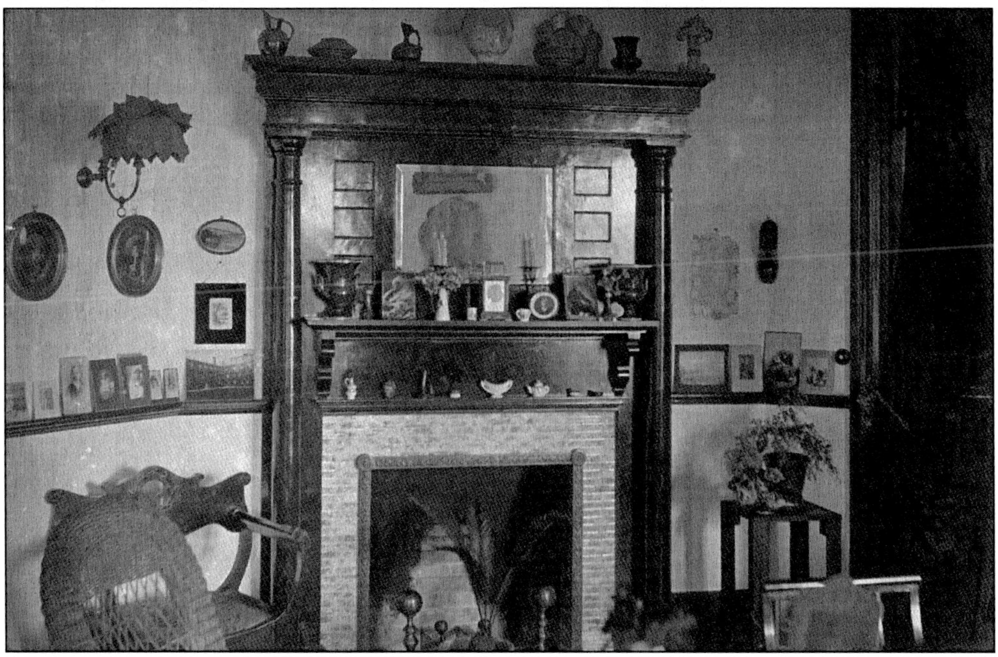

In 1902, Beatrice Alice Smyth sold property at the northeast corner of Magnolia Avenue and Washington Street to Clara Haden, who was apparently her sister. The Hadens built a house that they called Nightingale Lodge; the interior of which is seen here. Algernon Haden died in 1934, and Clara in 1939. By 1939, a gas station had replaced the Haden House. Today, high-rise office and condominium buildings occupy the site.

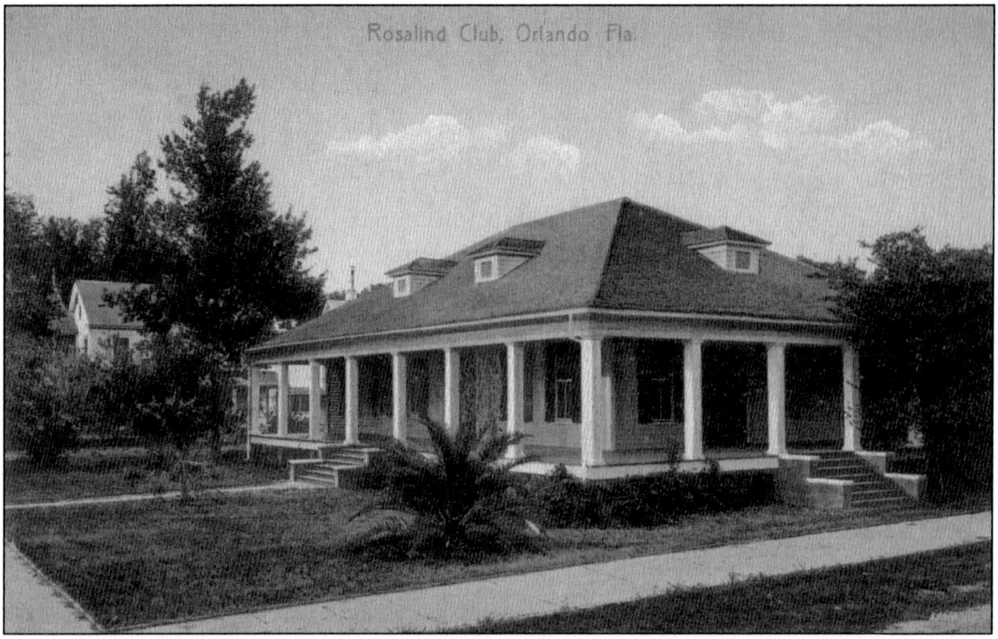

The Rosalind Club, an exclusive ladies' social club formed in 1894, built a clubhouse at the corner of Orange Avenue and Wall Street in 1903. They sold the property in 1919 and moved to Rosalind Avenue. The building was moved to Orange Avenue and Colonial Drive and became a rooming house before its demolition in 1952. The Angebilt Hotel occupies the original site of the Rosalind Club.

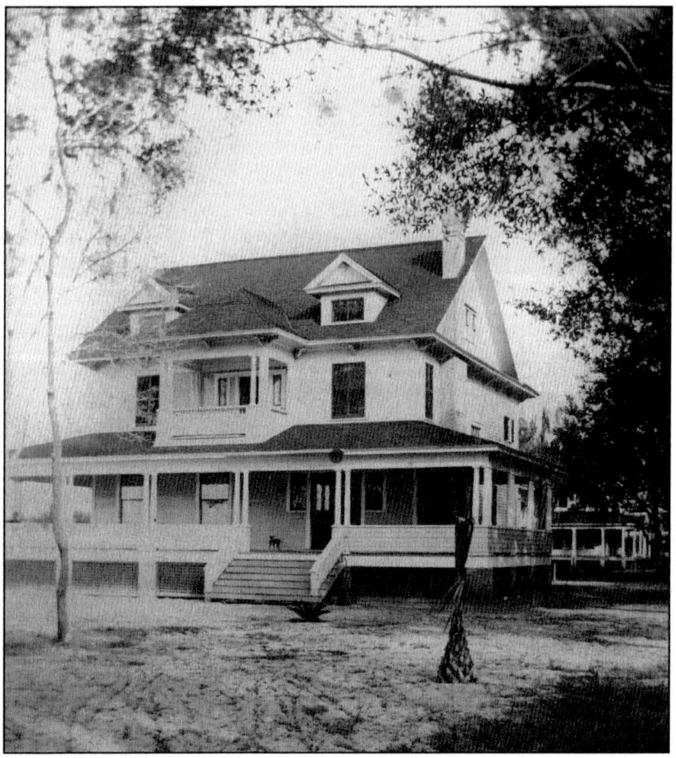

In 1904, S. Waters Howe built a house on Lake Eola, which he sold to Benjamin Drew of the Yowell Drew Department Store in 1907. Drew sold the home in 1920 to the Orlando Elks Lodge, and the Elks met in the Howe House until 1969. An apartment building opened on the site in 2000.

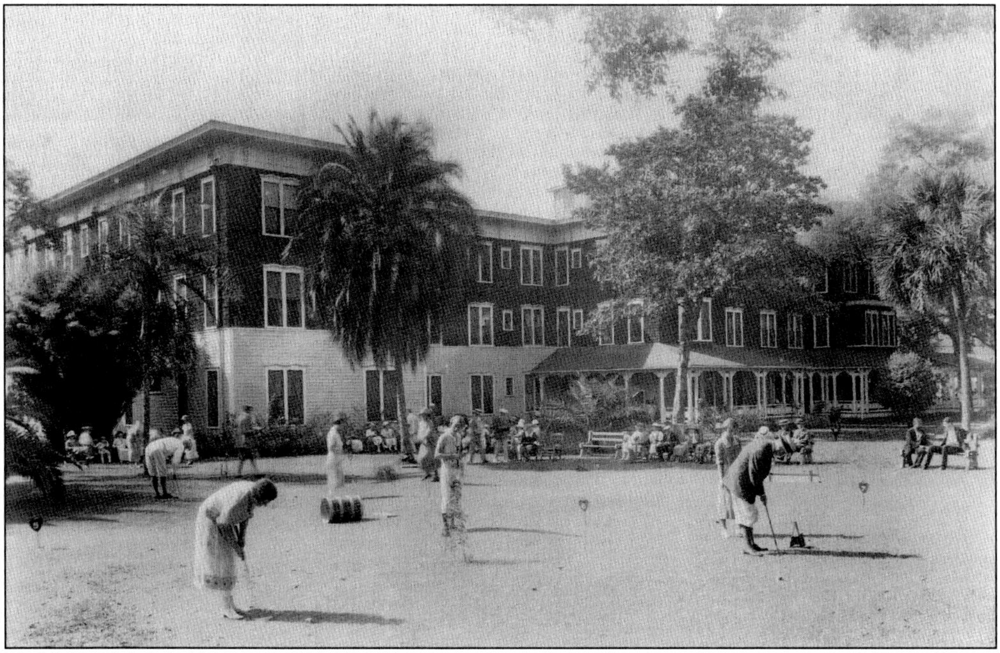

The Nat Poyntz House, constructed in 1886 on North Magnolia Avenue, became the Darrow Hotel in 1900. Albert Miller bought it in 1905, renamed it the Wyoming Hotel, and built a large addition in 1923. The hotel became famous for its gracious accommodations and select clientele during the winter seasons. Sold in 1955, the Wyoming Hotel was demolished in 1959. The Orange County Courthouse now occupies the site.

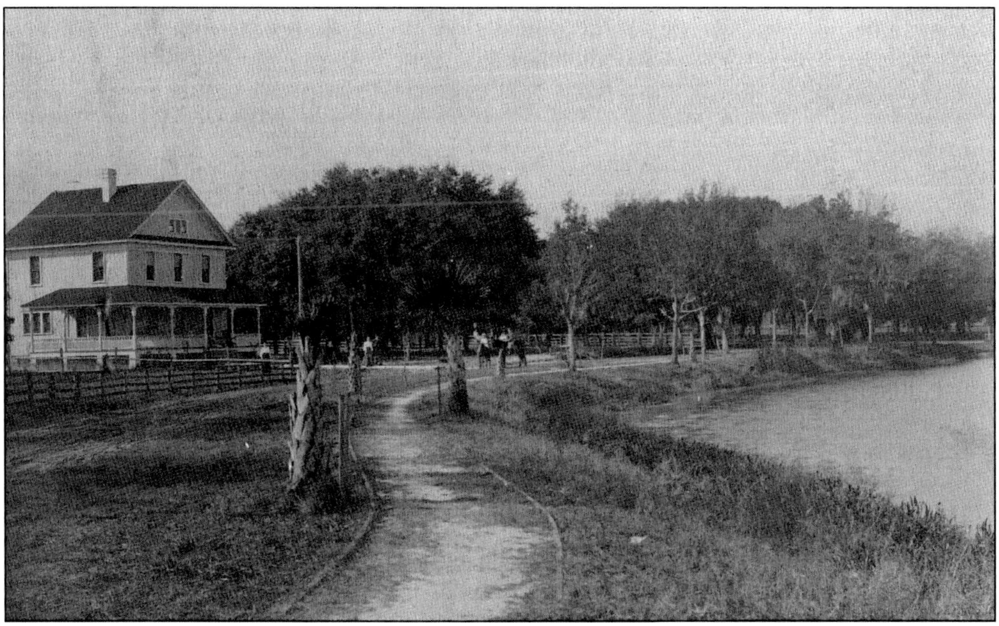

The house at 408 Lucerne Circle probably existed when Mary L. Reichard, wife of Dr. C.C. Reichard, bought the property in 1904. The family sold the house in 1937, and it was demolished between 1955 and 1970. The property changed hands several times, and in 1994, it became part of the Lucerne Medical Center. Today, it is part of the Orlando Regional Medical Center.

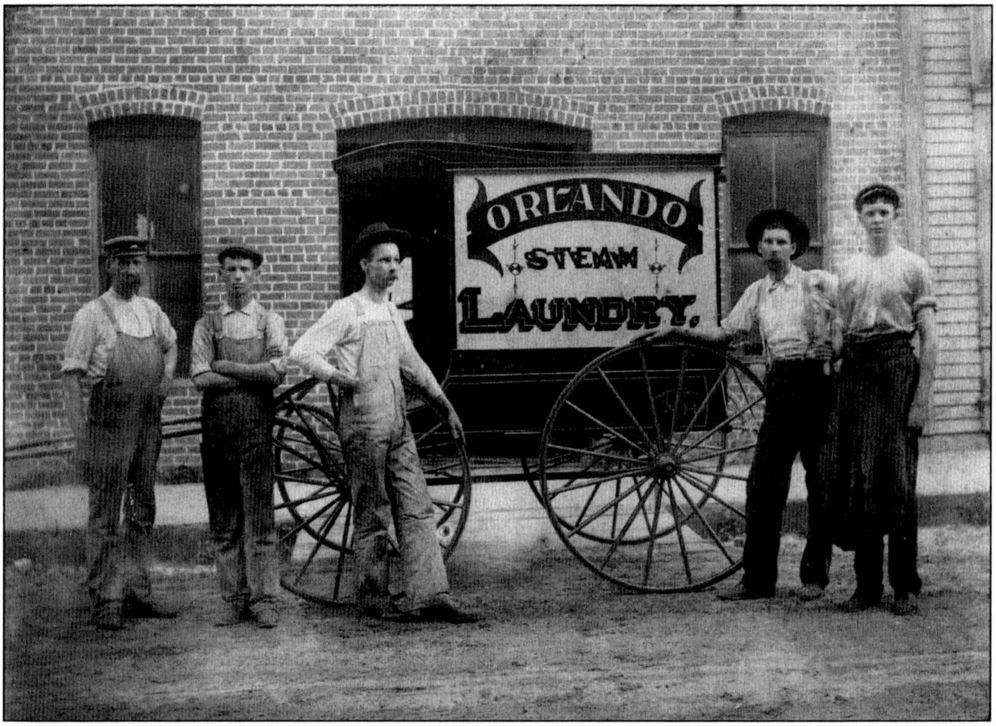

Ernest Holden took out a building permit in 1906 to erect a brick structure at 24 East Church Street for a steam laundry. His Orlando Steam Laundry grew to include cement block additions to the original building in 1910 and 1911. The Orlando Steam Laundry French Dry Cleaners attracted customers, and by 1916, the company employed 40 people. Holden sold the enterprise in 1919, and the new owner moved most of the operations to a larger site on West Concord Street in 1924; however, business continued in the building on East Church Street until 1946. Various businesses occupied the structure until 1969, when the entire block was demolished. A high-rise office building went up on the site in 1982.

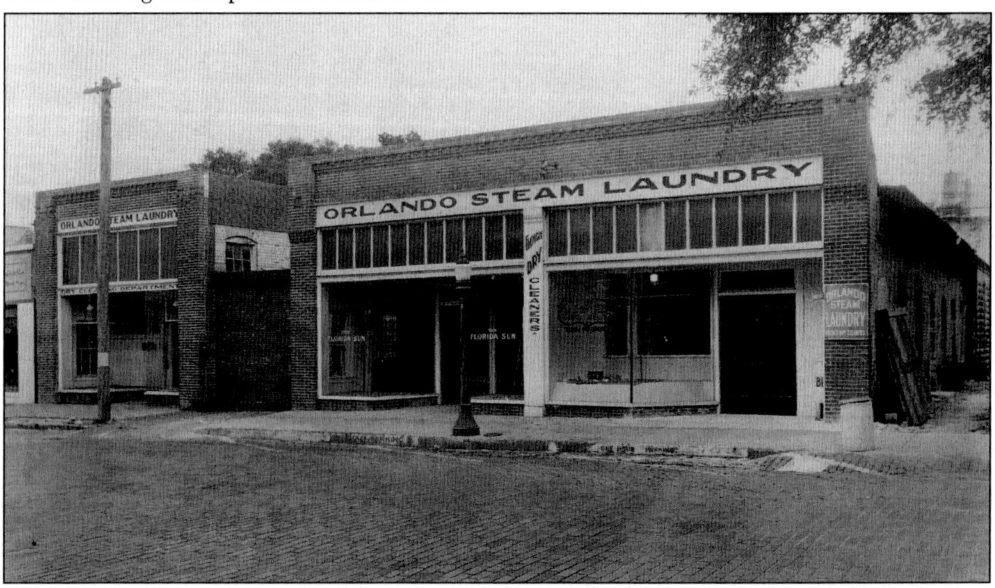

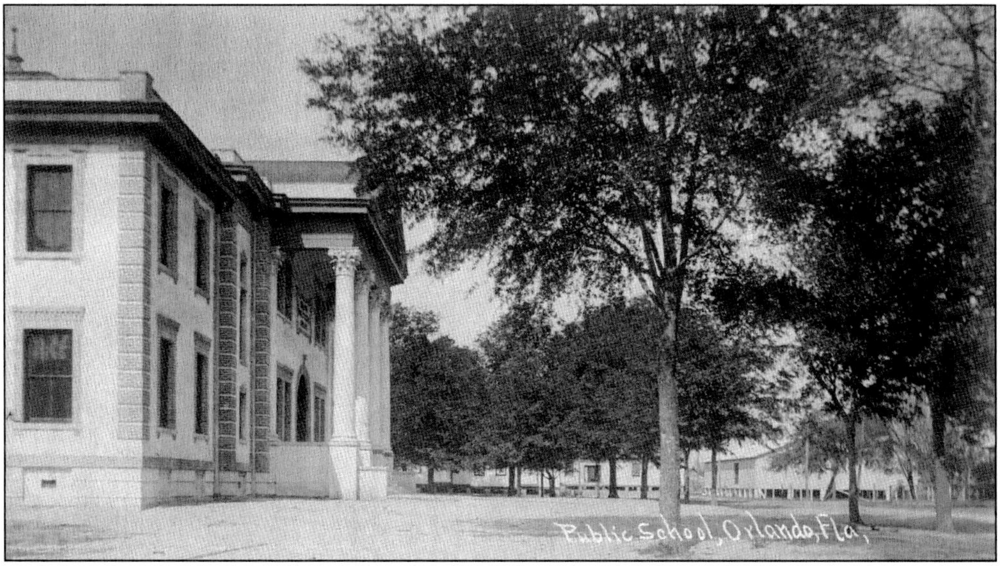

The Orlando Public School on South Orange Avenue was built of bricks in 1906 on the site of the original school, which burned in 1905. It served as the public school until 1922 and became city hall in 1924. When the city government moved out in 1958, it became the police headquarters. The building was torn down in 1972, and Orlando City Hall now occupies this site.

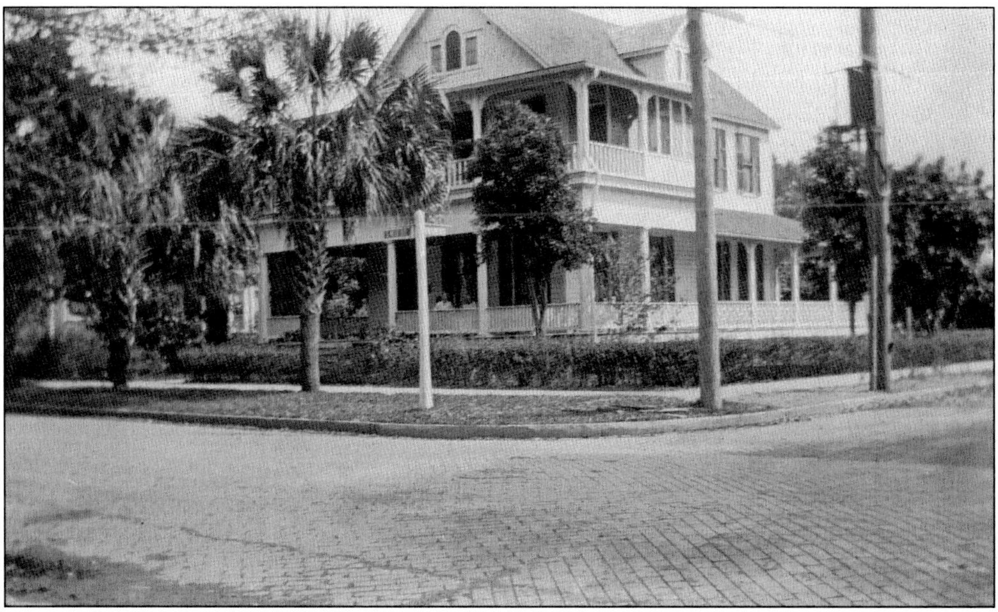

Edward Kuhl built several cottages between Jackson and South Streets about 1901, possibly including Joseph Meistermann's house at 307 Rosalind Avenue. Meistermann lived there in 1907 and cultivated pineapples. In 1919, Meistermann's widow, Charlotte, lived in the house with her niece Bertha Hamester, who continued to reside there for 40 years. The house was demolished by 1955 to build a gas station.

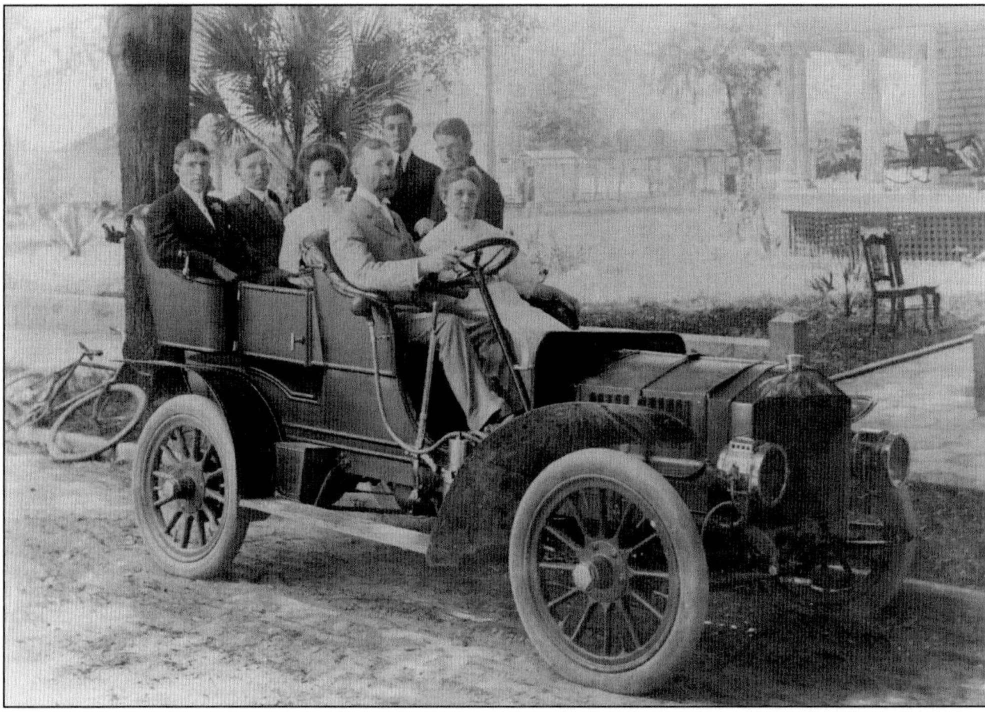

Joseph L. Guernsey, seen here with his family in front of their home, moved to Orlando from Kentucky in 1886 and bought a citrus grove. He traded his grove for Cassius Boone's hardware store in 1895, and went into the hardware business. Guernsey bought land on Lake Eola at East Central Boulevard and North Osceola Street in 1903, and by 1907, he had moved into a house on the property.

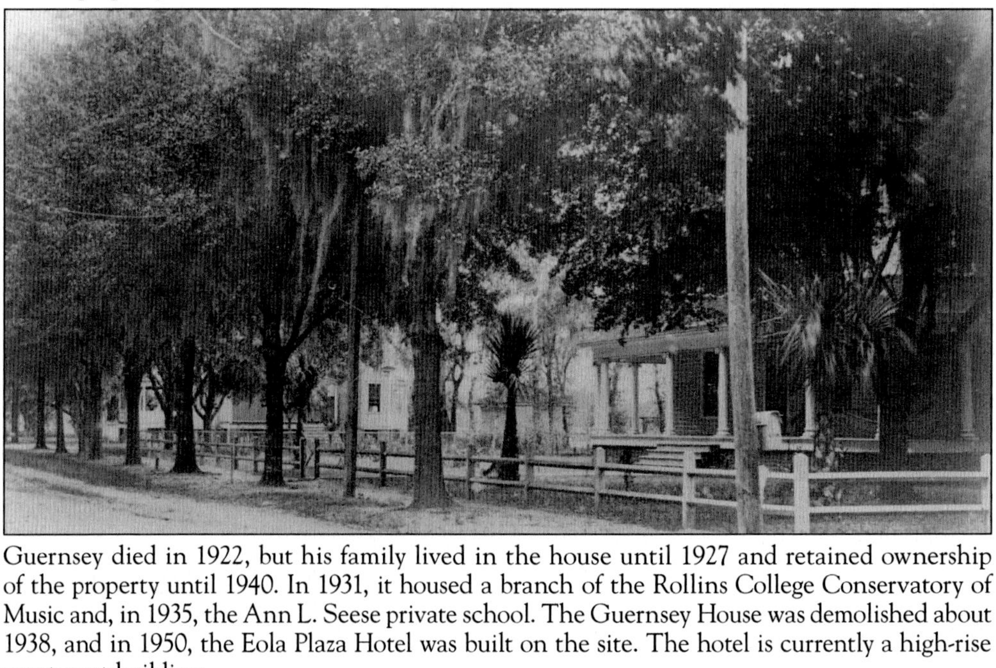

Guernsey died in 1922, but his family lived in the house until 1927 and retained ownership of the property until 1940. In 1931, it housed a branch of the Rollins College Conservatory of Music and, in 1935, the Ann L. Seese private school. The Guernsey House was demolished about 1938, and in 1950, the Eola Plaza Hotel was built on the site. The hotel is currently a high-rise apartment building.

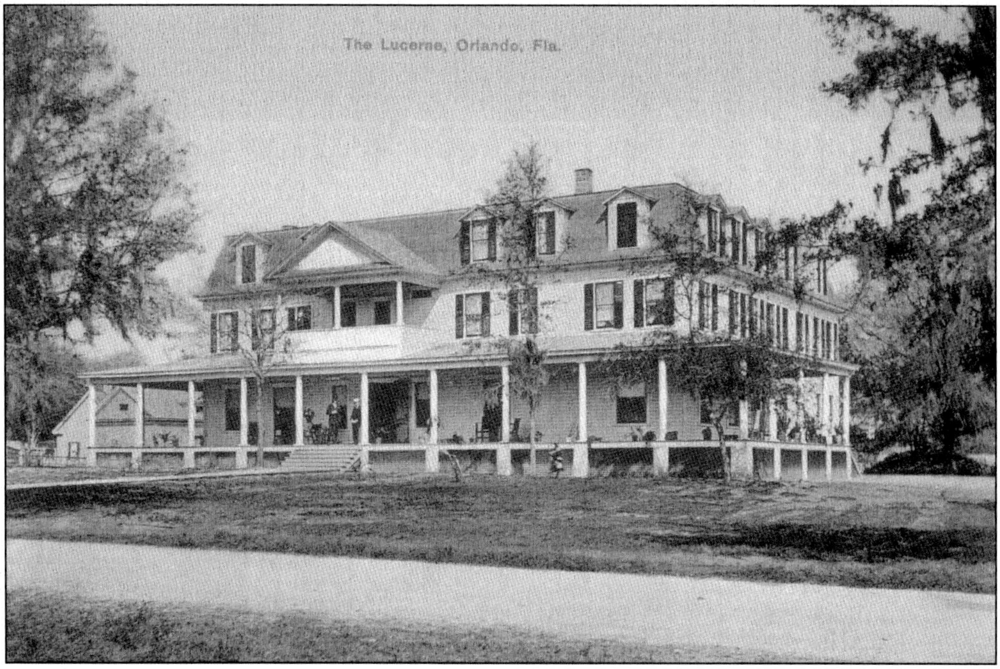

In 1907, Robert S. Rowland built the New Lucerne Hotel, seen in this undated postcard, at the southeast corner of Magnolia Avenue and South Street. His wife, Annie J. Rowland, bought the property in 1904, and in 1911, the Rowlands spent $8,000 to add 30 rooms to the hotel, which is visible in the photograph above. They operated the hotel until 1933, when they sold to Herman Hillman, who in turn sold to Fred Hillman in 1939. Twenty years later, Fred Hillman's wife, Elsie, added her three daughters to the property deed. In 1967, Wayne Harper, husband of one of the Hillman daughters, signed the demolition contract for the New Lucerne Hotel. The First United Methodist Church of Orlando acquired the property in 1988 and sold it to the City of Orlando in 2009 for the Dr. Phillips Center for the Performing Arts.

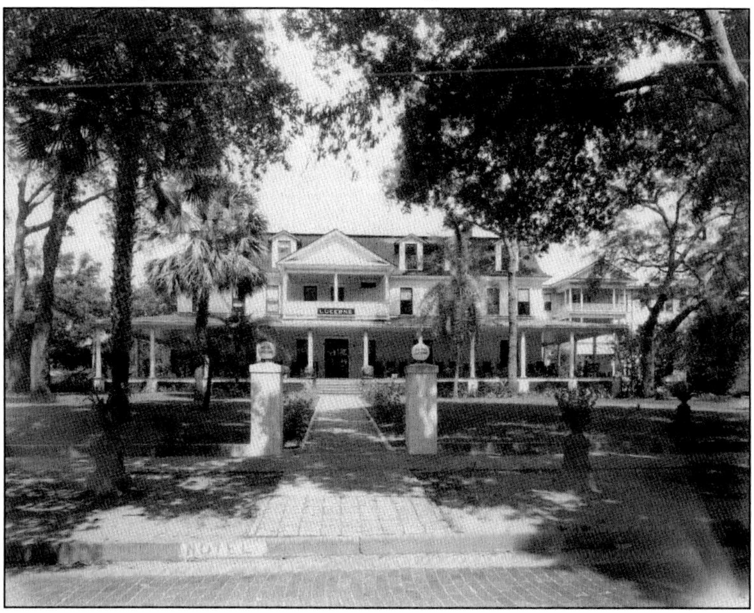

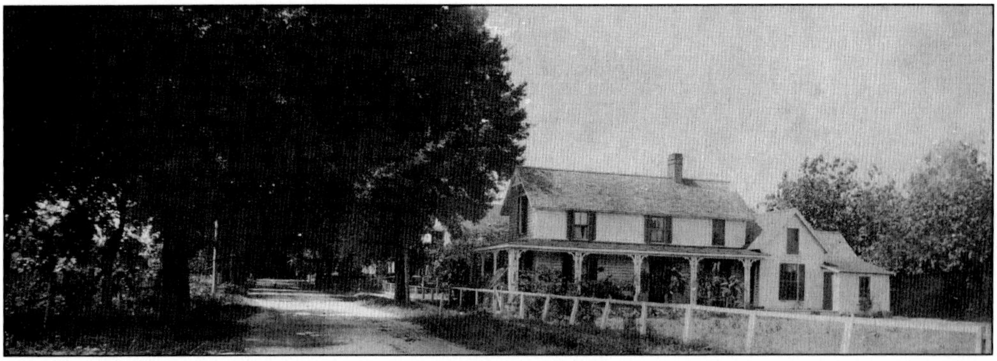

The house at 404 Boone Street appears for the first time in the 1912 city directory as a bowling alley owned by W.M. van Brunt, seated in the elevated chair visible at the far right in the photograph below. This interior shot shows Augusta Wright, left, and Beth Branham standing at the end of the lanes as they enjoy a game of bowling with friends at van Brunt's. J.W. McElroy owned the structure in 1916, but no evidence suggests he operated a bowling alley. By 1919, a brick building housing the Lewis-Chitty Wholesale Grocery covered the whole block, and the long, narrow house was gone.

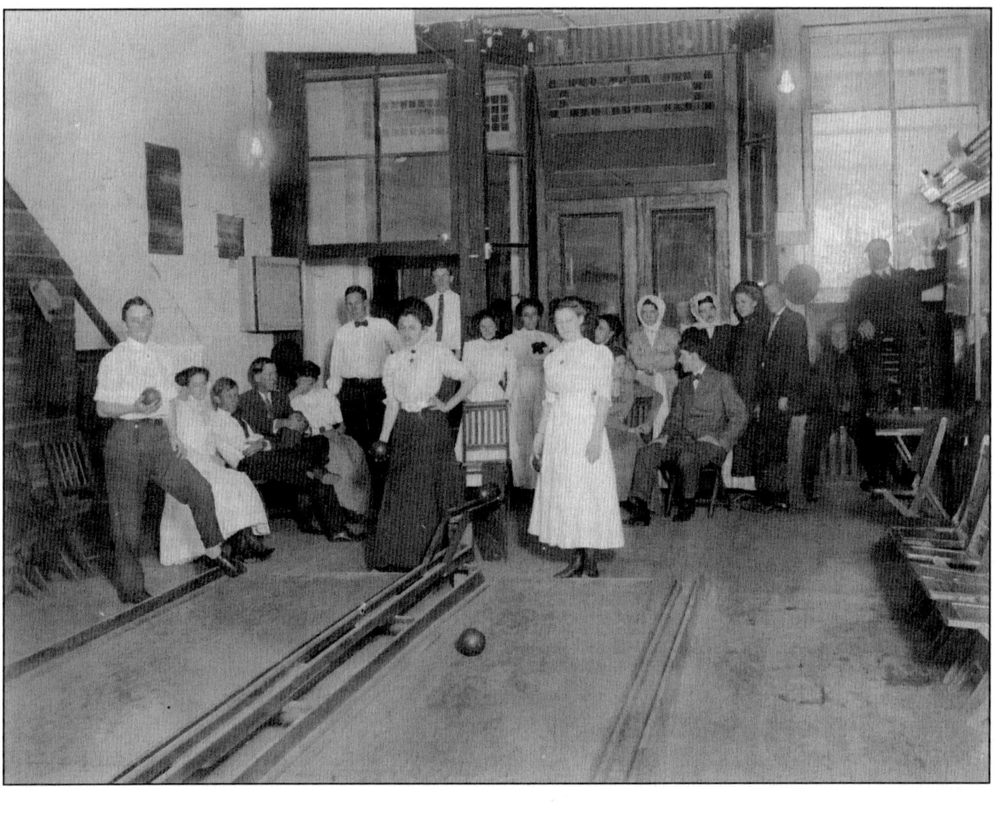

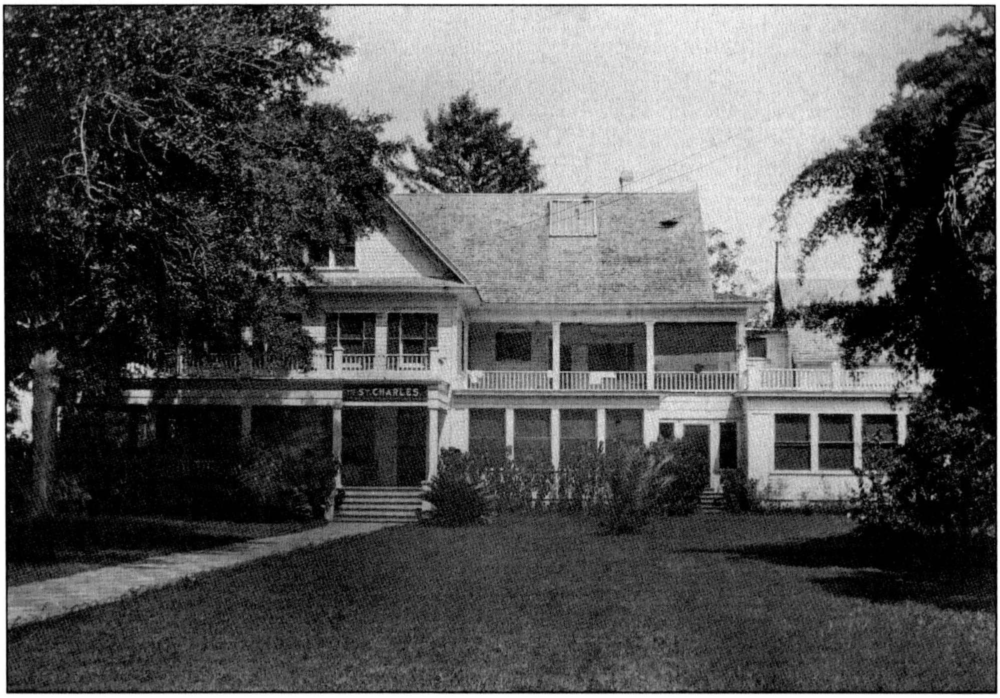

Anna Hilpert opened the St. Charles Hotel in 1908 in a former hospital on Washington Street that she bought from Dr. R.L. Harris; however, the building was probably there when Doctor Harris bought the property in 1901. Hilpert sold it in 1925, and part of the building was demolished. In 1929, the remaining portion became part of the three-story Fidelity Building at 60 North Court Street.

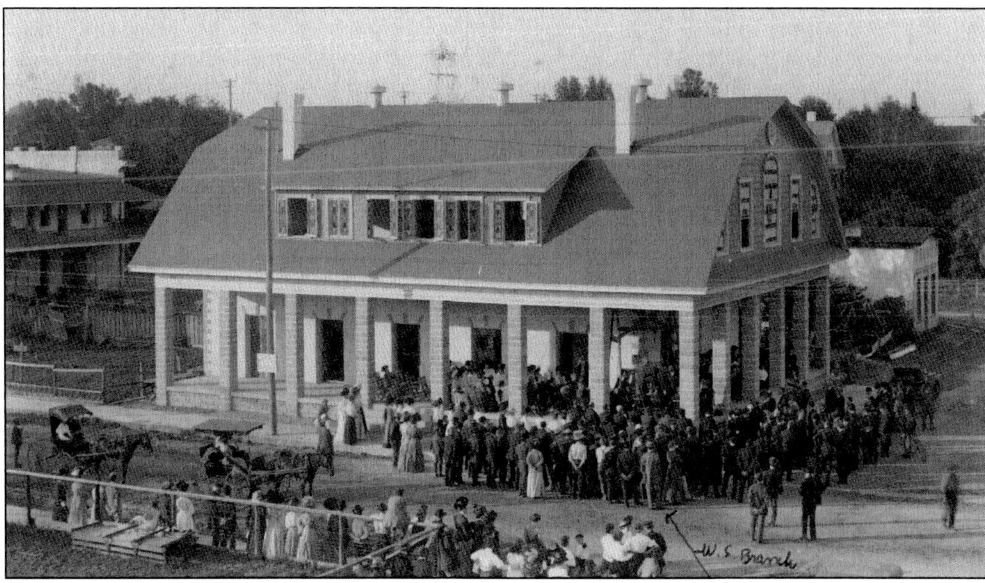

The Elks Club organized in 1907 and dedicated their lodge building on East Central Boulevard at Court Street in 1908. They remodeled the structure in 1918, adding stores on the first floor, and moved to a new location in 1919. The old Elks lodge was demolished in 1957, when Court Street was relocated to make space for the Courthouse Annex.

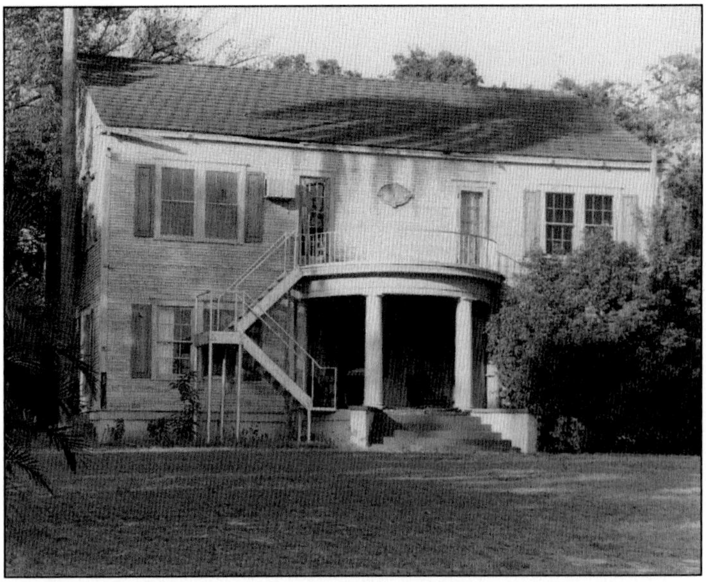

Harold Bourne, one of a group of immigrants known as the English Colony, came to Orlando in 1882. In 1920, he bought a large, two-story frame house that W.E. Wright built on the north side of Lake Cherokee about 1908. A citrus grower in the Conway area, Bourne hosted memorable gatherings in the house, where he lived until 1951. In 1982, the Cherokee Place Condominiums replaced the Bourne House.

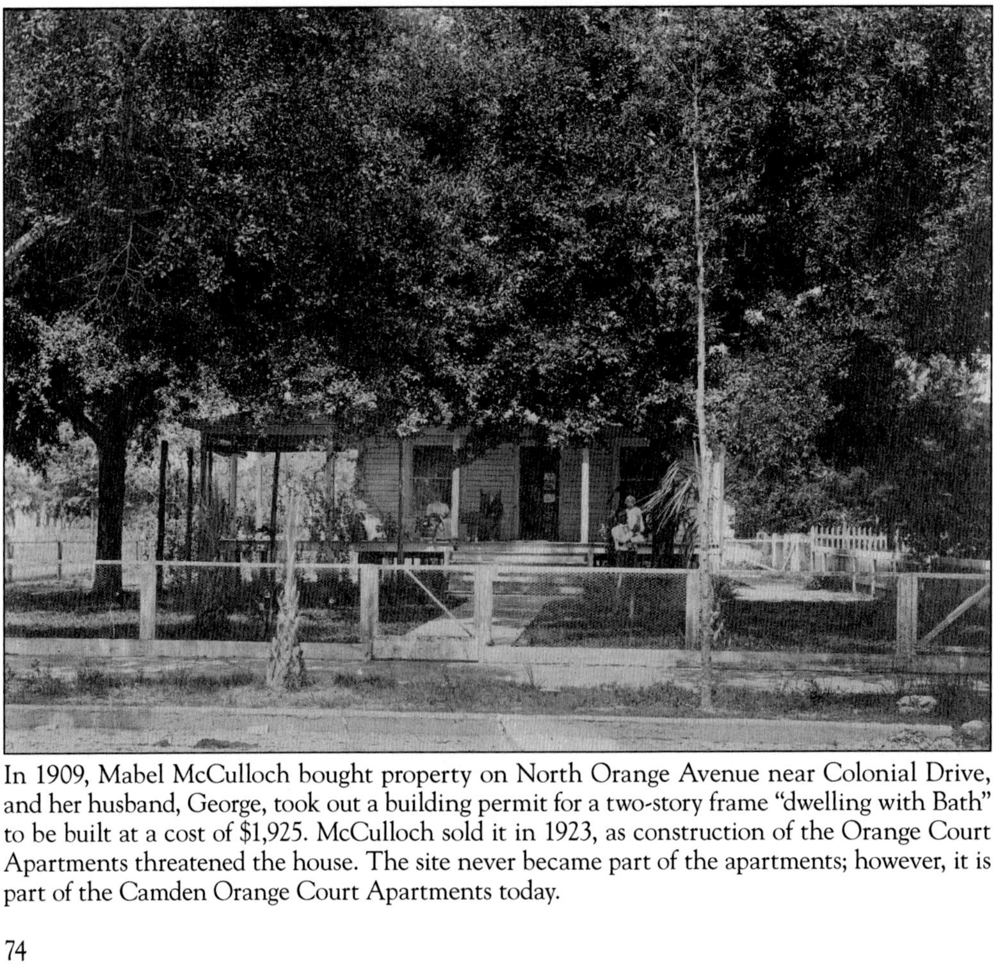

In 1909, Mabel McCulloch bought property on North Orange Avenue near Colonial Drive, and her husband, George, took out a building permit for a two-story frame "dwelling with Bath" to be built at a cost of $1,925. McCulloch sold it in 1923, as construction of the Orange Court Apartments threatened the house. The site never became part of the apartments; however, it is part of the Camden Orange Court Apartments today.

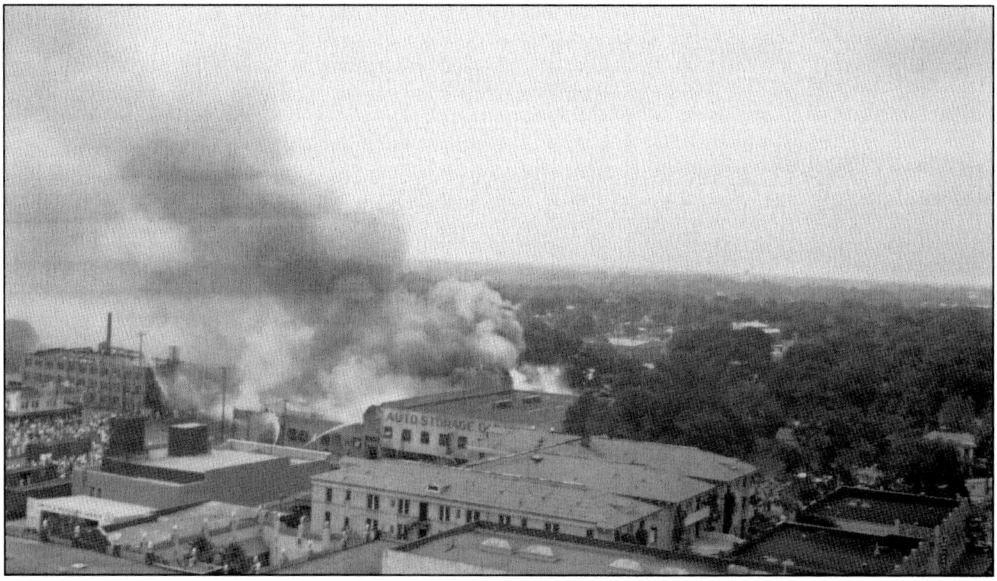

Constructed about 1909 between Jefferson Avenue and Robinson Street at the railroad, the Dr. Phillips packinghouse went up in a spectacular blaze in 1936, as seen in this photograph. Dr. Phillips became the largest of the great citrus companies, with packinghouses lining the railroad from Amelia to South Streets. The Dr. Phillips Company still owns the property, which is now occupied by office buildings and garages constructed in the 1940s.

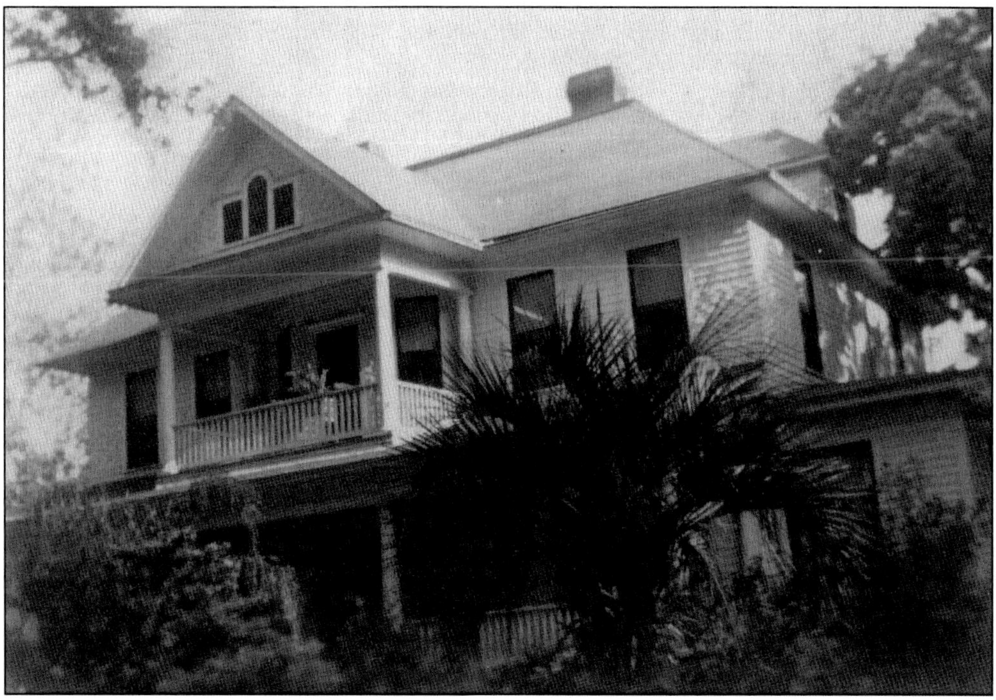

Eugene Duckworth bought property on East Jackson Street in 1904, where he built a house that he sold to Newton Yowell in 1909. The Yowell House was demolished in 1950, and the property was sold to the Methodist Church in 1955. The church sold the property to the City of Orlando in 2009, and today, it is part of the future Dr. Phillips Center for the Performing Arts.

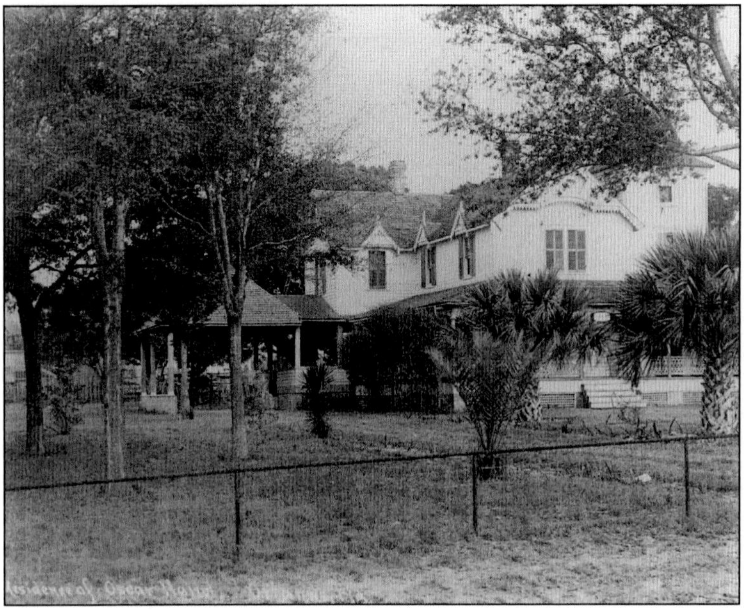

W. Brown probably built the Oscar Hand House on Lake Ivanhoe in the 1880s. In 1911, Hand bought it from William Daniels, and in 1948, the house became the Hand Apartments. It remained in business as the Shady Oaks Apartments until 1963. Interstate 4 now crosses Lake Ivanhoe near the site.

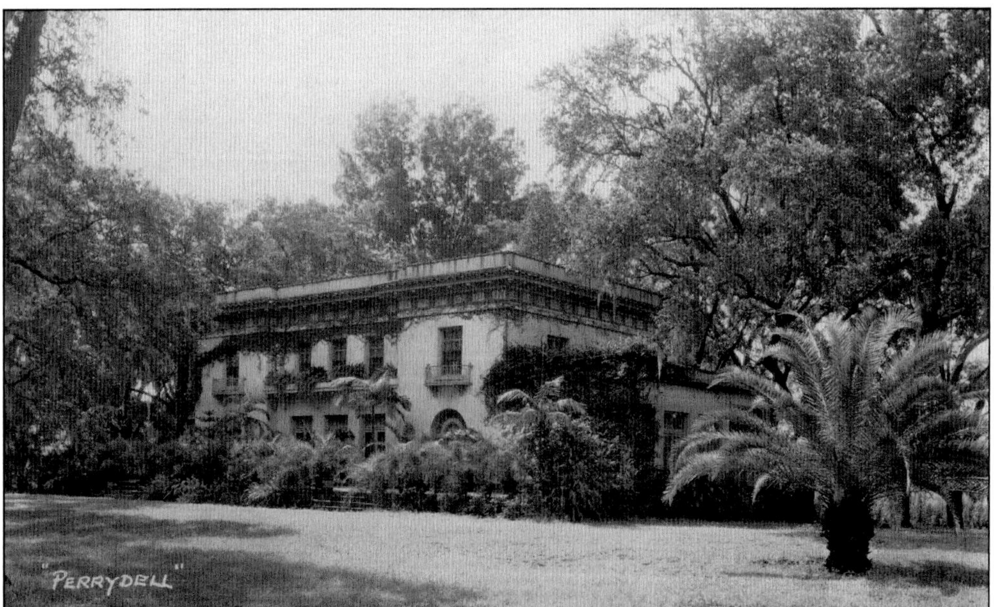

In 1911, Harry L. Beeman of Beemans Chewing Gum built a $12,000, 10-room house on Gore Street. His family lived in the house until 1930. By 1936, it had become the Perrydell Tea Room, shown in this photograph by T.P. Robinson. In the 1970s, the Hampden DuBose Academy acquired the mansion. It was demolished by 1988 to make room for the expansion of Orlando Regional Medical Center.

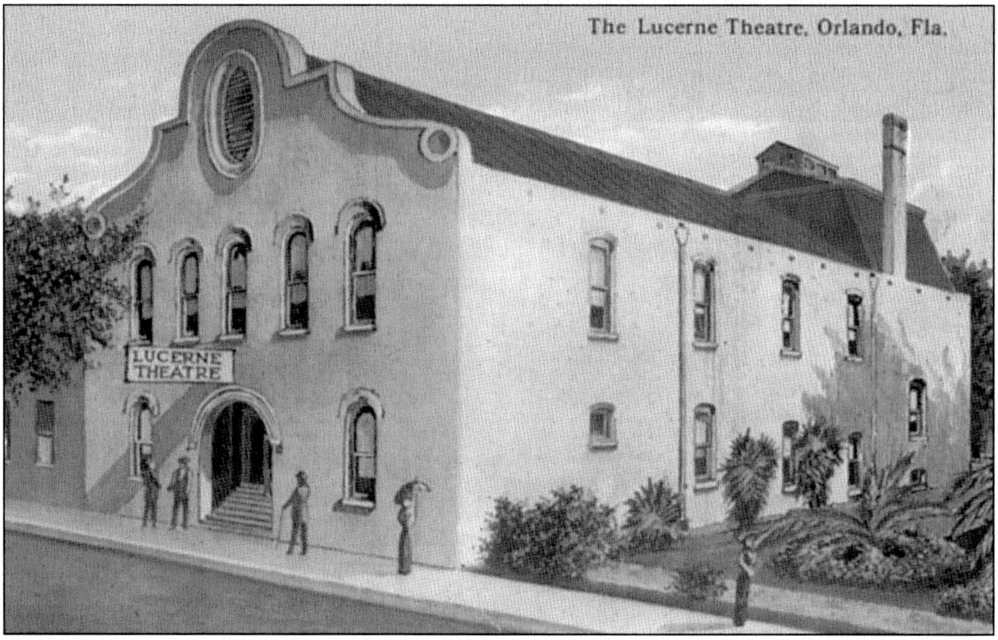

Orlando's second opera house, the Lucerne Theatre, opened in 1911 on South Magnolia Avenue. Built to seat 1,000 people with designated sections for African Americans, the theater offered high-class vaudeville. It was remodeled into stores in 1925 and designated a local historic landmark in 1973. Unused and boarded up, it was demolished in 1997. Today, high-rise condominiums and a parking garage have replaced it.

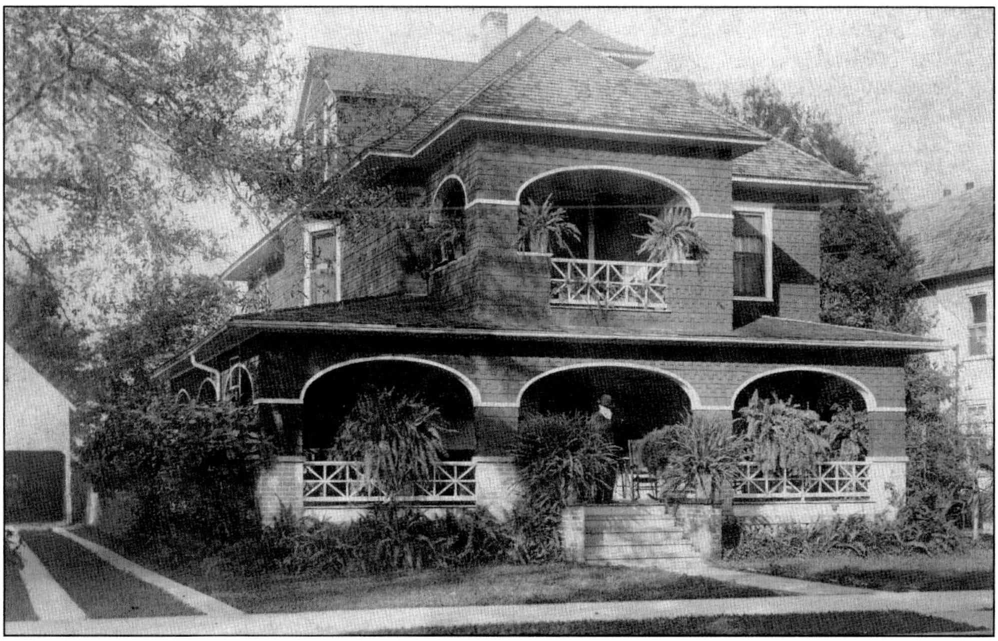

Maria Chapman built a frame house with a metal roof on Orange Avenue in 1912 at a cost of $3,500. Sometime before she sold the house in 1922, she married James Mainland. A parking lot occupied the site by 1927, and by 1955, new commercial blocks replaced all residential structures in that block of North Orange Avenue. Today, the site provides parking for St. James Cathedral.

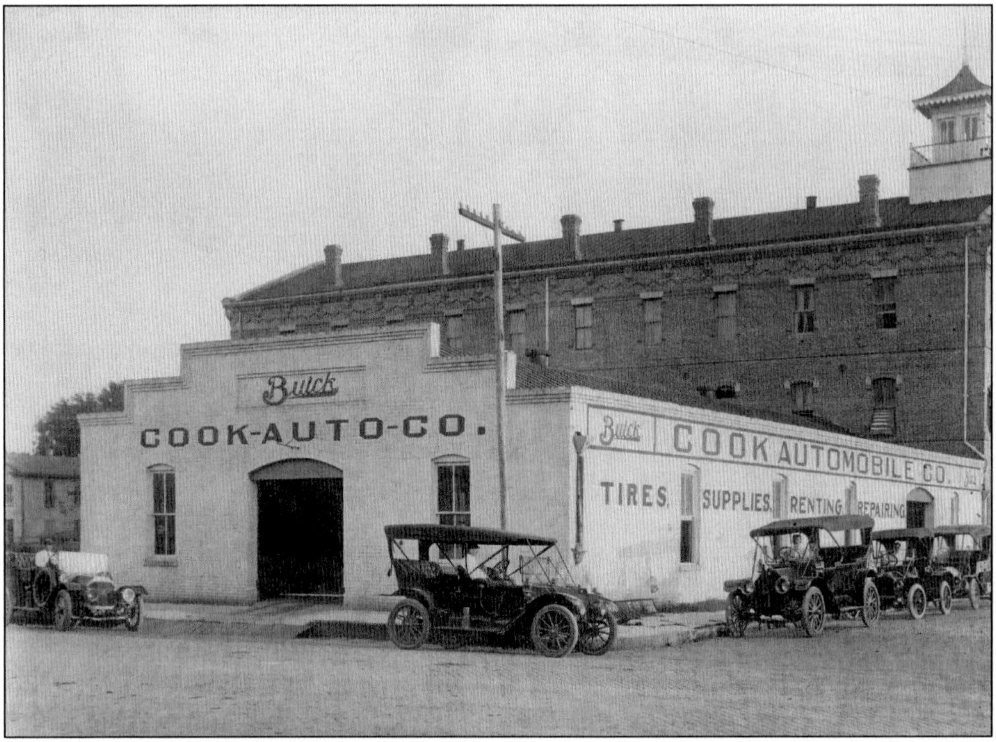

John Cook, born in Orlando in 1874, had a reputation as the city's premier blacksmith. With the popularity of the automobile in the early 1900s, Cook left the blacksmith trade to become Orlando's first auto mechanic. In 1905, he incorporated the Cook Automobile Company and secured a Buick and Cadillac franchise. Over the ensuing years, Cook operated repair shops at several locations in downtown Orlando. With B.C. Abernathy, Cook bought the property on Central Boulevard in front of the Armory in 1914. There, he operated a garage and Buick salesroom. They sold the building in 1917, and it was demolished to construct an arcade in 1925.

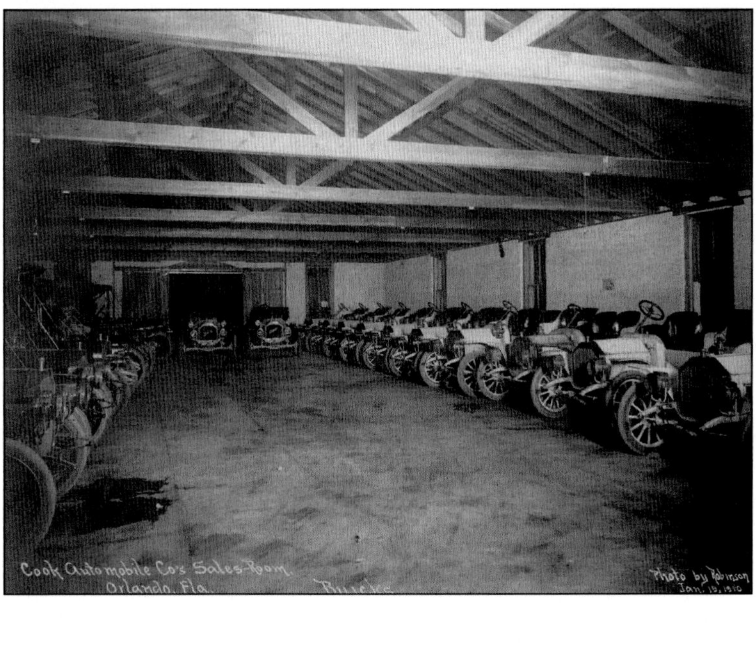

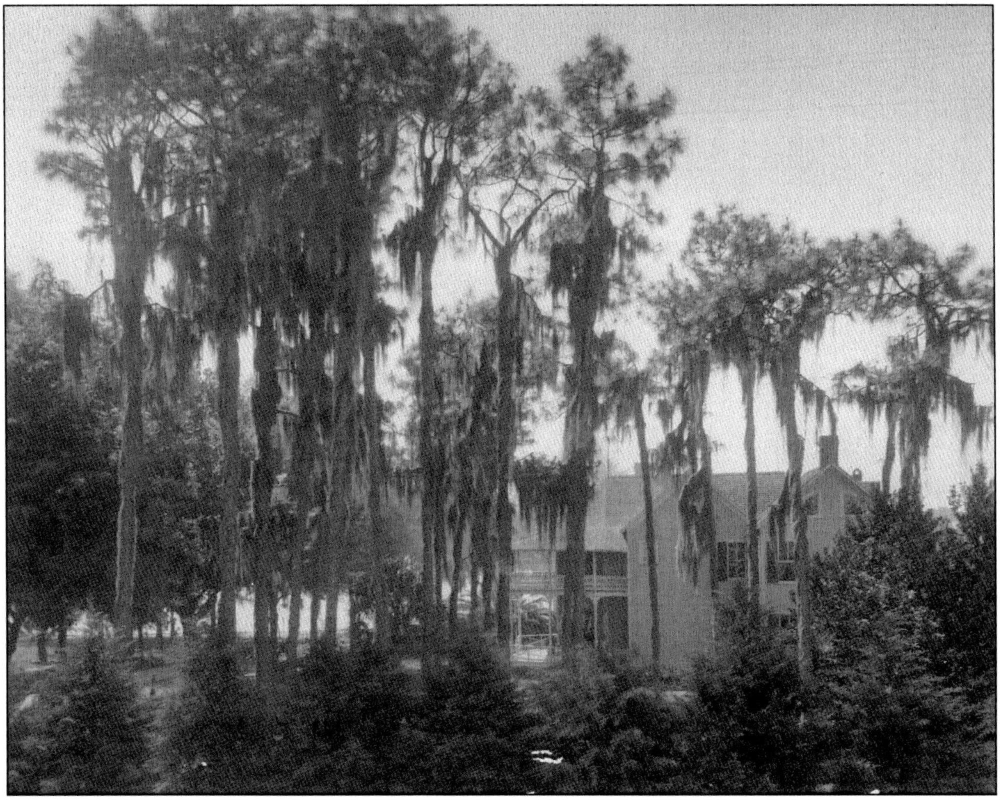

Dr. Calvin Christ and his wife, Elizabeth, lived at 504 South Orange Avenue in a large frame house that resembled a riverboat. Doctor Christ came to Orlando in 1906 to practice medicine. He married in 1911 and moved to the house in 1912. Doctor Christ died in 1938 in his office at the medical clinic he opened on Lucerne Circle, located around the corner from his house.

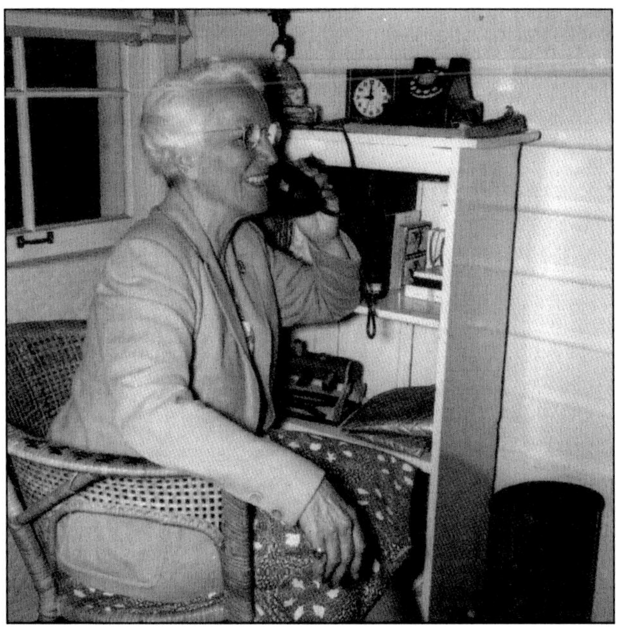

Elizabeth Abbott Christ, shown at right, founded the Girl Scouts in Orlando. This photograph was most likely taken in her home. Elizabeth lived in the house for 10 years after her husband's death. An office in 1948, then a youth center in the 1950s, the house was finally razed in 1967 to clear the space for construction of the Orlando Utilities Building.

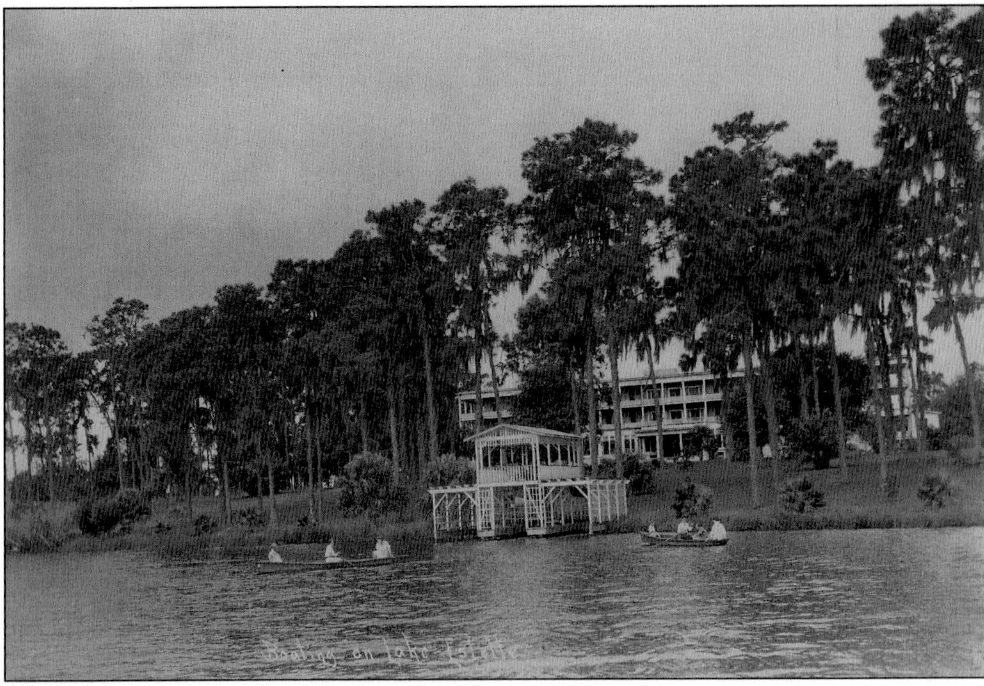

The Florida Seventh Day Adventist Church constructed the main building of the Florida Hospital and Sanitarium in 1912. Dr. R.L. Harris started the hospital about 1900 as a tuberculosis sanitarium in a farmhouse on 52 acres of land on Lake Estelle. In 1908, he sold the property to the Southeastern Seventh Day Adventist Conference. The farmhouse remained the main building until 1912, when the hospital erected the new 2.5-story, concrete block structure. The 1912 building remained unchanged from 1918, when it was enlarged to three stories and doubled in length, until its demolition in the 1960s. The hospital changed its name to Florida Hospital in 1970.

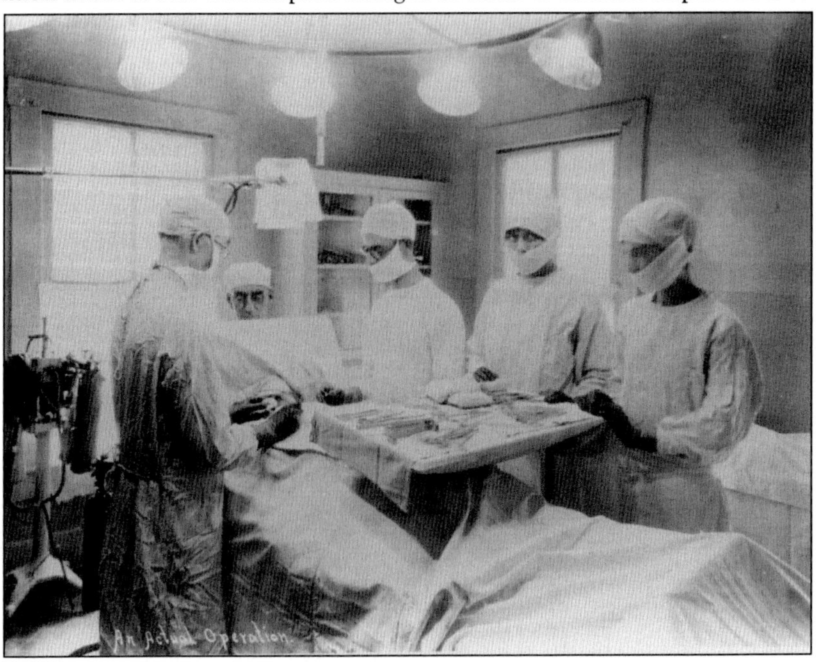

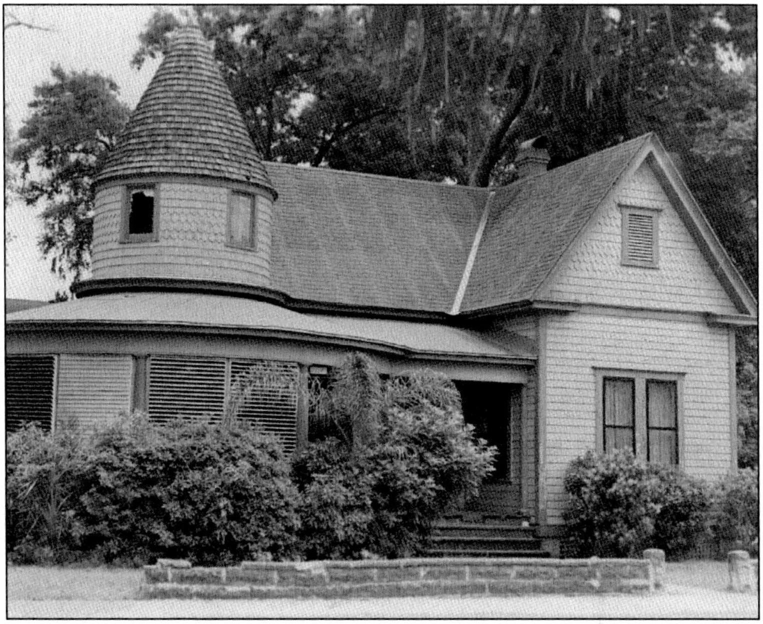

Orlando alderman W.T. Sims lived on Liberty Street in 1912 in a frame house with a distinctive tower and rounded front porch. After Annie Sims sold the house in 1914, it was rented as apartments until 1978. The Sims House was razed by 1984 for the Lutheran Towers retirement complex.

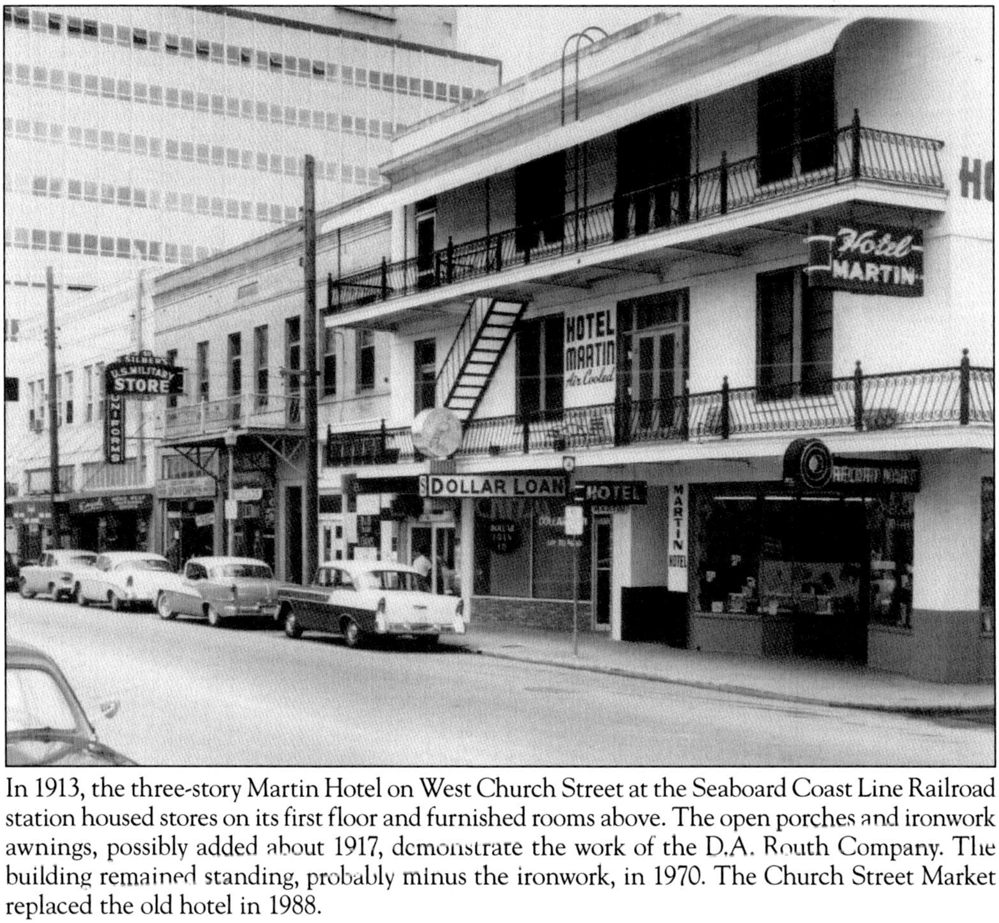

In 1913, the three-story Martin Hotel on West Church Street at the Seaboard Coast Line Railroad station housed stores on its first floor and furnished rooms above. The open porches and ironwork awnings, possibly added about 1917, demonstrate the work of the D.A. Routh Company. The building remained standing, probably minus the ironwork, in 1970. The Church Street Market replaced the old hotel in 1988.

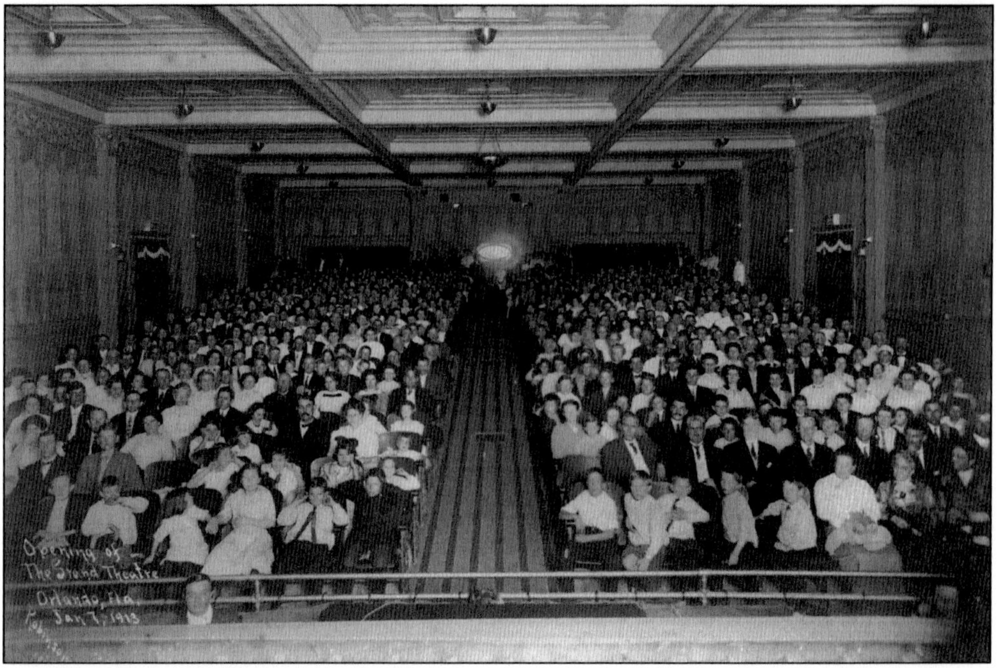

In 1911, Colonel Watkins began construction of the Grand Theatre in the Nashville Block, built in 1886 on West Pine Street. Pictured here on January 7, 1913, the theater opened to much excitement, as evidenced by the packed house. By December, the Montgomery Moving Picture Company took possession of the Grand Theater and brought in crews to make *Romance in Orlando*. The film was shown at the theater in January 1914; advertisements for which are visible outside the building. The theater underwent several operation and ownership changes before becoming the Astor Theatre in 1953. Prior to demolition in 1965, the theater was closed for many years. A nightclub now occupies the site.

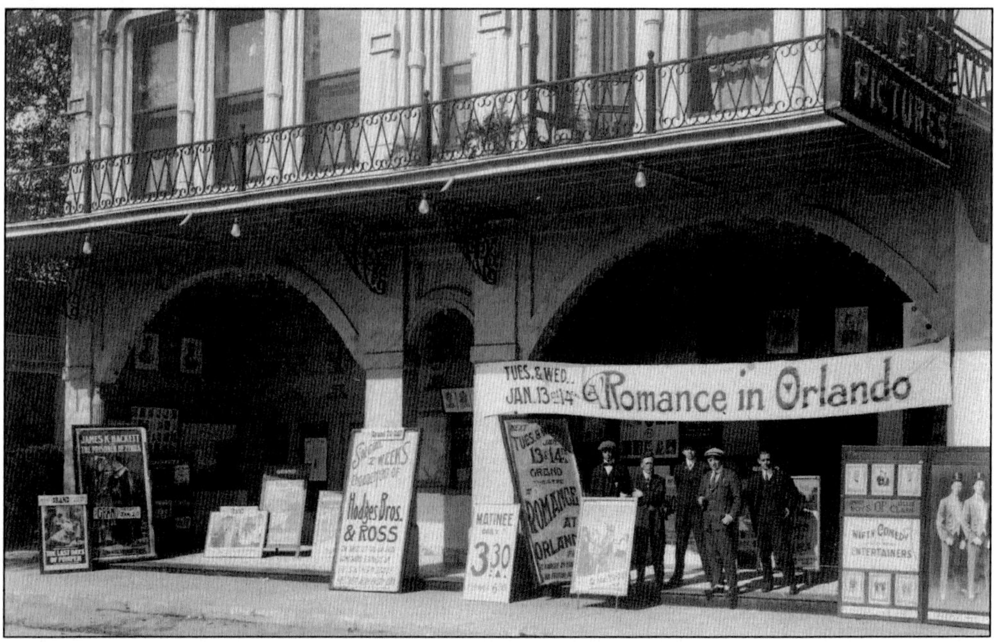

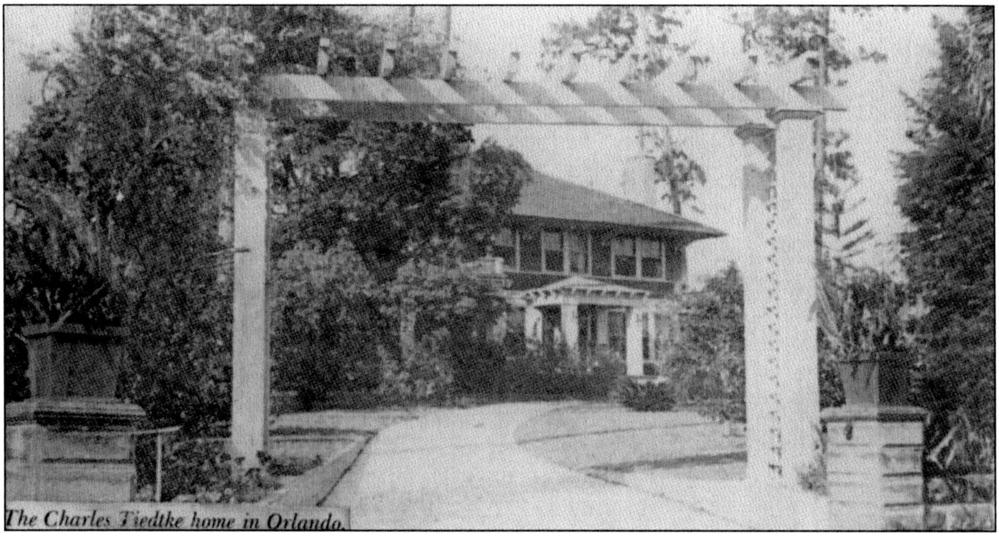

Charles Tiedtke built his house at 103 Hillcrest Street in 1913. The Tiedtkes sold the house in 1936, and it operated as the Carlyn Manor Hotel from 1937 until 1951 when the Young Women's Community Club bought it. The Tiedtke House was razed to clear space for new buildings in 1975. Today, the Coalition for the Homeless occupies the site.

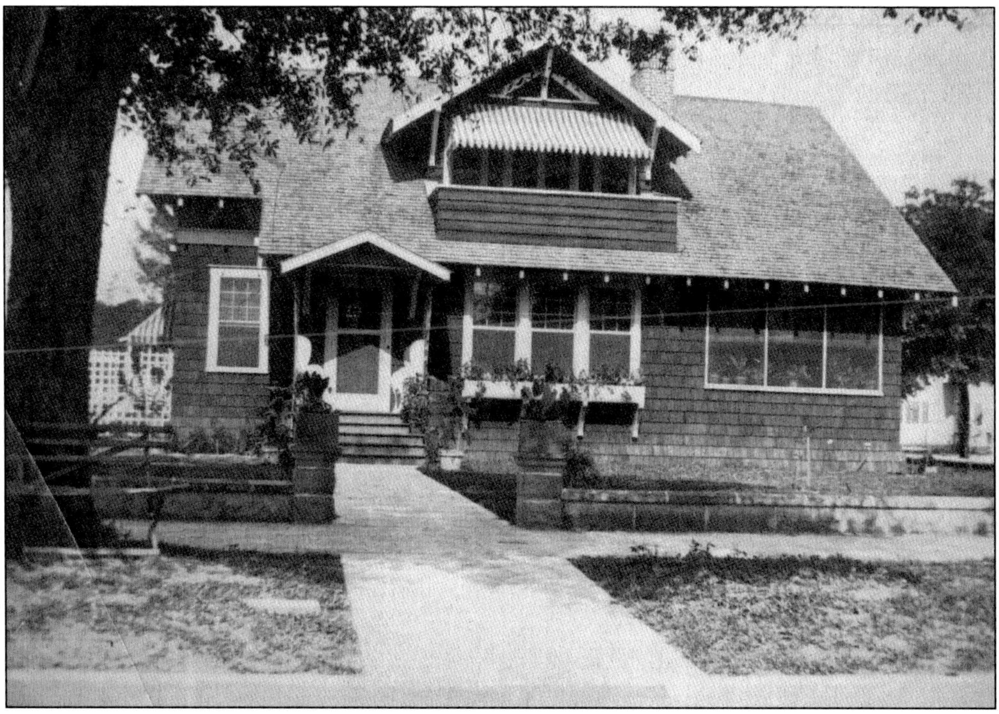

Orlando artist Lu Halsted Tieman designed the house constructed at the corner of Magnolia Avenue and Concord Street in 1914. Listed as the Concord Art Shop with second-floor apartments in the 1920s, it became the Carrigan Apartments in the 1960s. In 1979, the house was sold to the *Sentinel Star*. The Tieman House was demolished in 1978, and the *Orlando Sentinel* now occupies the site.

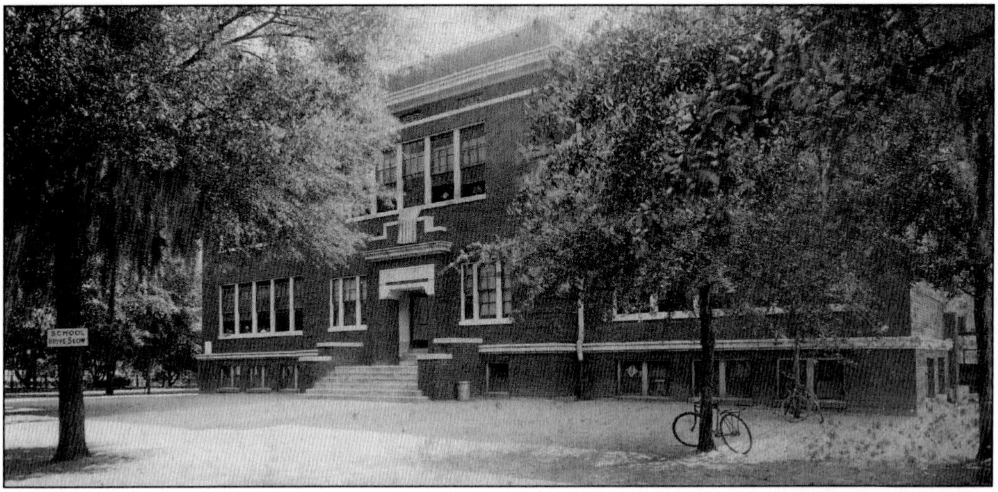

Magnolia School opened in September 1914 on Magnolia Avenue, now 325 Palmetto Avenue, as Orlando's first elementary school. The city purchased five million bricks from the Copeland -Ingles Shale Brick Company of Birmingham, Alabama, to construct the three-story building. The plumbing cost $2,958, and the wiring was $545.75. During the 1920s, the building served as the high school until the completion of Orlando High School, now Howard Middle School, in 1927. From 1938 to 1981, the building served as the Orlando Vocational School. It even housed the Orlando Junior College for three years in the early 1940s. On October 10, 1982, fire raced through the building. Flames could be seen from Interstate 4. Vacant commercial structures now occupy the site.

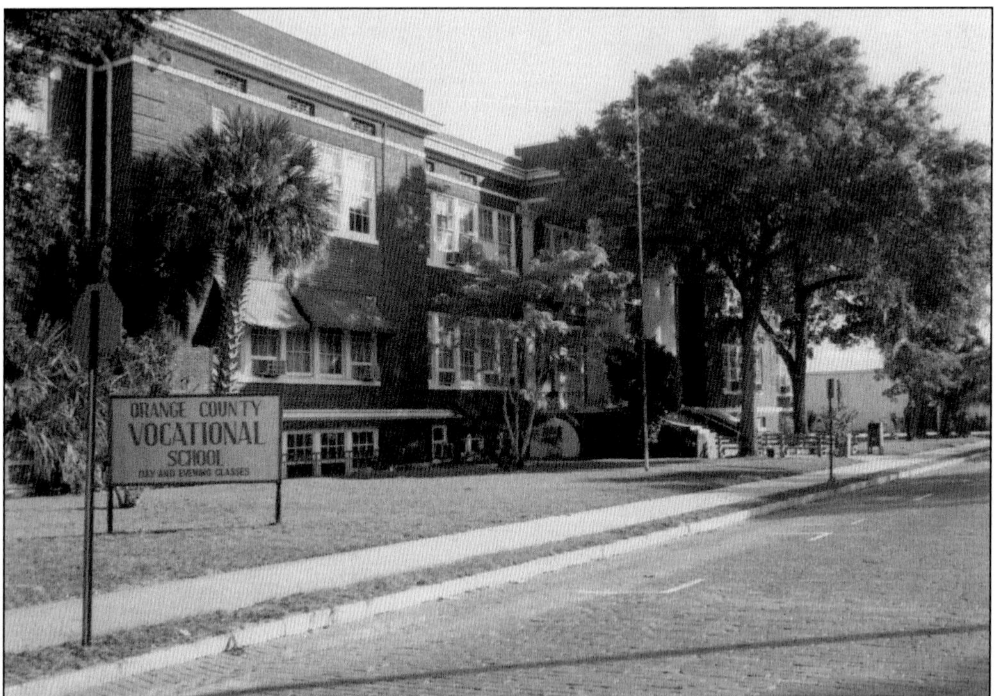

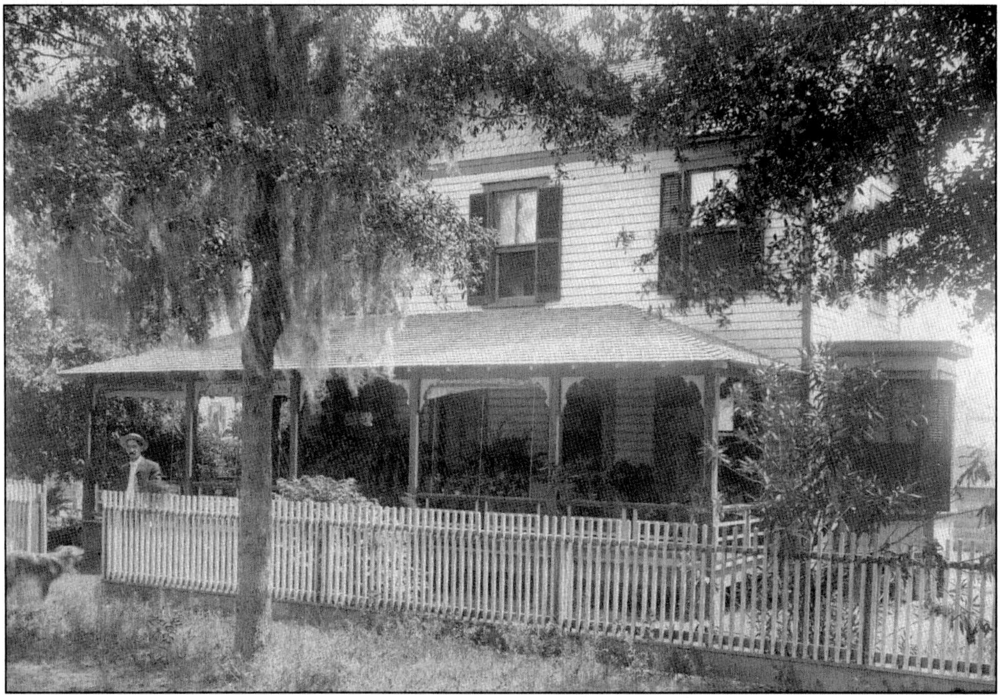

Orlando photographer T.P. Robinson was born in Holly Springs, Mississippi, in 1870. In 1875, he moved with his family to Zellwood, Florida, where his father began growing oranges. Robinson married Mary Sherman Field in 1899 and took up photography as a hobby. In 1906, he opened a commercial photography studio and soon became one of Orlando's most prolific photographers. Many of his photographs can be seen throughout this book. Robinson and one of his beloved collies appear in the image above in front of the home he purchased on Weber Street in 1915. Fittingly, the Downtown Pet Hospital now occupies the site.

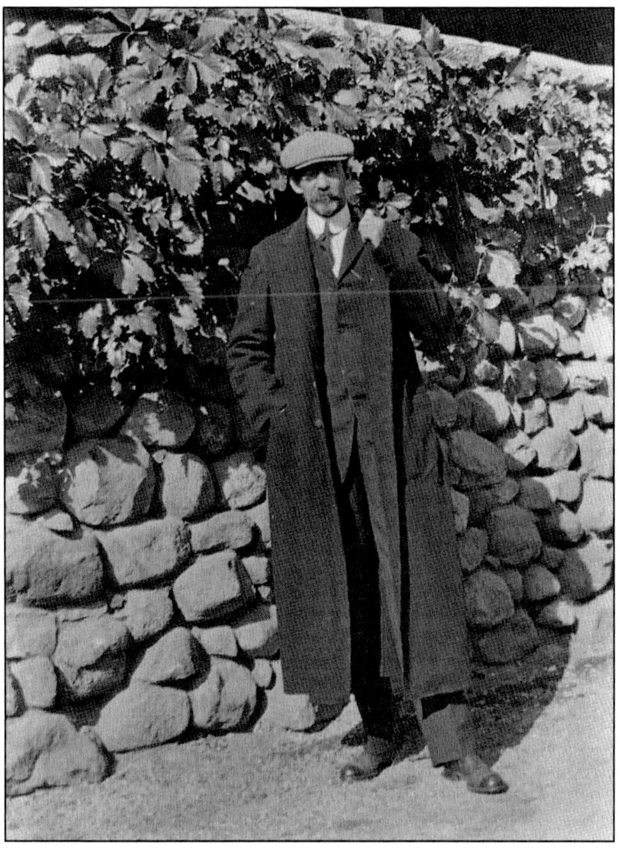

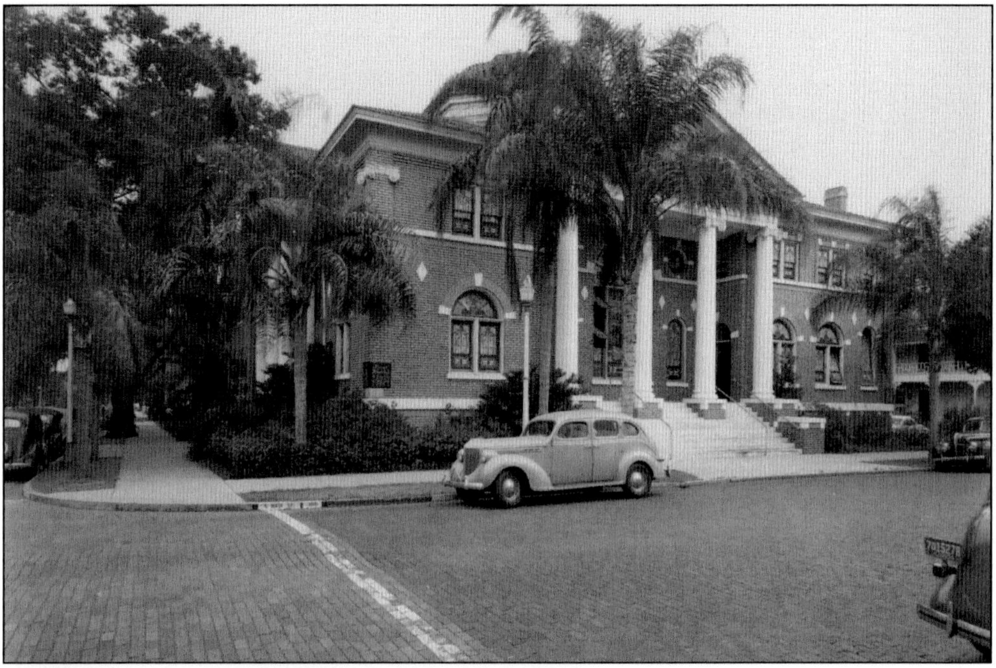

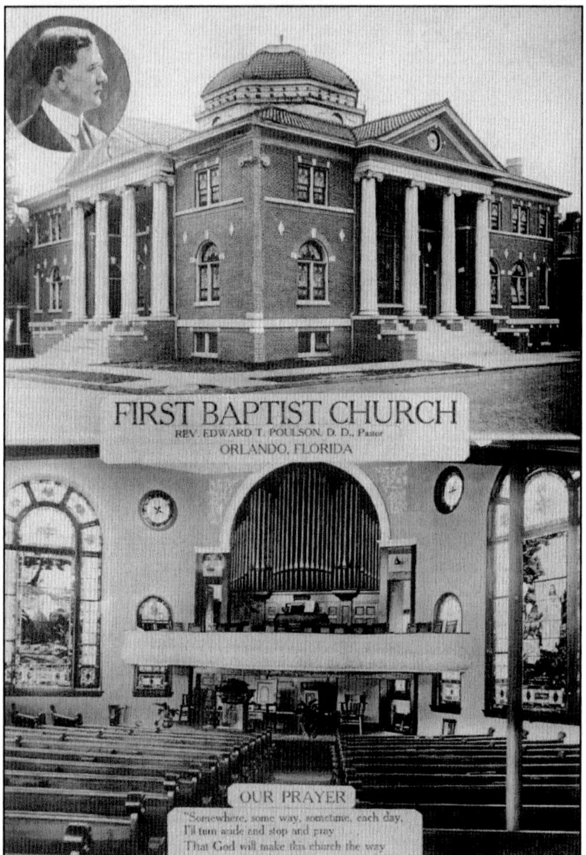

Dr. E.T. Poulson, seen in the upper left corner of the postcard at left, became pastor of the First Baptist Church in 1913. Poulson soon determined that the church needed a new building to better serve the spiritual needs of Orlando's growing tourist population. The congregation laid the cornerstone for the new brick structure, located at the corner of Pine Street and Magnolia Avenue, on October 14, 1914. They dedicated the new 1,200-seat church, which replaced a frame church built in 1897, on May 30, 1915. That year, church membership reached 494, and it continued to grow. After a fourth new church was dedicated in 1961, the 1915 church served as a recreation center until its demolition in 1975 to clear space for the Christian Life Center.

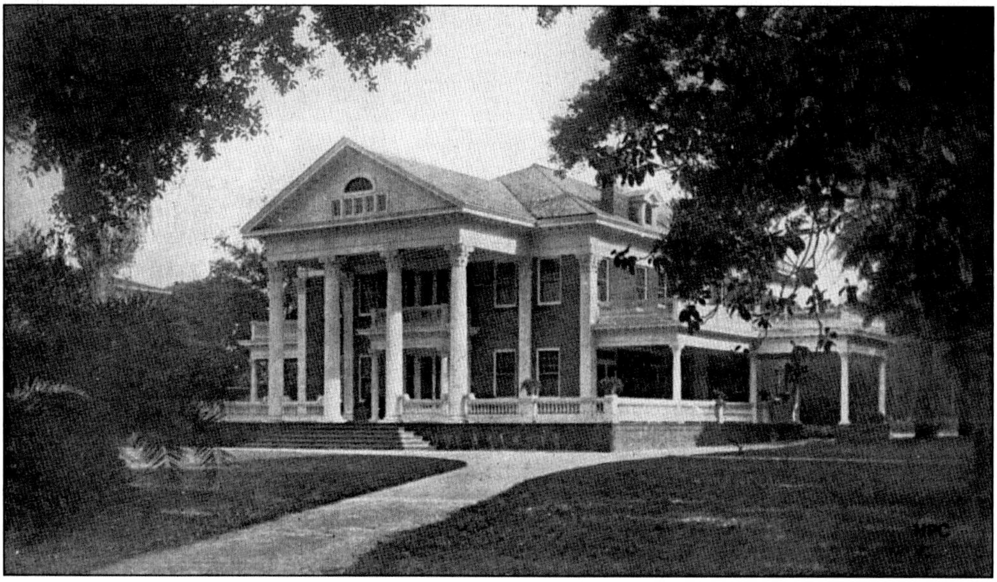

Moses Overstreet, state senator from 1920 to 1928, built a three-story house in 1916 at Rosalind Avenue and East Central Boulevard overlooking Lake Eola. A showplace for many years, the Overstreet House was razed in October 1954 for a parking lot. Today, the Embassy Suites Hotel occupies the site.

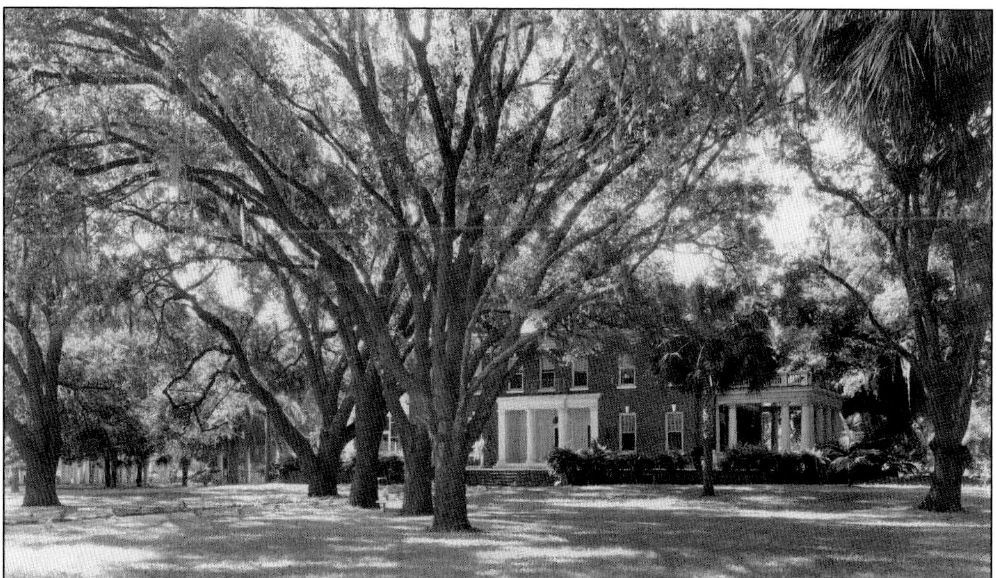

Six-term Orlando mayor James L. Giles built the house he called Oakleigh on Lake Lucerne in 1916. He sold the house in 1945, and it was converted to apartments. In 1961, the Lucerne Towers residential high-rise was built on the site. This photograph, taken in 1932, was included in a proposal written by Brass & Condict Realtors to the motion picture industry, highlighting various sections of Orlando.

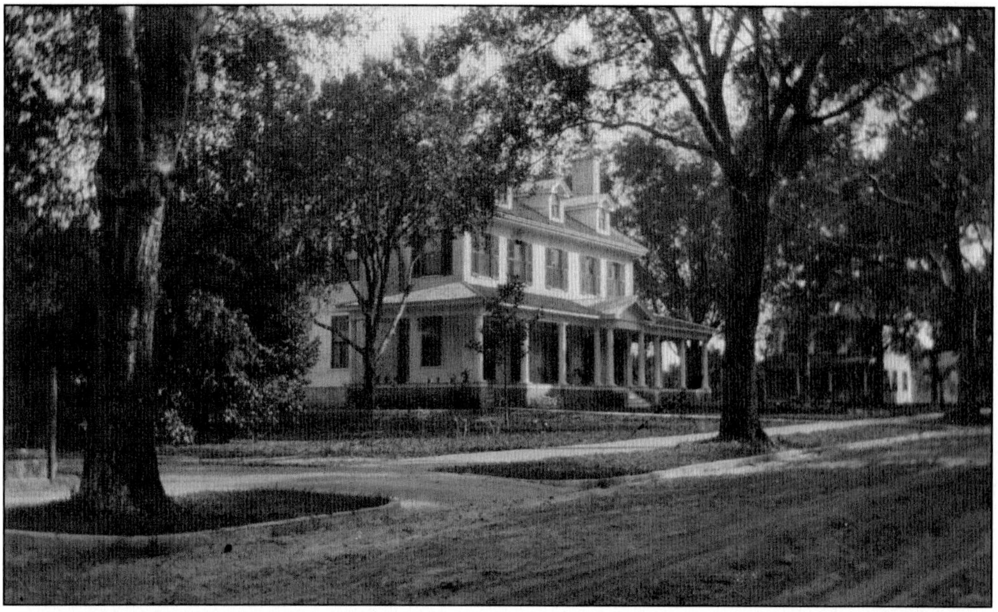

Frederic Henry Rand hired Henry Green to build the stately frame house at 5 North Osceola Avenue. Completed in 1916 at a cost of $6,500, the house had eight bedrooms (many with fireplaces) and a master suite with a bathroom. The house and a barn dating to a previous owner occupied half of the city block. The Rand House was demolished in 1972. A city park now occupies this site.

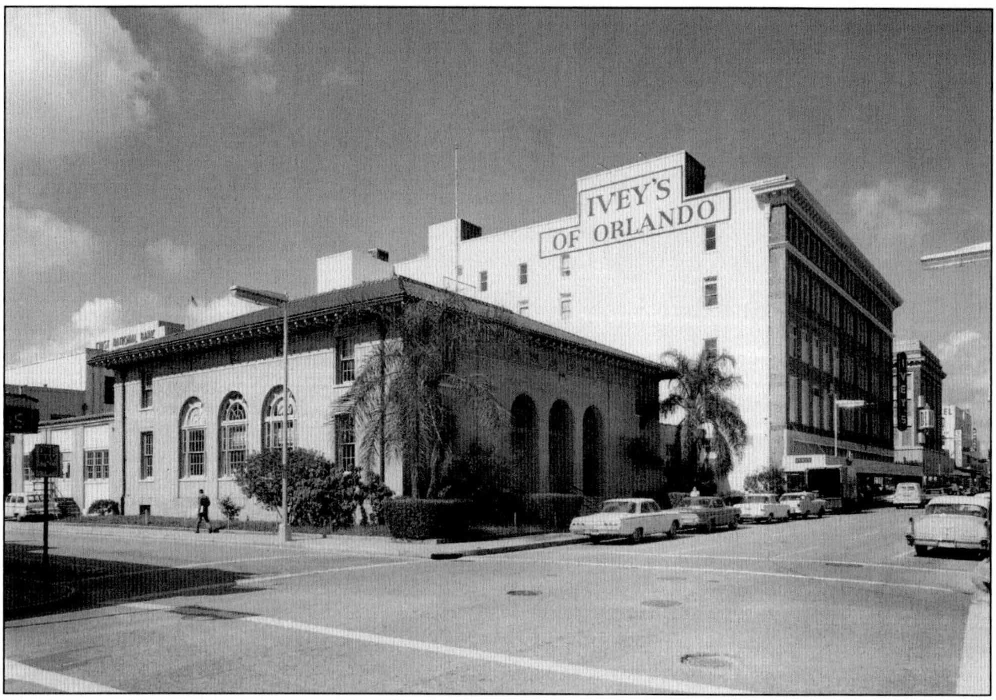

The first building in Orlando specifically designed to be a post office opened in 1917 at the corner of South Court Avenue and East Central Boulevard. Despite an addition in 1928, the post office outgrew the building by 1935 and moved to a new building on Robinson Street in 1941. The post office was razed in 1962 for a parking lot. Today, a commercial building sits at that corner.

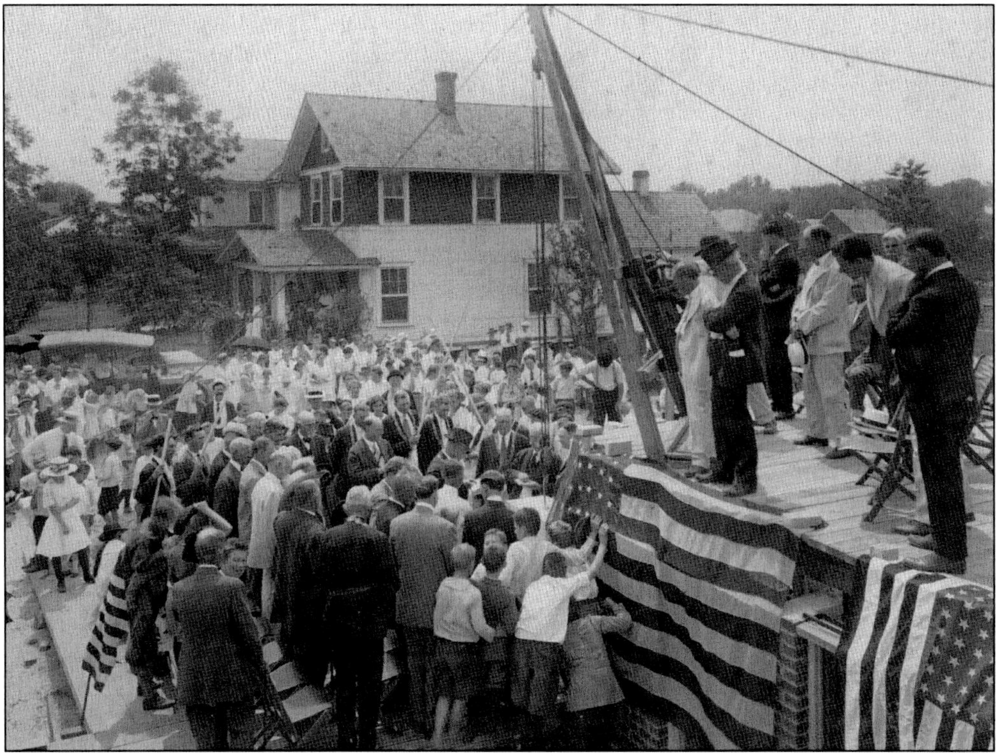

West Central Elementary School, seen above during the laying of the cornerstone and after completion around 1920 below, opened in 1917 at 728 West Central Boulevard. During the 1921–1922 school year, 12 teachers worked at the school, earning a total monthly salary of $1,150. The number of teachers remained steady during the 1930s, with ten in 1930, eleven in 1931, and ten in 1932. In 1957, the school closed, and the building became home to the Orange County Health Department. A spectacular fire destroyed the former school building in 1973, and a new health department building was erected on the site.

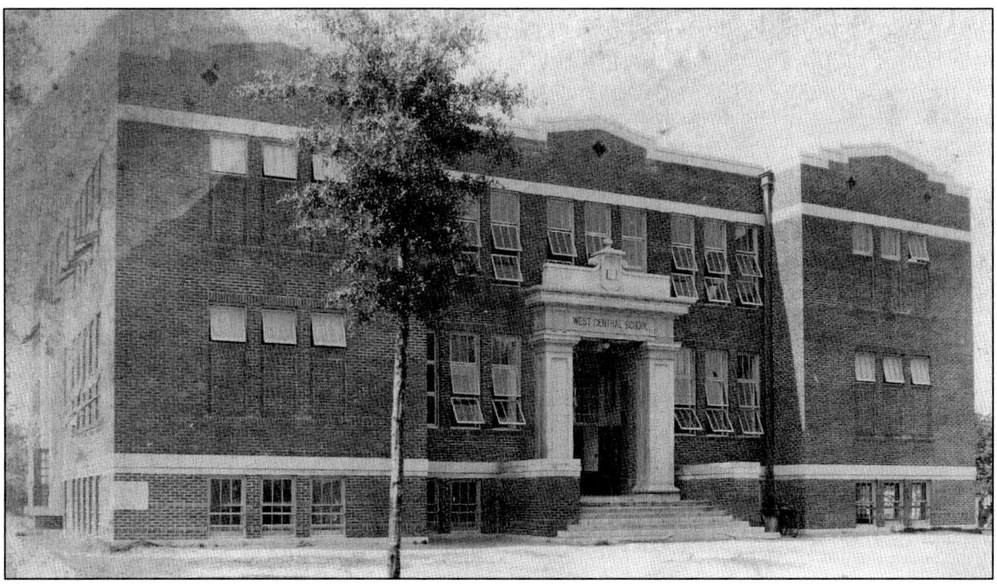

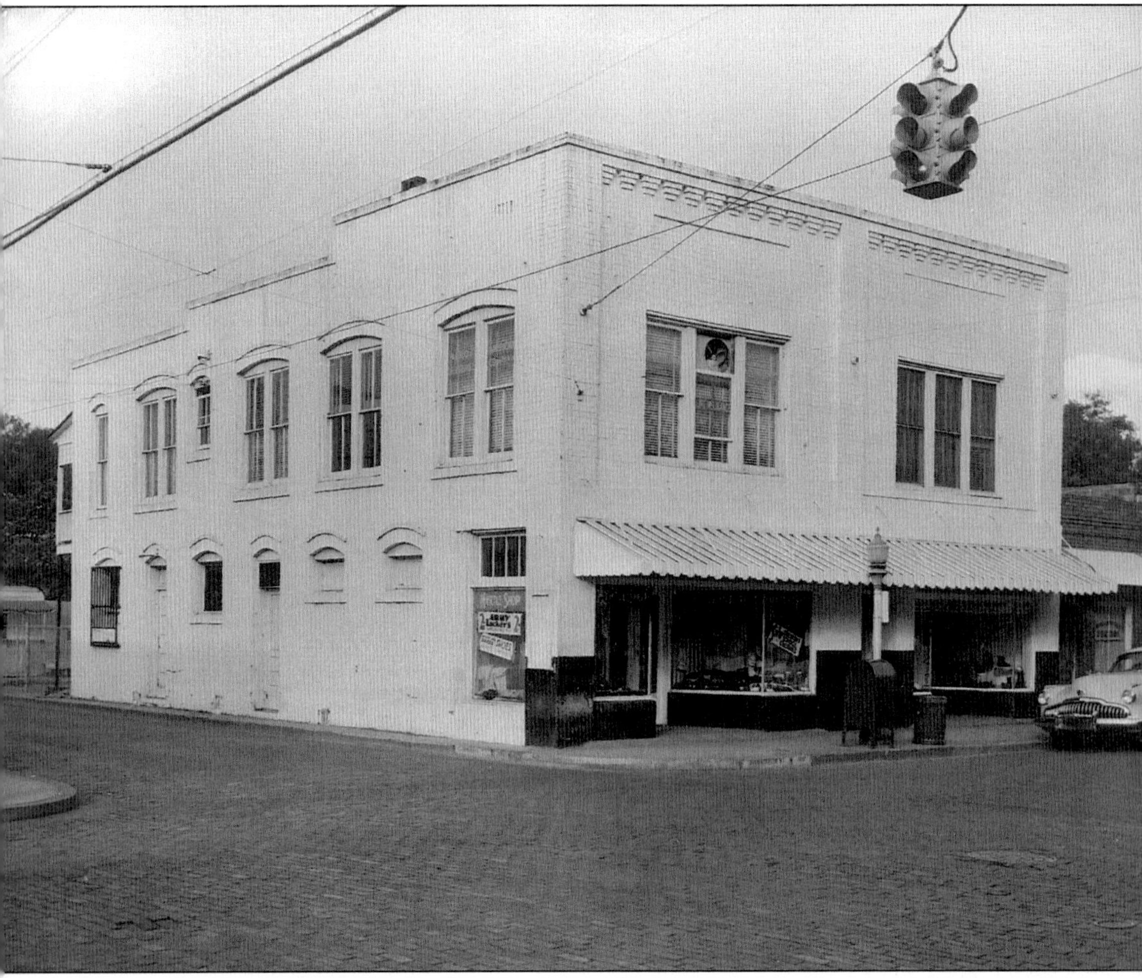

Adams and Taylor built the two stores on West Church at Division Street in 1917. Taylor's Drug Store occupied one of the storefronts. From 1921 through 1934, African American physician Dr. William Monroe Wells had an office on the second floor. Probably the building's most important tenant, Doctor Wells delivered more than 5,000 babies in Orlando's African American community. He constructed the South Street Casino and the Wells' Built Hotel when segregation restricted African Americans to the black neighborhood of Parramore, located west of the railroad. Downtown clubs and theaters relegated blacks to undesirable seats or refused to admit them at all. Hotels closed their doors to African Americans. Located in the Parramore African American business district, the building later housed the Myrtle shop, which specialized in men's, women's, and children's clothing for the black community. A parking garage was built in 1989 on this corner.

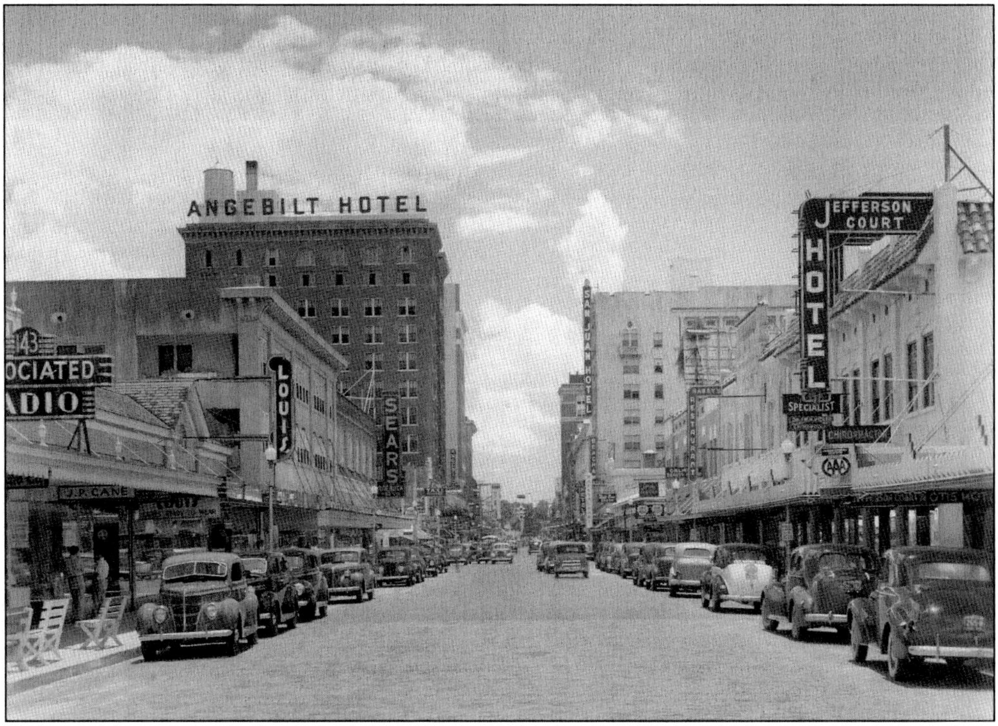

Designed by architect George Krug, the Jefferson Court Hotel opened at the corner of Orange Avenue and Jefferson Street in 1918. The three-story E-shaped building cost $125,000 and was sponsored by a group of 25 businessmen under the corporate title of Orlando Investment Company. In early 1925, W.W. Rose purchased the Jefferson Court Apartments for $250,000. The apartments were sold later that year for $500,000 to Marvel Holding Corporation of Chicago with plans to build a business structure in front of the complex. By 1954, the land was needed for commercial development, and the Jefferson Court was demolished.

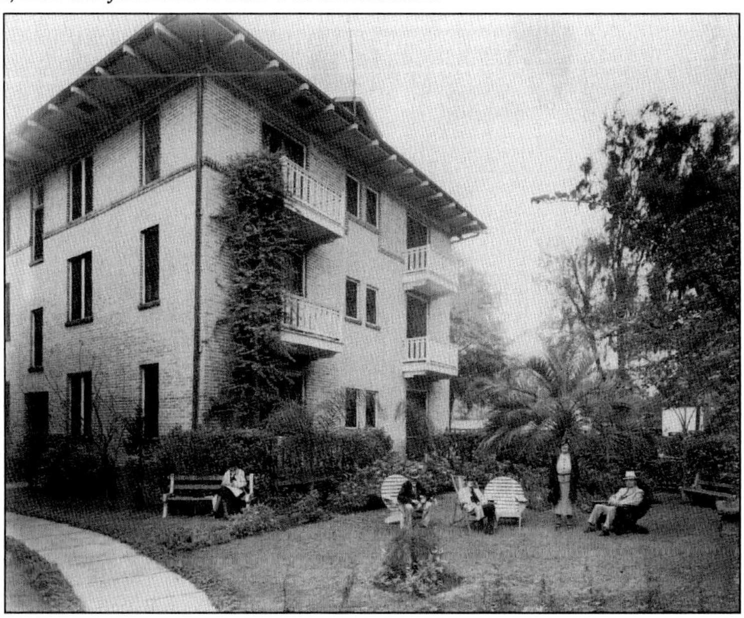

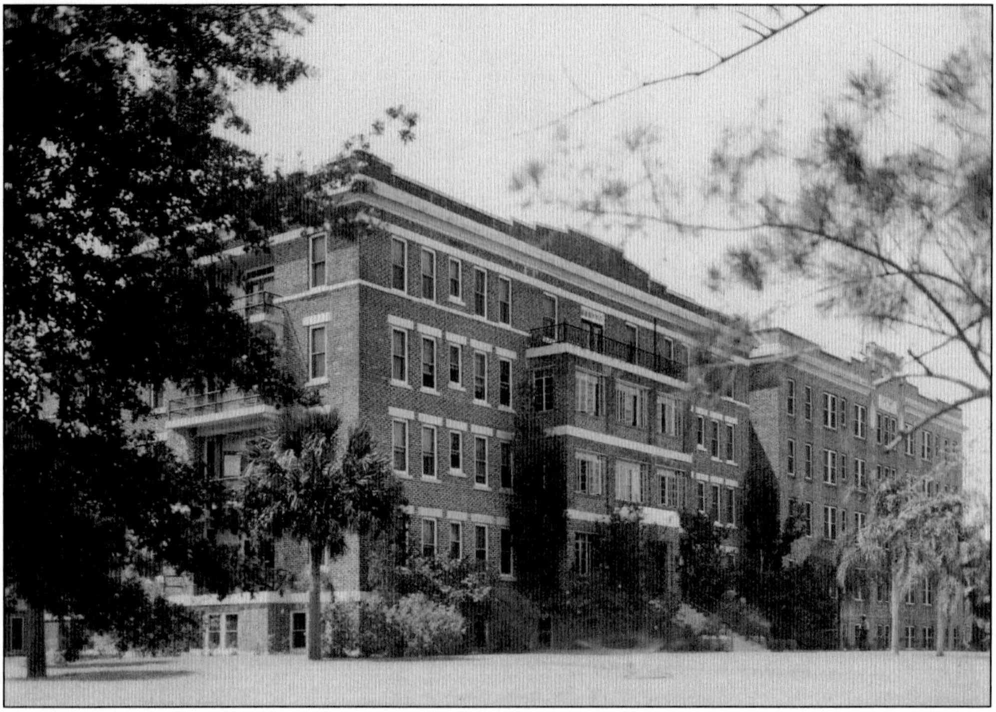

In 1916, James L. Giles, Dr. John McEwan, and Dr. Gaston Edwards started a campaign to build a new hospital, with each man donating $1,000 toward the cause. They set a goal of building a 100-bed hospital for $150,000 and selected an elevated lot on South Orange Avenue. A contract to build the hospital was awarded in November 1916; however, World War I delayed construction, and Orange General Hospital did not open until 1918. On May 30, 1946, the hospital's name was changed to Orange Memorial Hospital to honor the men who died in World War I, as well as the institution's founders. The building was demolished in 1990 as a part of an Orlando Regional Medical Center expansion project.

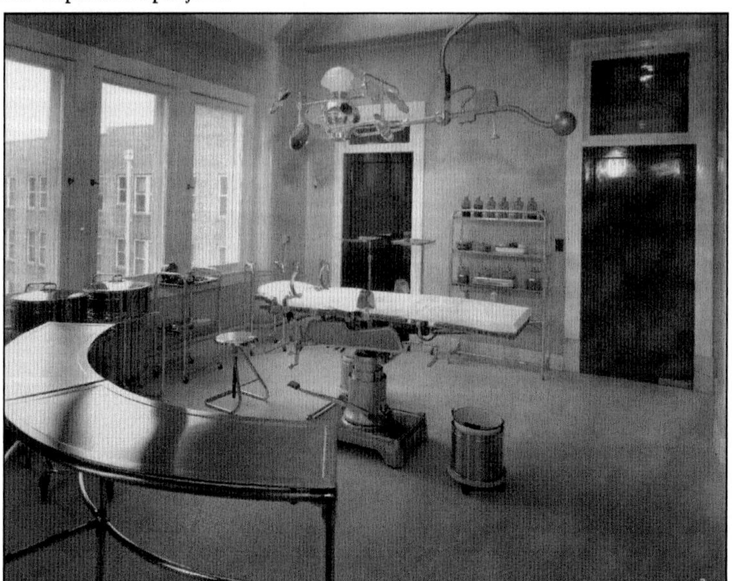

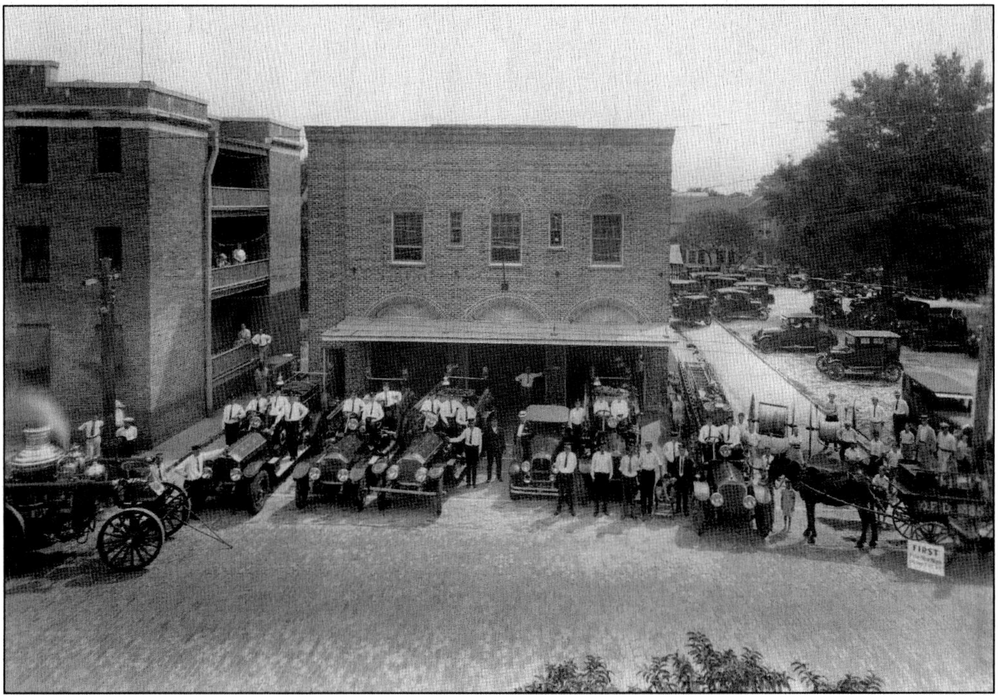

The City of Orlando obtained a building permit for a new fire station on July 18, 1919. Architect Fred Trimble designed the two-story brick building to be constructed by C.C. Hanner at a cost of $17,780. The new Station No. 1 opened on March 25, 1920, across Magnolia Avenue from the courthouse, replacing the old building on Wall Street. Three years later, all Orlando Fire Department firefighters became paid employees, and Chief Dean, in his 16th year of service to the department, became the first paid fire chief. In 1960, the fire station moved to South Magnolia Avenue, and the building on North Magnolia Avenue was demolished for a parking lot. The Orlando Public Library now occupies the site.

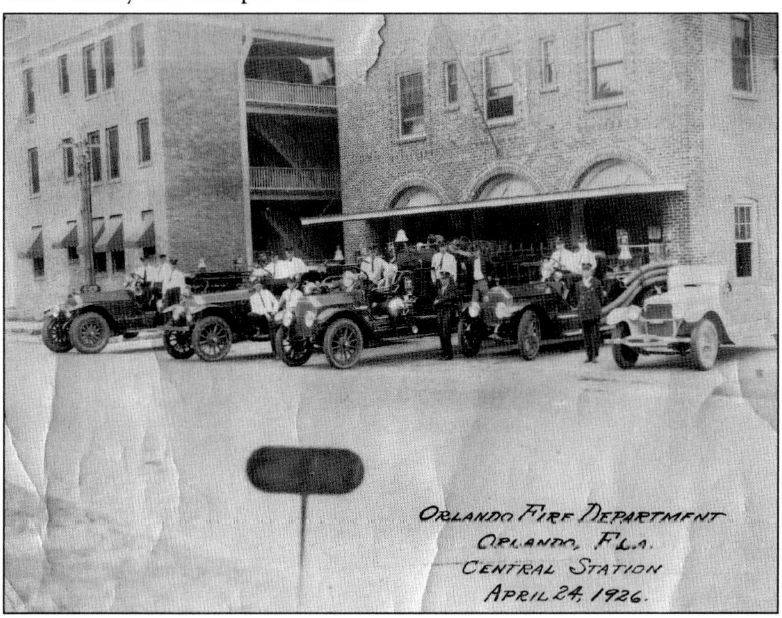

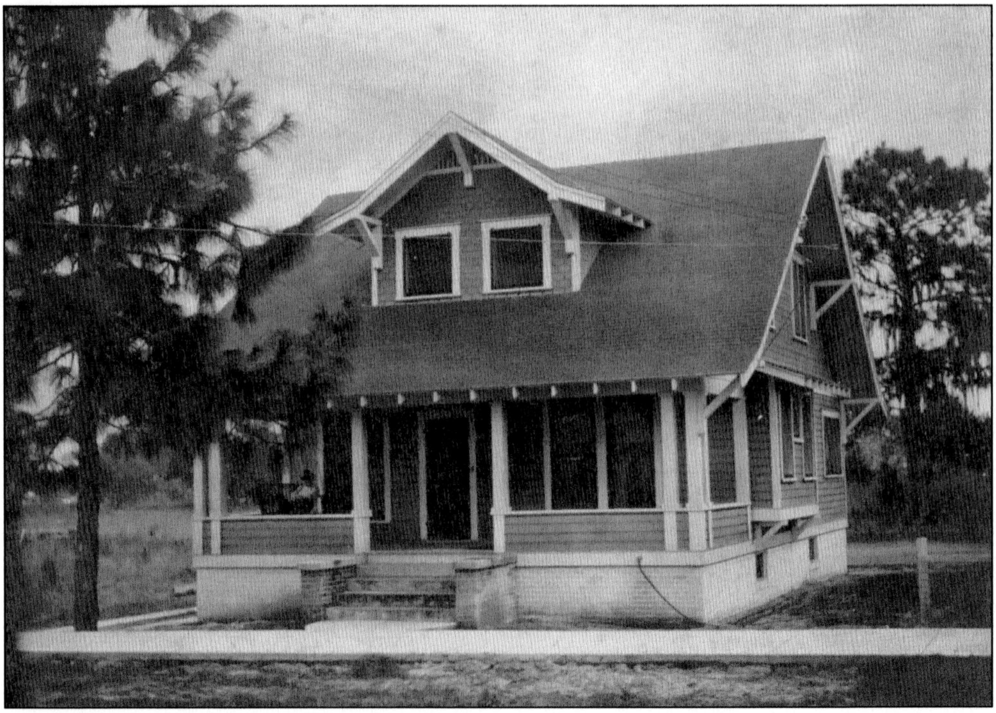

T.W. Matthews built a two-story frame house costing $3,500 on North Magnolia Avenue in 1919. Helen Pratt bought the house from Matthews in 1922. She lived there until 1955, when her daughter Dorothy Pratt sold the house. It was demolished in 1957 to make way for construction of the Midtown Building. Today, it is the site of the Boys and Girls Clubs.

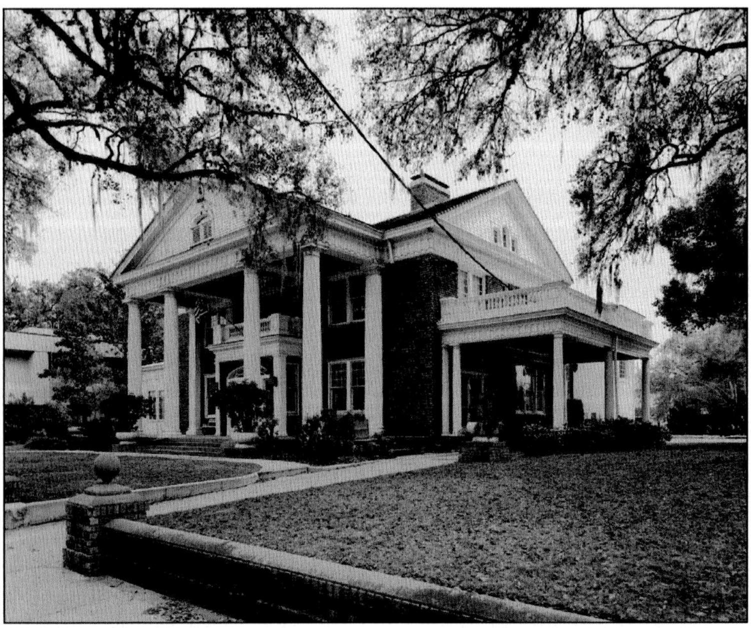

Orlando architect Murry King designed the palatial W.H. McRainey House on East Central Boulevard in 1920. Mary McRainey sold it in 1939 after her husband's death, and in 1960, it became the offices of the Anderson and Rush law firm. Anderson and Rush sold the home in 1999, and it was demolished to build the 22-story luxury apartment building, the Waverly.

Four

1921–1950

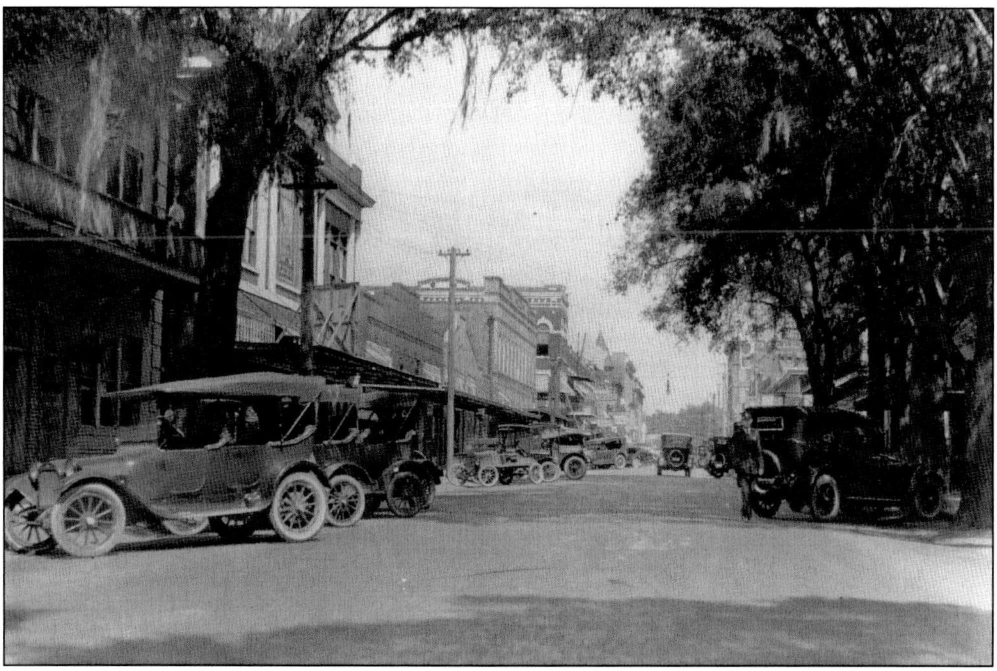

Orlando saw great growth between 1921 and 1950. The Great Florida Land Boom, the Great Depression, and World War II all contributed to the expansion. Government and business remained downtown. Wealthy people built their imposing houses on the city's outskirts, and institutions, especially schools, followed the residential city as it grew and shifted to less congested areas.

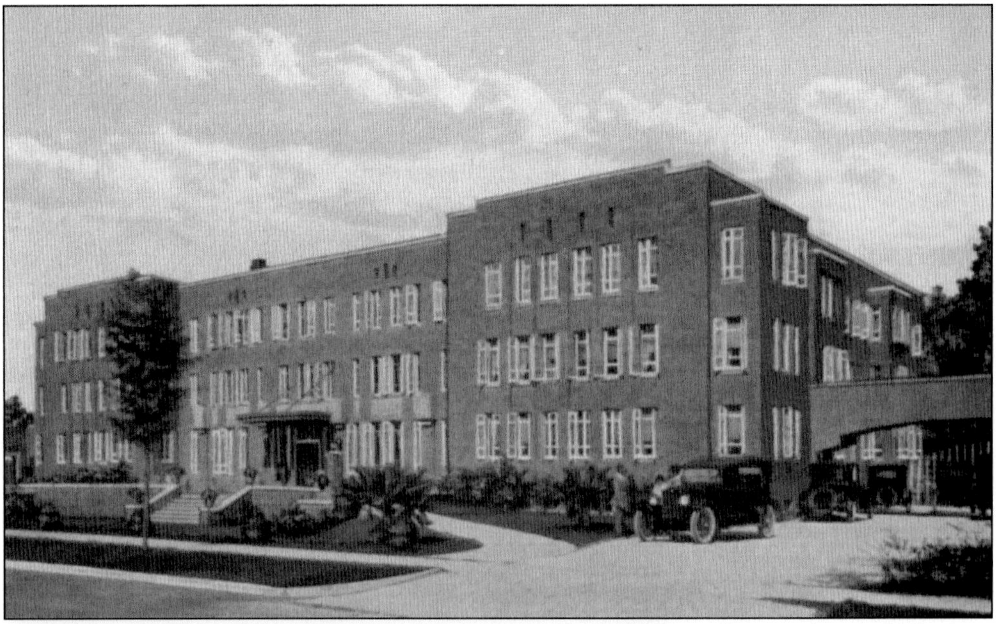

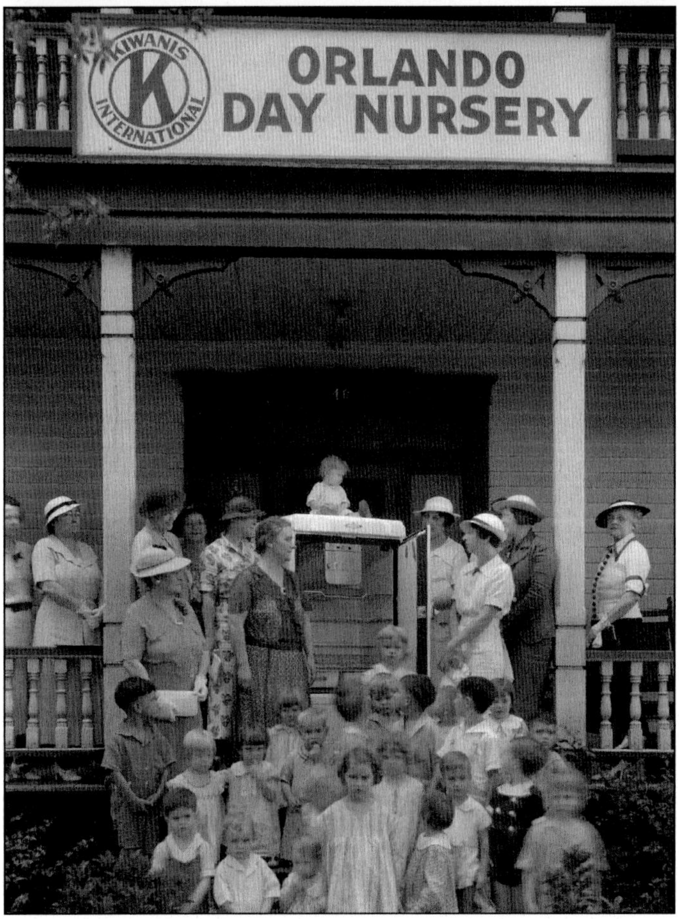

Ida Ryan designed the Amherst Apartments, built in 1922 at 325 West Colonial Drive. Once the most prestigious apartment building in Orlando, the Amherst Apartments had elegance and charm. The widening of Colonial Drive in the 1950s eliminated the landscaping and circular driveway. These losses, combined with age, made the apartments less desirable to residents. The building was demolished in 1986.

George Macy built a large house on the southeast corner of Hughey and South Streets, probably in the early 1880s. It operated as a rooming house when the Orlando Day Nursery Association bought the Macy House for $15,000 in 1922. In 1960, the house, in the way of Interstate 4 construction, was demolished.

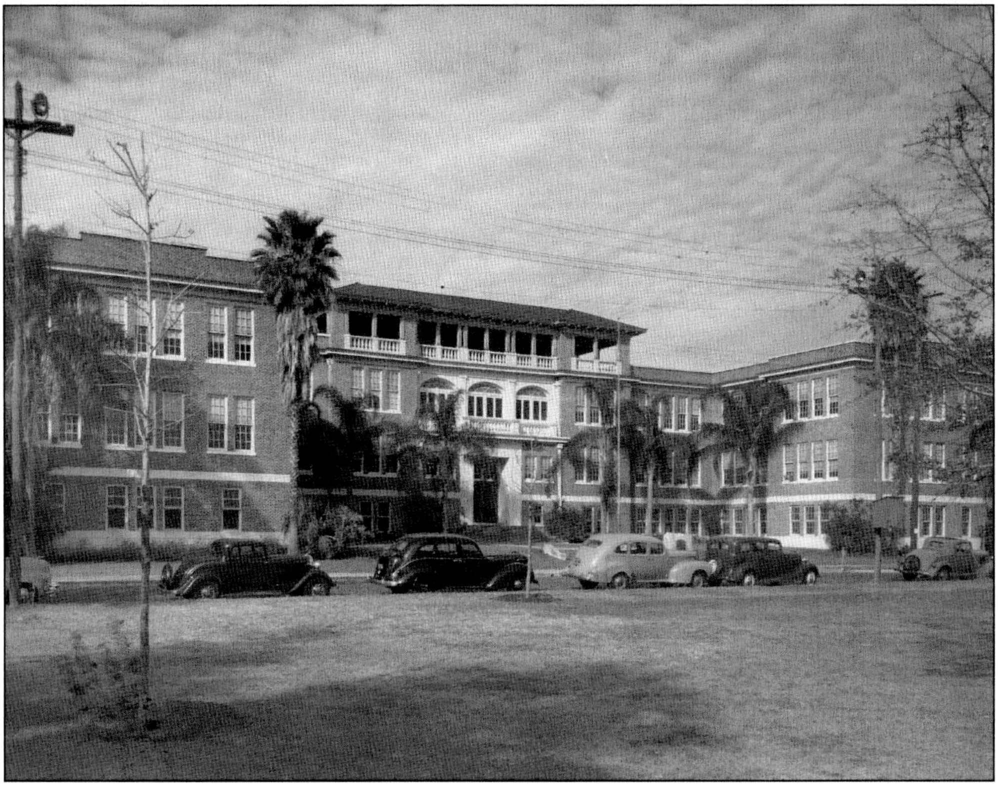

Memorial Junior High School, dedicated to veterans of all previous wars, opened in 1922 on Rosalind Avenue facing Lake Eola. At that time, the school was the only one in Florida dedicated solely to grades seven, eight, and nine. From 1922 until 1925, the senior high occupied the south wing of the building while waiting for completion of Orlando High School, and the junior high occupied the north wing. The center section housed the auditorium and gymnasium. In 1926, the senior high moved to Magnolia School, and the structure became Memorial Junior High School. The building was sold in 1961, and a hotel was constructed in its place. Today, the hotel operates as condominiums.

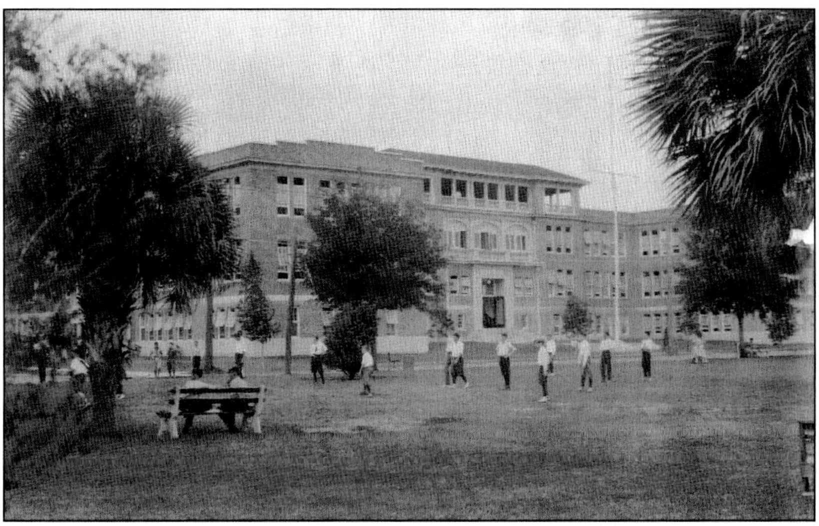

In 1920, Capt. Charles Albertson, a retired New York police inspector and Orlando winter resident, offered his collection of 12,000 books to the City of Orlando, provided that a suitable library be constructed to house them. Designed by Orlando architect Murry King, the concrete and steel Albertson Public Library opened in 1923 on East Central Boulevard. The building was demolished in 1963 to erect the new Orlando Public Library.

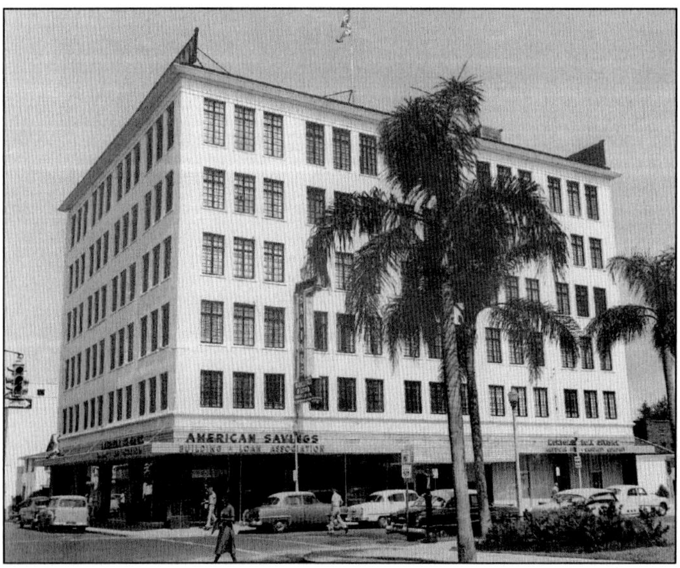

Built in 1923 at Orange Avenue and Jackson Street, the six-story, steel and reinforced concrete American Building, seen here in January 1955, opened as a garage and car dealership. Converted to offices, it housed an insurance company in 1928. In 1946, the American Fire and Casualty Company bought the property, and it became the American Building; later, it was the American Pioneer Life Insurance Building. It was demolished in 1995.

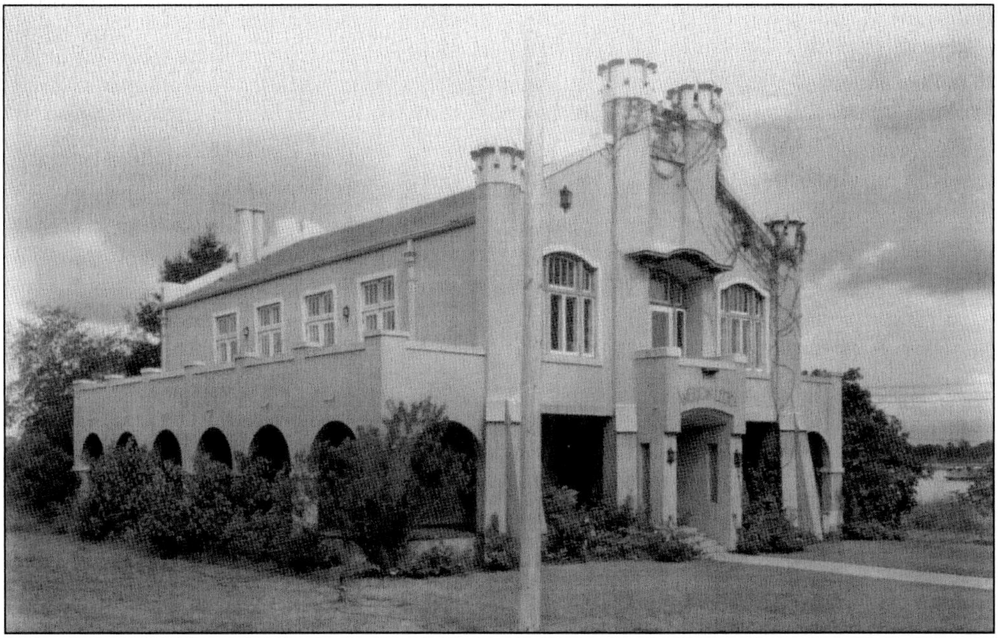

Orlando's American Legion organized in 1919. In 1921, the city gave them property on Lake Ivanhoe for a headquarters building, constructed in 1924. The American Legion demolished the structure in 1938 to clear the way for a new building. An office building now occupies the site.

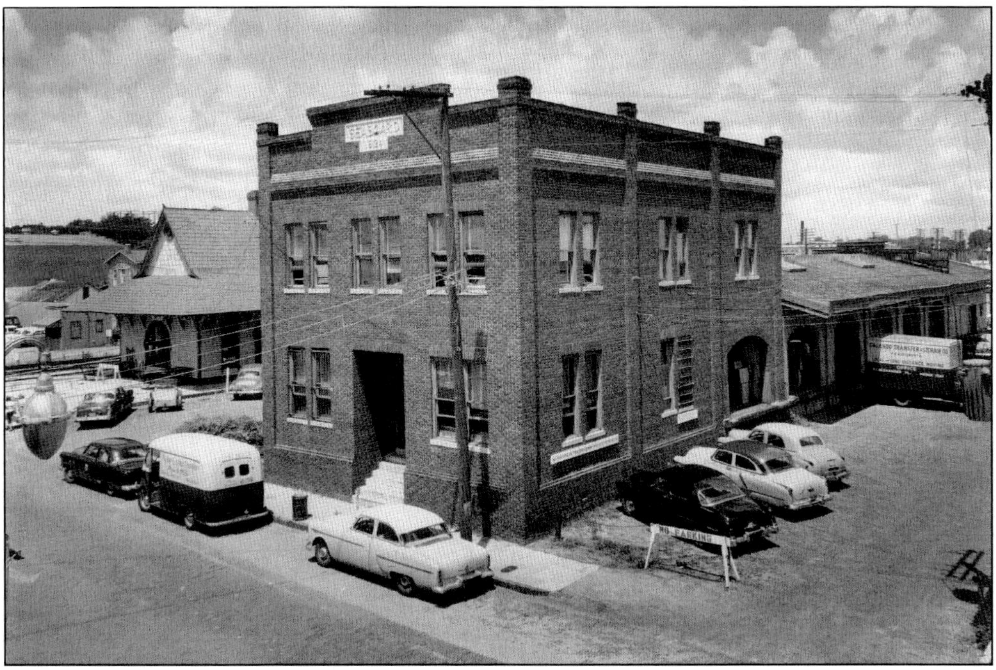

The Seaboard Air Line Railroad demolished its freight office in 1924 and replaced it with a two-story brick building near its passenger station. The passenger station, built in 1896, and the 1924 freight office shared the railroad property between West Washington Street and West Central Boulevard along the railroad until both were demolished in 1955 for a parking lot. A city parking garage stands there today.

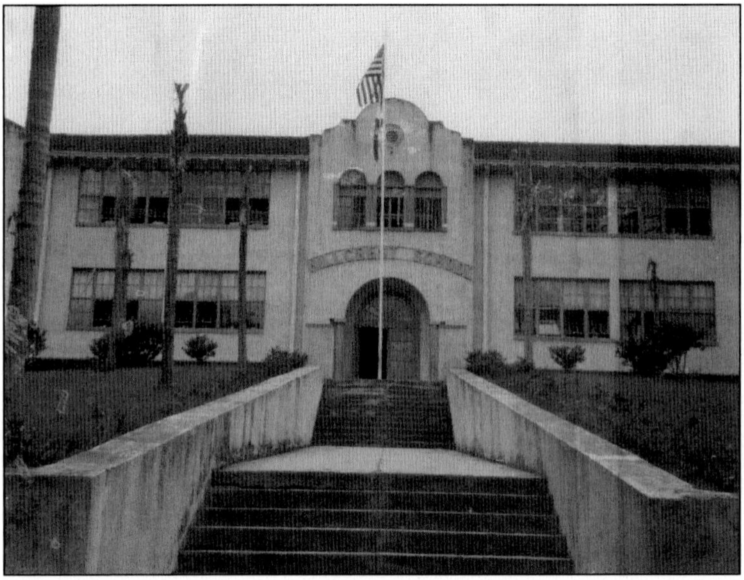

Hillcrest Elementary School opened in February 1924 at 706 Concord Street. The school caught fire on December 22, 1963, requiring 10 Orlando Fire Department pumpers and three aerial trucks to bring the three-hour blaze under control. The building was a total loss, and a new Hillcrest School was built on the site in 1964.

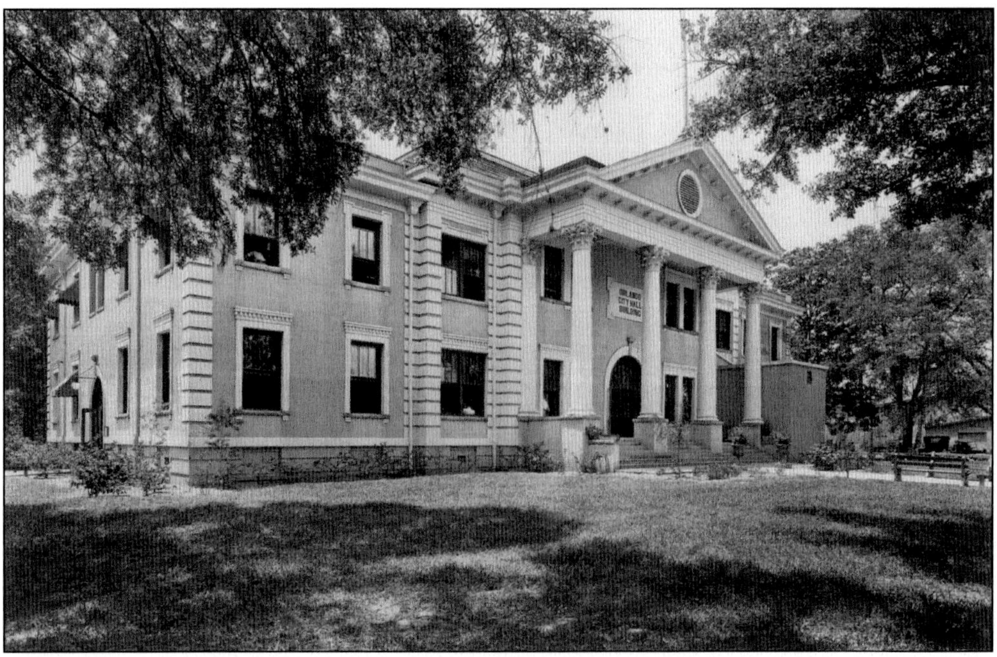

In 1924, the city bought the old high school, built in 1906 on South Orange Avenue, for its city hall. The police department went into the basement, and the utilities commission rented offices on the first floor. The city government was there until 1958, and the police department remained until 1972, when the building was demolished.

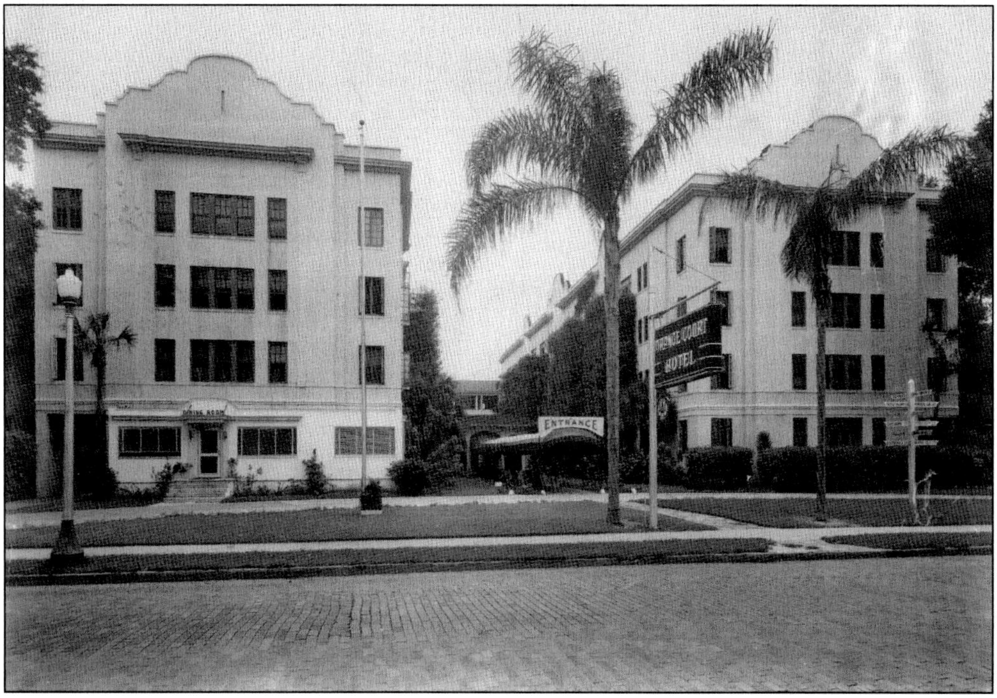

In February 1923, several old buildings along North Orange Avenue were torn down to make room for the Orange Court Hotel. The hotel opened at 650 North Orange Avenue on March 4, 1924. It consisted of three buildings, two of which were four stories tall. Over the years, the hotel was known as the Orange Court Motor Lodge and the Orlando Motor hotel. After many years as a popular lodging place, the hotel closed in the 1960s. It was demolished in 1990 because the aging structure could not be brought up to code. Today, the Camden Orange Court Apartments occupy the site.

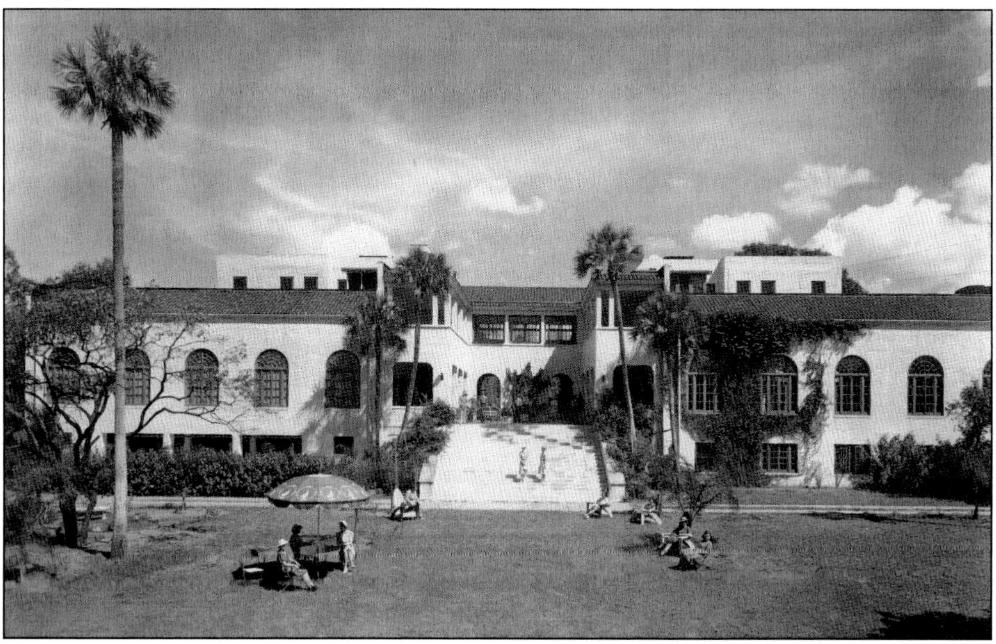

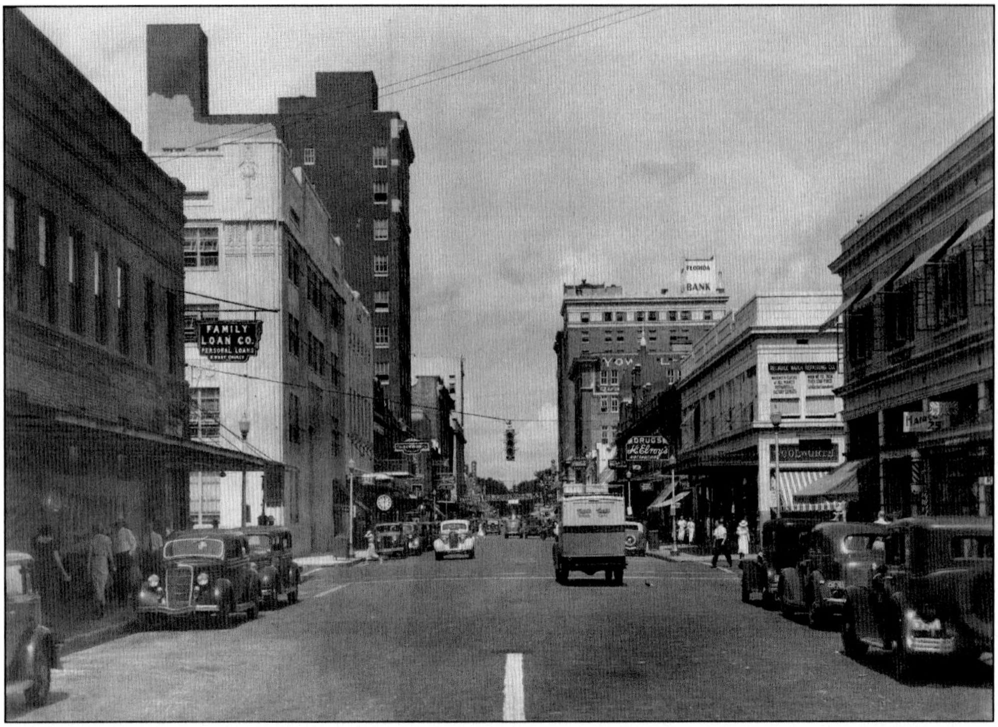

The Woolworth Company leased the Guernsey Block on South Orange Avenue at Pine Street in 1923 and demolished the building a year later to construct a new five-and-dime store. McCrory's opened a new five-and-dime on South Orange Avenue at Church Street in 1942. Both stores closed when the buildings' owners evicted them in December 1990. By 2003, the structures, then known as the Jaymont Block, were declared unsafe by the city's code enforcement board, which allowed the City of Orlando and developer Cameron Kuhn to take advantage of a loophole in the historic preservation code. Over the protests of preservationists, the block was demolished starting late at night on December 8, 2003, to make way for the Plaza Complex.

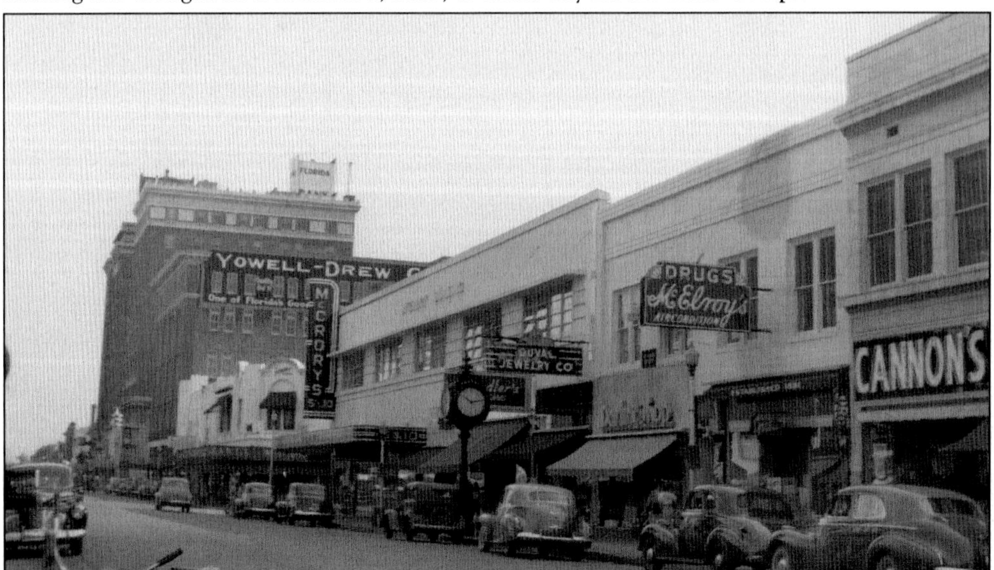

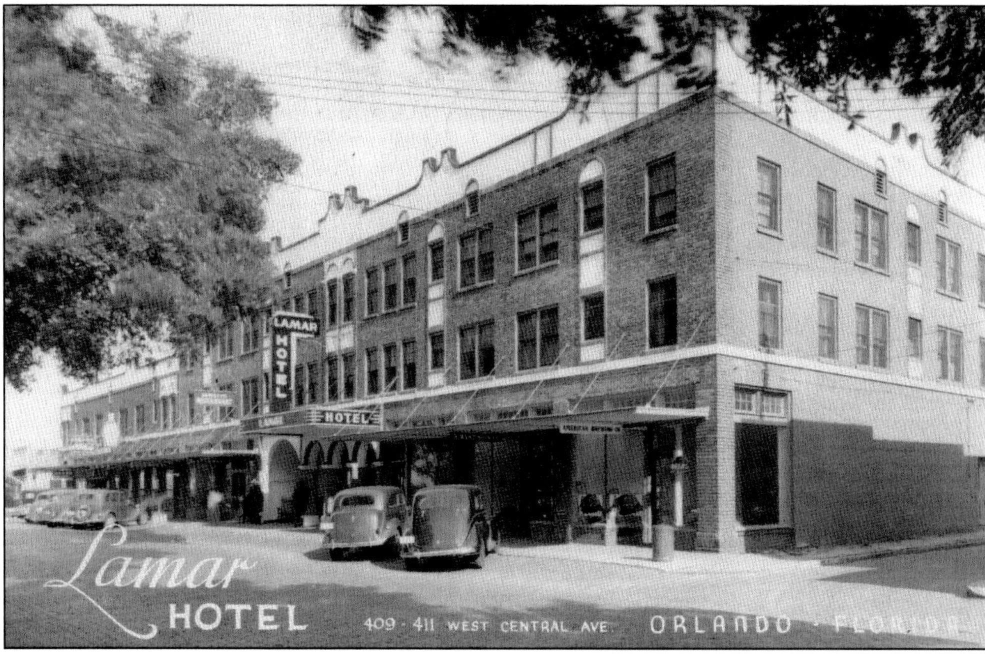

The Lamar Hotel opened on West Central Boulevard in 1924 as the Hotel Roberts. C.A. Roberts sold the building to L.B. McLeod in 1938, and it was renamed the Lamar Hotel. It was demolished in 1997 for expansion of the federal courthouse. Lamar Hotel manager B. Willox mailed this postcard in 1939 to hotel patrons, thanking them for their business.

The building on the northeast corner of West Pine Street at the railroad shows the decorative metalwork of the D.A. Routh Company. Established at the corner of East Church Street and Magnolia Avenue in 1913 as Routh and Caldwell, the business moved to East Pine Street about 1925 and later to South Hughey Avenue as the D.A. Routh Company. Today, Orlando Fire Station No. 1 occupies the site.

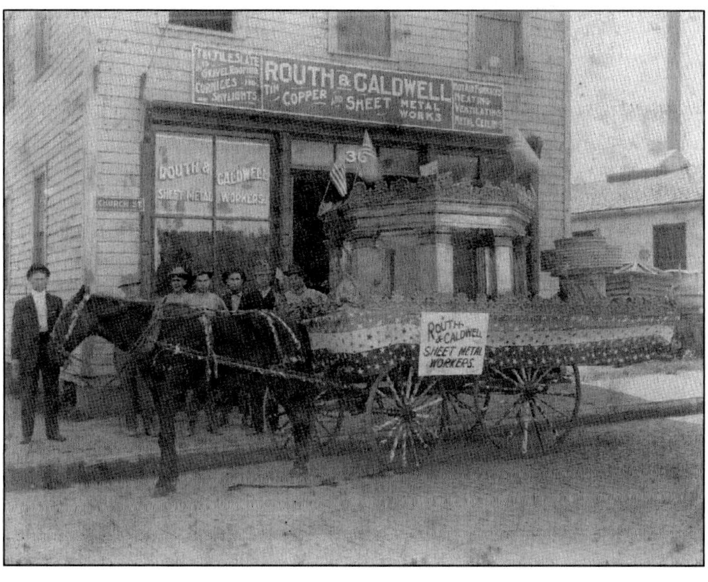

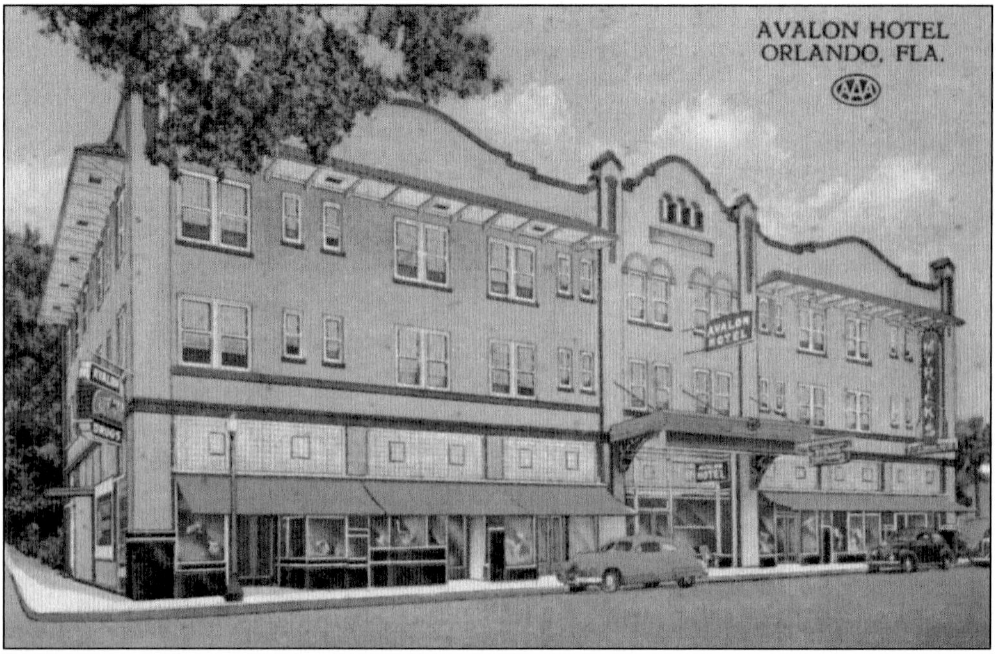

The three-story frame and brick Avalon Hotel opened in 1925 at the corner of North Orange Avenue and Amelia Street. The 60-room hotel, a favorite of traveling salesmen, was destroyed in a spectacular fire in 1955. Today, the courthouse parking garage occupies the Avalon Hotel site. This postcard boasts free parking, "air cooling," and steam heating for those staying at the hotel.

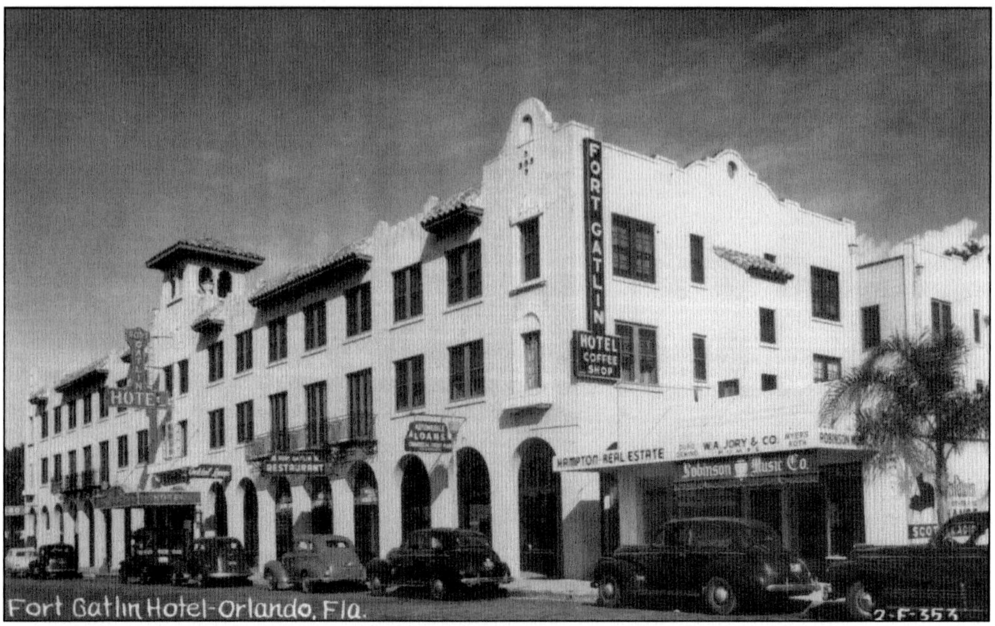

The Fort Gatlin Hotel opened in 1926 on North Orange Avenue and featured 150 rooms, each with its own bath. The Orlando Broadcasting Company operated Orlando's first radio station, WDBO, from the hotel beginning in 1927. The *Orlando Sentinel* bought the hotel in 1964 to secure the entire block between North Orange and Magnolia Avenues. The hotel was closed and demolished in 1965 to provide parking for the newspaper offices.

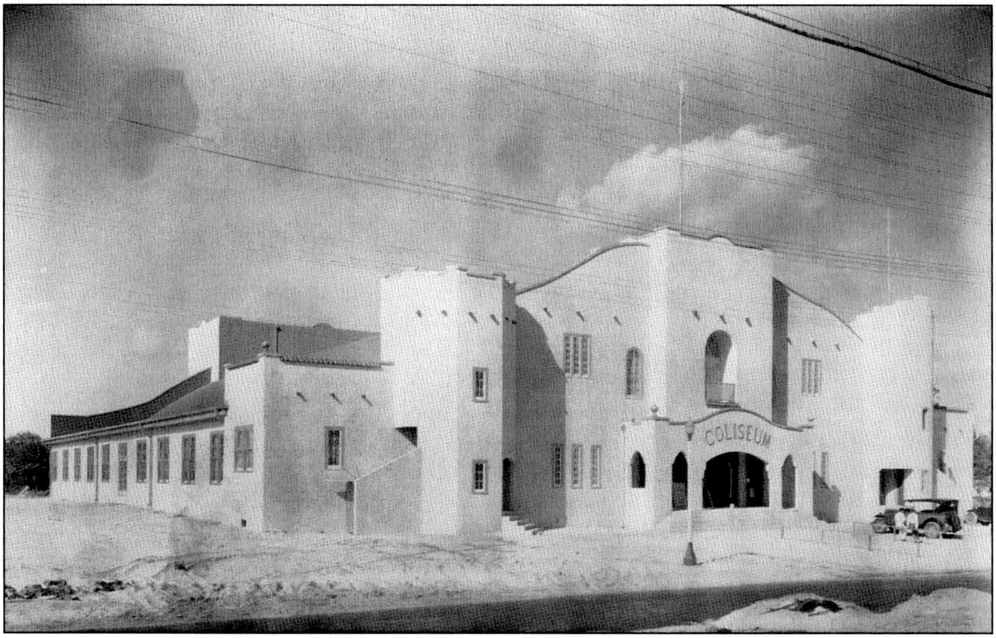

The Coliseum opened on North Orange Avenue near Lake Ivanhoe in 1926. More than a theater, it included Orlando's first public swimming pool and a large exhibition hall. The Coliseum hosted big-band dances, auto shows, and rock concerts, among other events. In 1932, Brass & Condict Realtors submitted these photographs to the motion picture industry with the "intention to select from buildings located in Orlando that which most nearly conformed with the requirements of the Motion Picture Industry." The building and land were being offered for sale for $30,000, a "depreciated value because of the desire of the owner and the City of Orlando to meet present depressed conditions and offer real dollar value." In 1937, new owner Bill Kemp added a bowling alley. It was demolished in 1972, and the site is now warehouses and parking lots.

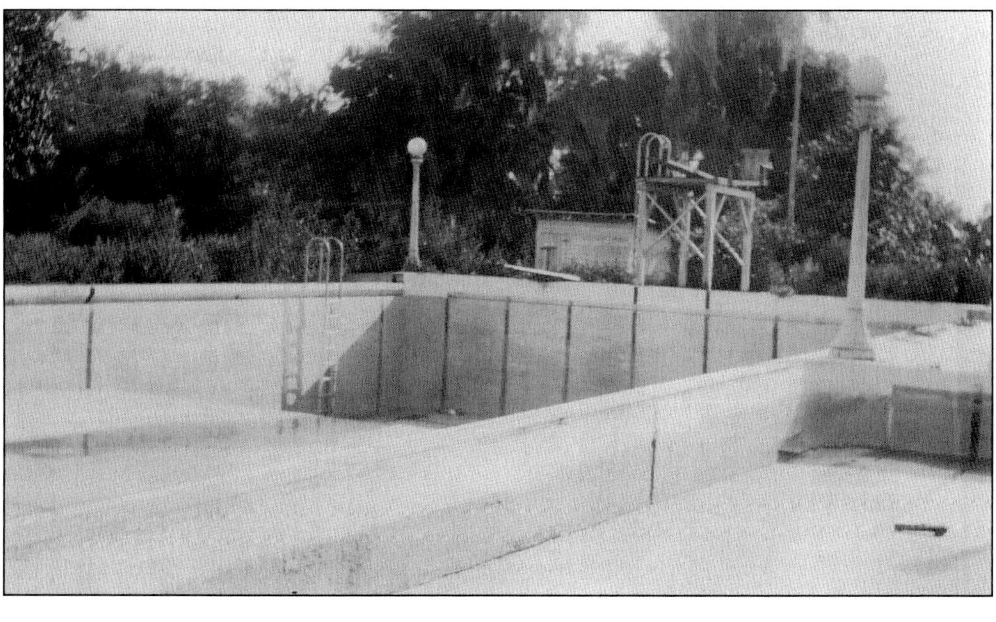

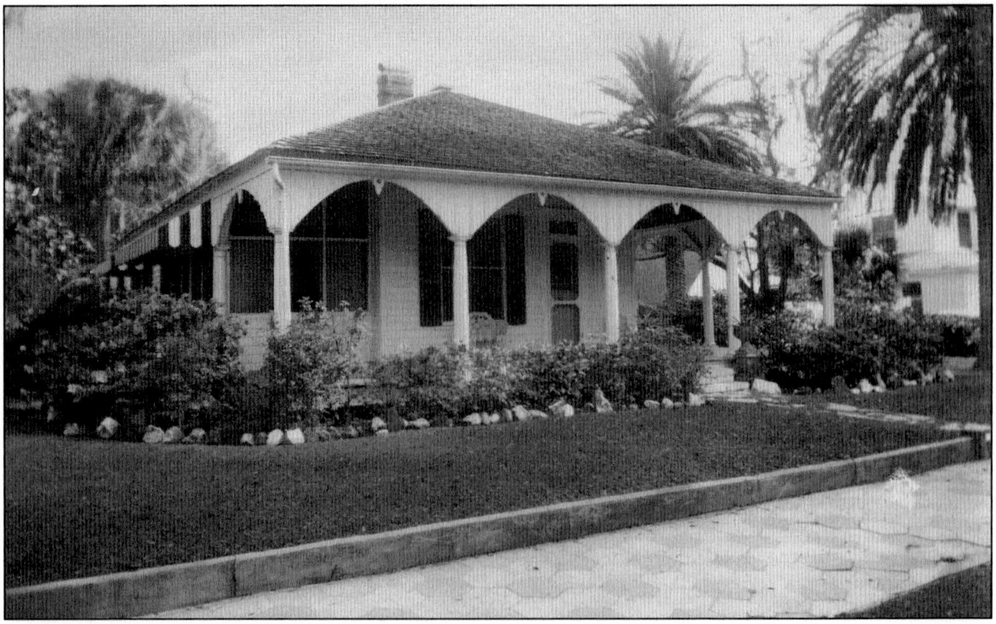

Robert Rowland probably built the Dunn House on South Magnolia Avenue near Lake Lucerne soon after his wife bought the property in 1925. Rowland's family lived there from 1926 until 1965, when his daughter Nellie Dunn Van Anden sold it to the Magnolia Towers. A high-rise apartment building replaced the charming frame dwelling in 1966.

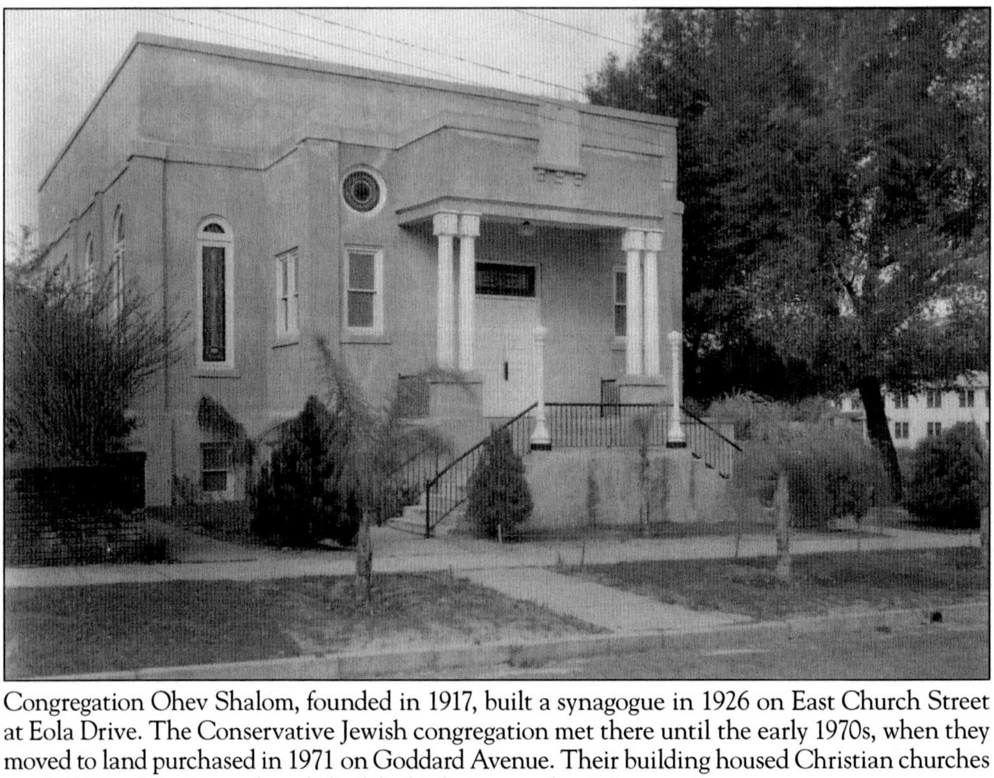

Congregation Ohev Shalom, founded in 1917, built a synagogue in 1926 on East Church Street at Eola Drive. The Conservative Jewish congregation met there until the early 1970s, when they moved to land purchased in 1971 on Goddard Avenue. Their building housed Christian churches until 2002, when it was demolished for high-rise condominiums.

In 1926, V. Baylarian built a $14,000 house at 216 East Miller Street. The house featured a reinforced concrete foundation, solid brick walls, walnut woodwork, and a baked-clay green tile roof. Baylarian sold the house in 1936, and it became the Holiday House Convalescent Home. It later became the Holiday Hospital, which merged with the Orlando Regional Medical Center in 1978. In 1980, the property was sold, and the house was demolished.

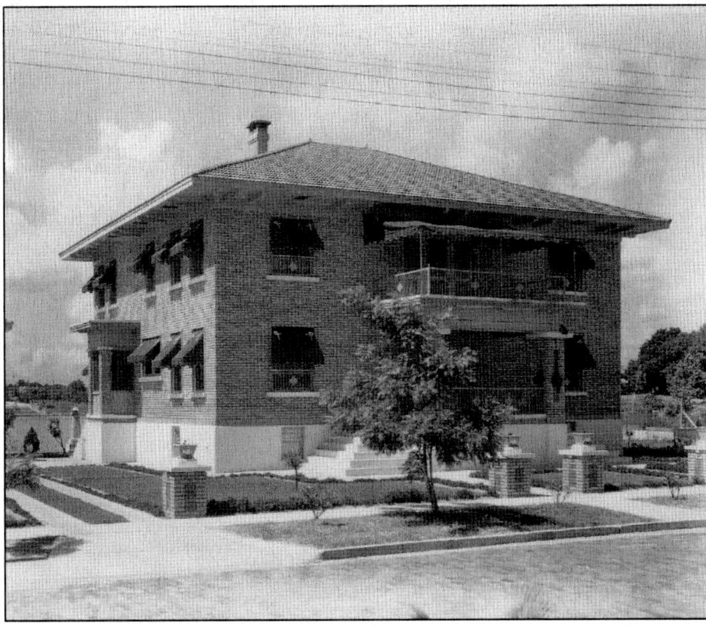

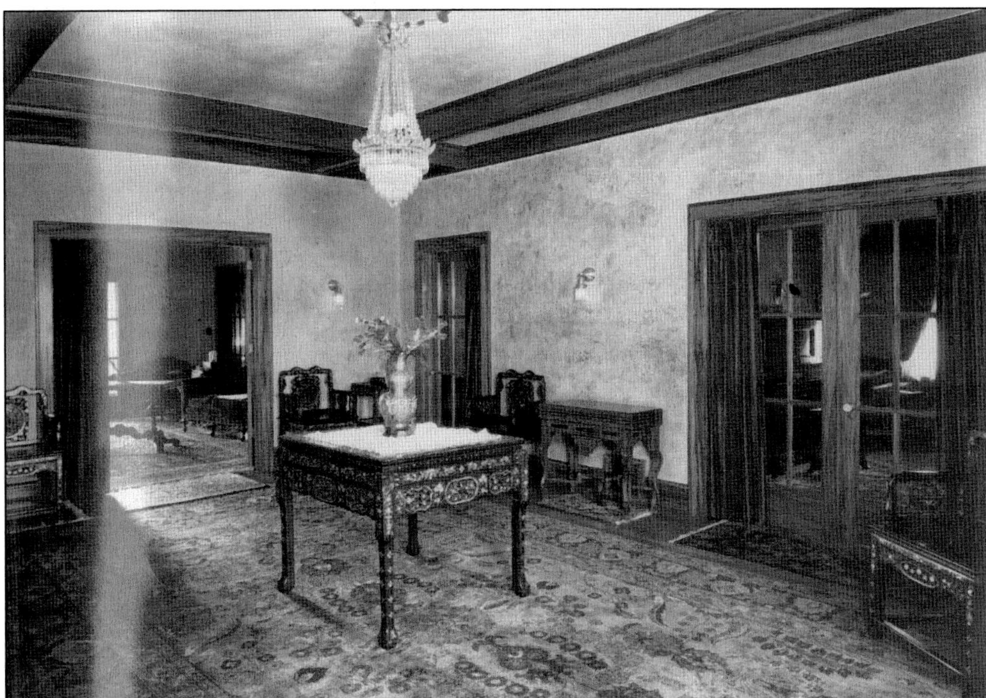

The Baylarian House's reception room featured 10-foot high ceilings, Tiffany mottled-gold walls, a Bohemian crystal chandelier, and silver fixtures. The floor was covered with an 18-foot-by-24-foot, handmade Persian rug. The six chairs and two tables were made of solid ebony with mother-of-pearl inlay. A hand-hammered, solid brass, electric floor lamp and brass Chinese flower vase rounded out the furnishings.

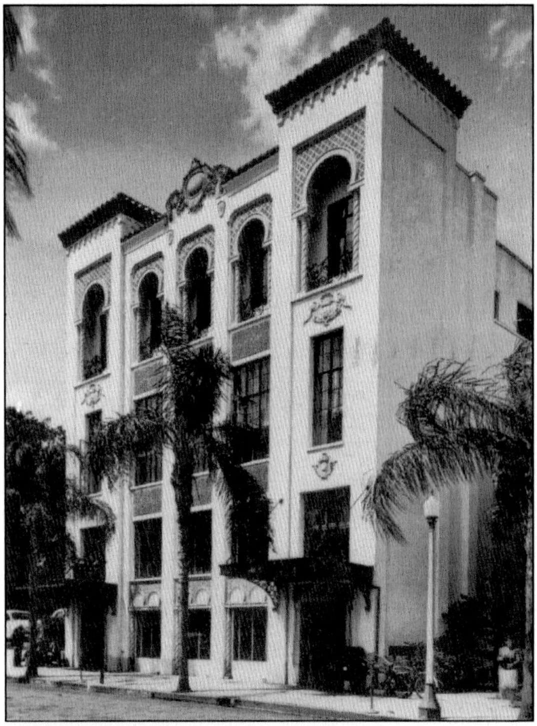

Architect Howard M. Reynolds designed the new chamber of commerce headquarters on East Central Boulevard in 1926. The four-story steel and tile structure, built by Fred Ley, Inc., featured an ornate exterior and a columned lobby with plants and a fountain. In 1935, artists with the Florida Artist Project of the Federal Emergency Relief Administration painted murals in the auditorium. The chamber of commerce traded the property to the city in 1967, accepting in return a site for a new headquarters on Ivanhoe Boulevard. When the chamber moved out of the old building in 1968, the city leased it to the junior chamber of commerce. The Jaycees remained in the building until 1983, when it was demolished to clear the block for an addition to the Orlando Public Library.

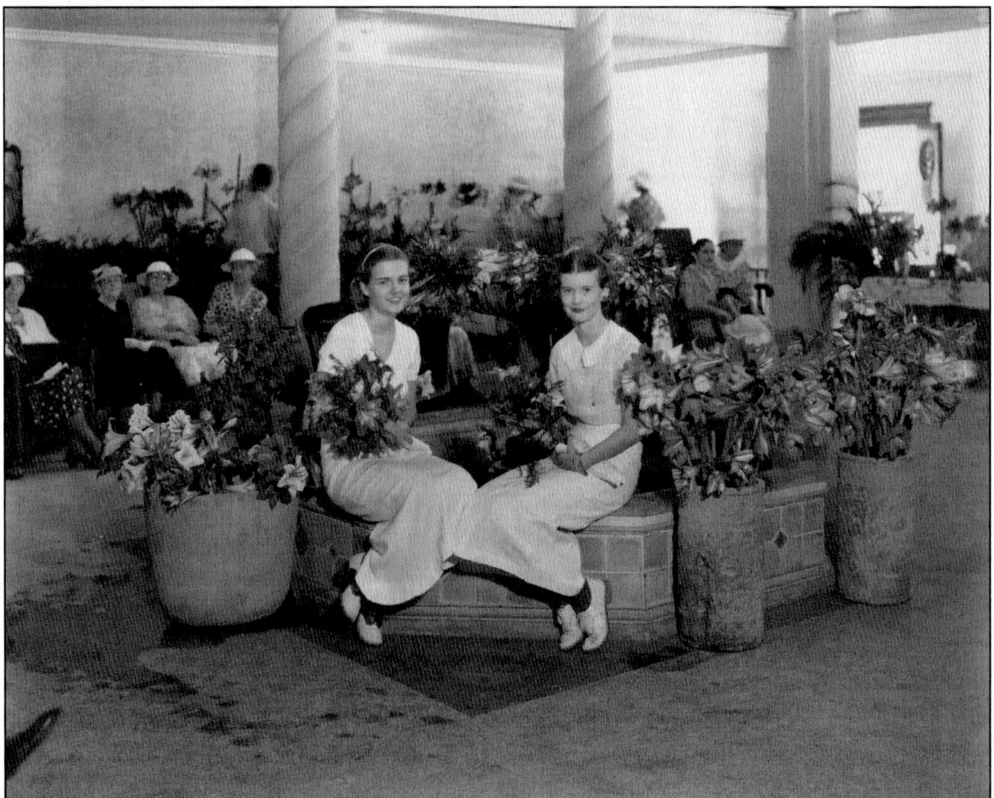

In 1927, St. Mark's African Methodist Episcopal congregation completed a new $15,000 church, seen here on August 20, 1940. The concrete tile building on Avondale Avenue at Conley Street, which replaced an earlier frame church at the same location, was demolished in 1971 to make way for the East-West Expressway.

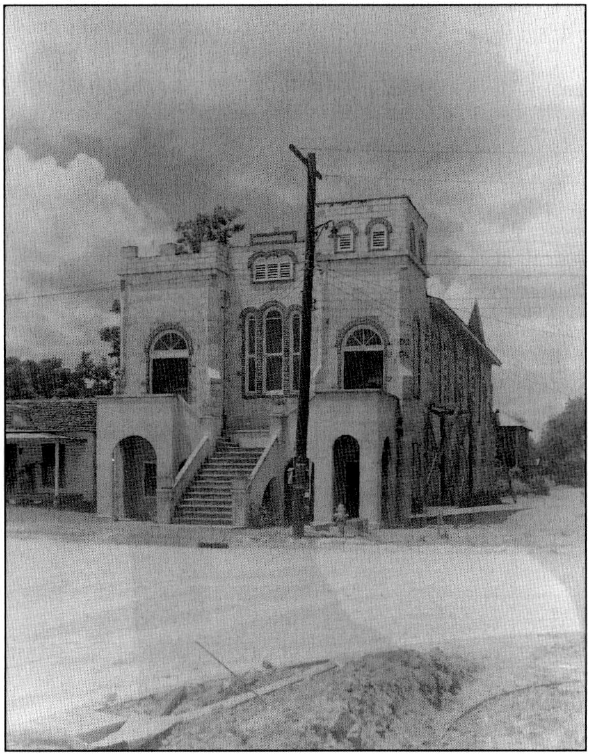

The Salvation Army came to Orlando in 1920 and opened a citadel on East Central Boulevard in 1928. They sold the land on East Central Boulevard to the City of Orlando in 1967 and dedicated a new citadel at Lake Dot in 1969. The Orlando Public Library was built on the former Salvation Army site.

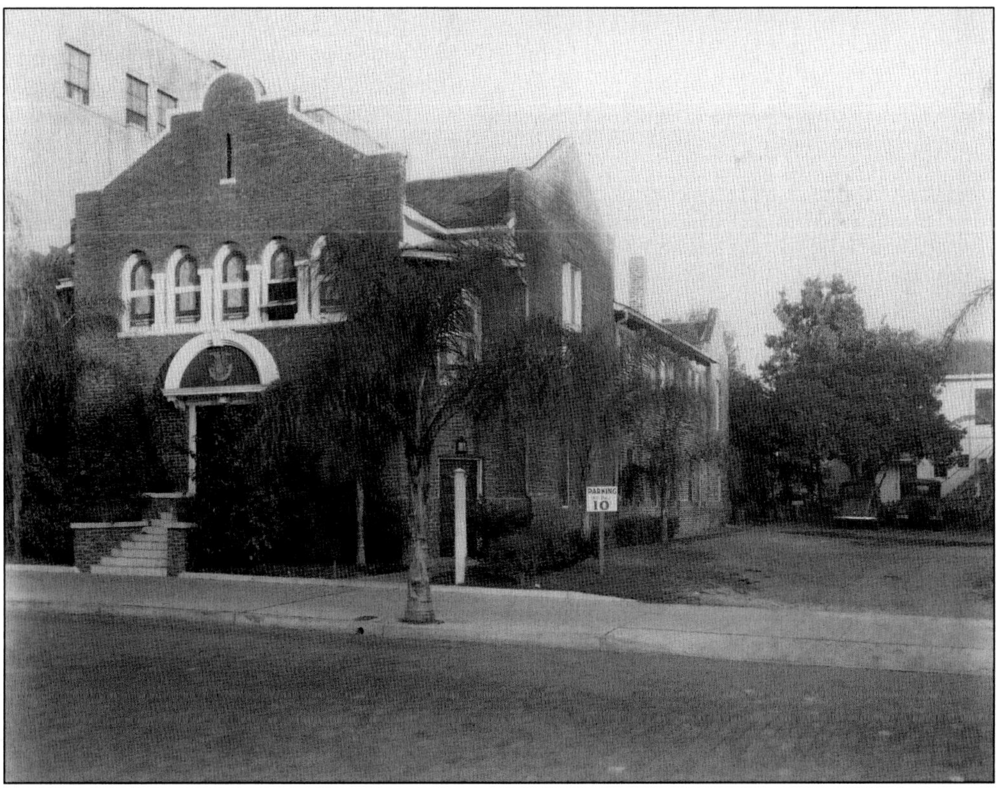

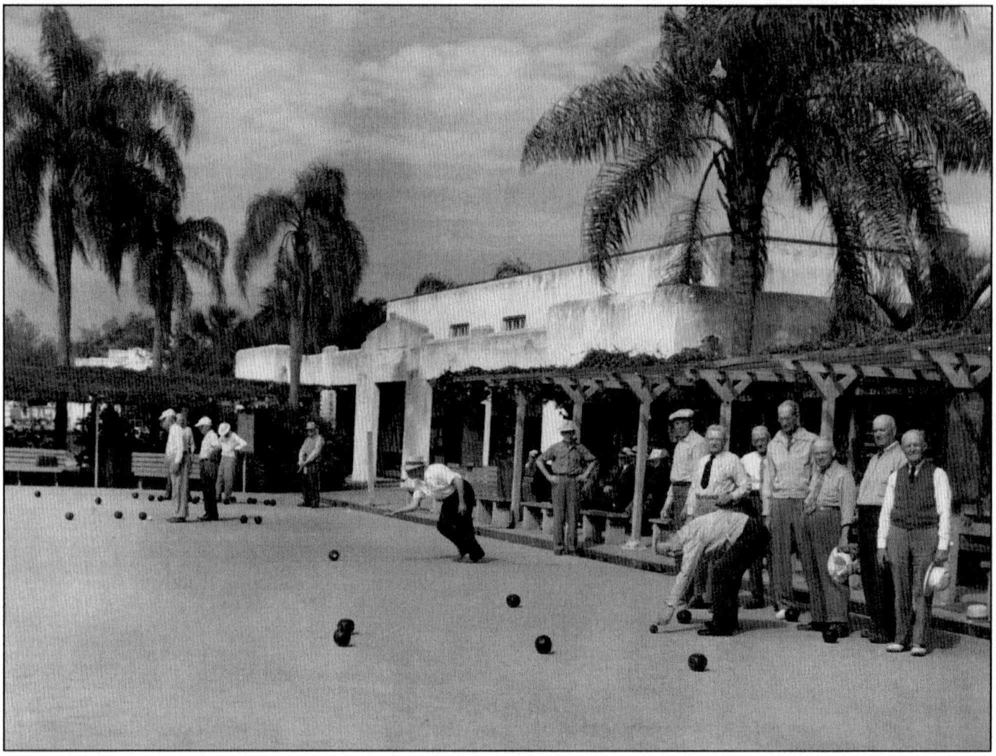

The Orlando Lawn Bowling Club was organized on December 11, 1922. The club used lawn bowling courts located on East Central Boulevard until the city moved the facilities to West Livingston Street in October 1923. In 1934, the club built its second clubhouse, seen here, at Exposition Park. The building was demolished for Interstate 4 expressway construction in 1959.

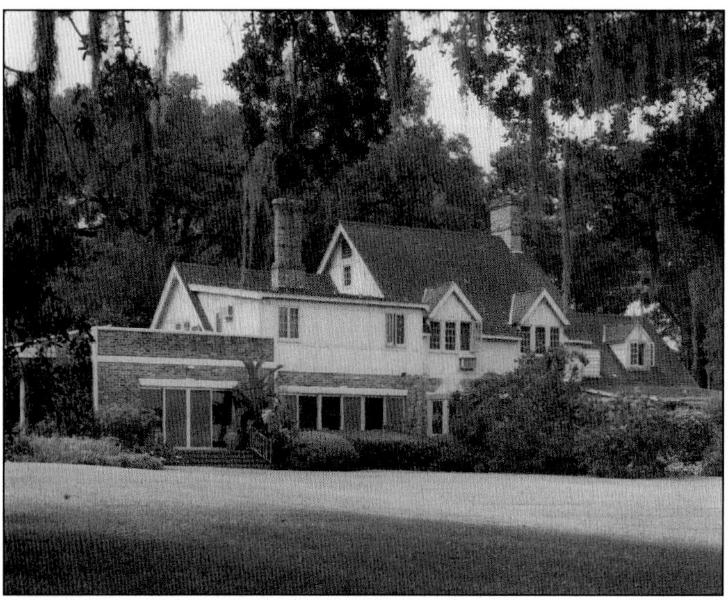

Noted architect James Gamble Rogers II built the house on Lake Concord in 1935 for Laura and John Huttig. The English Tudor design was unusual for the architect. The Huttigs died in the 1980s, and the house remained vacant for several years. It was restored in the 1990s and listed in the National Register of Historic Places in 1993. Despite this, the house was demolished in 2006.

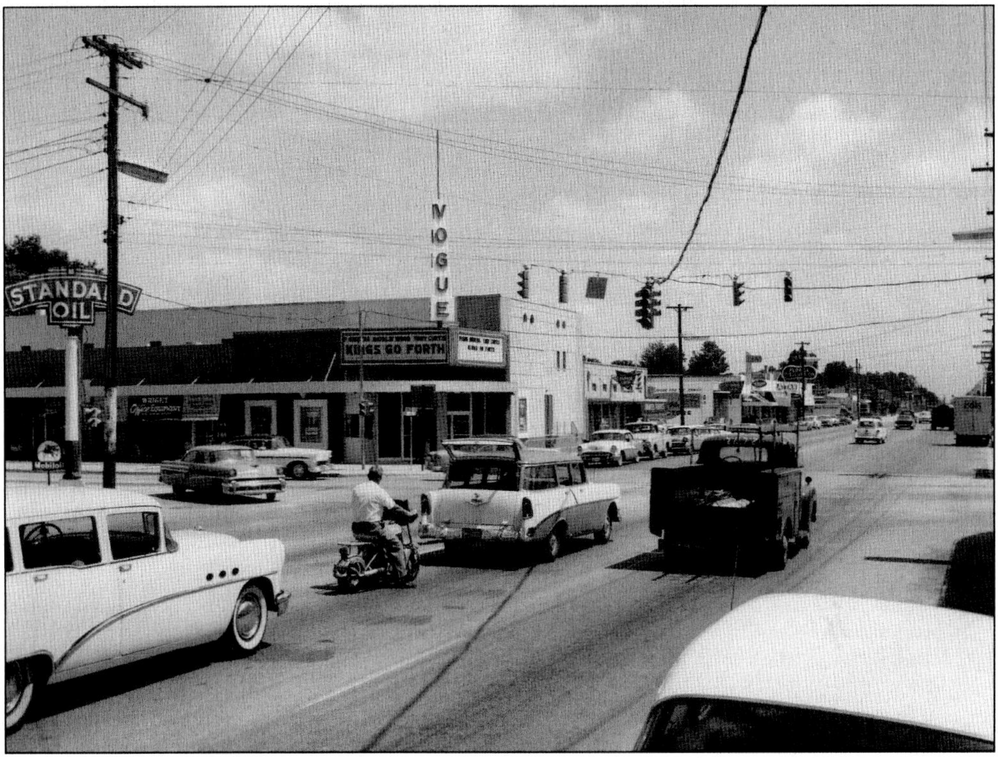

The Vogue Theatre, specializing in second-run movies, opened about 1936 in a building at the corner of Mills Avenue and Colonial Drive. The popular, air-conditioned theater offered family and general audience films on its 50-foot-high silver screen until the 1960s. Unable to compete with big theater chains, the 625-seat Vogue turned to art films. The theater closed in 1971 and was demolished to be replaced by a gas station.

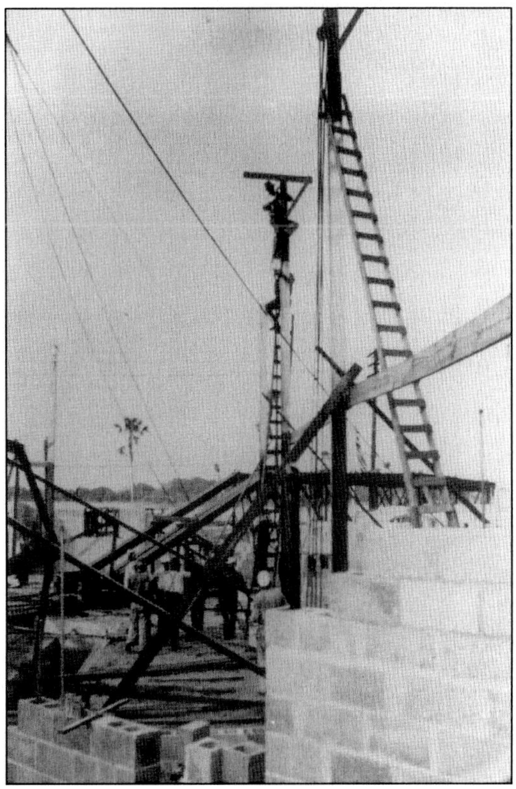

In 1938, the American Legion Post No. 19 laid the cornerstone for a new building on the former site of its old headquarters on North Orange Avenue. The Works Progress Administration constructed the new home on city property. The city and the American Legion signed a 60-year lease agreement that granted the American Legion $1-per-year rent with an option for an additional 30-year renewal.

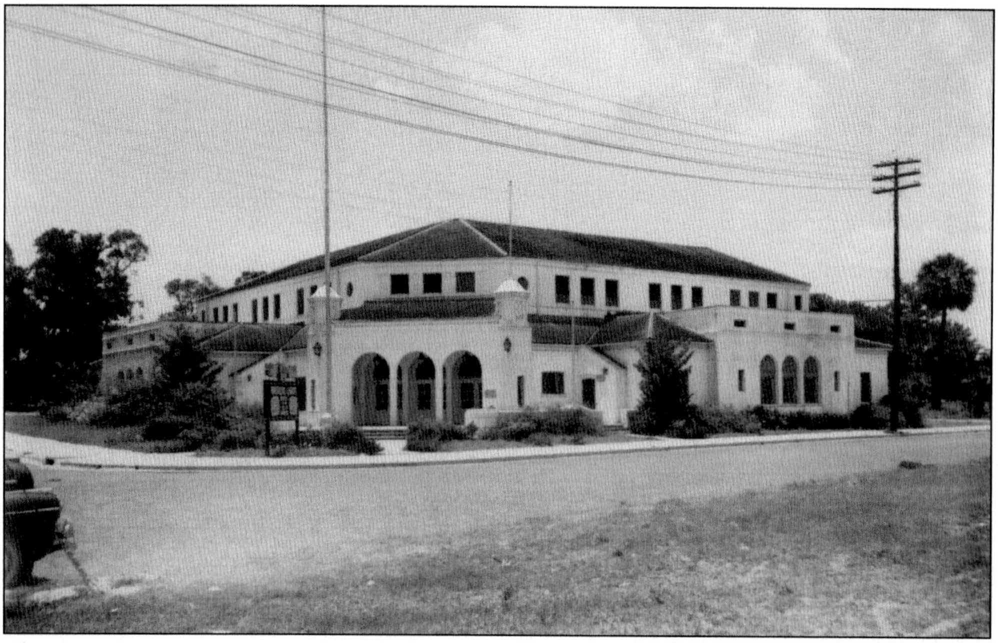

The American Legion finally leased and dedicated the building in 1949. In 1987, the city sold the land for an office building. To satisfy a $1-per-year lease that did not expire until 2008, the American Legion moved to a new property on city-owned land near the Ben White Raceway. The Bank of America Center now occupies the North Orange Avenue site.

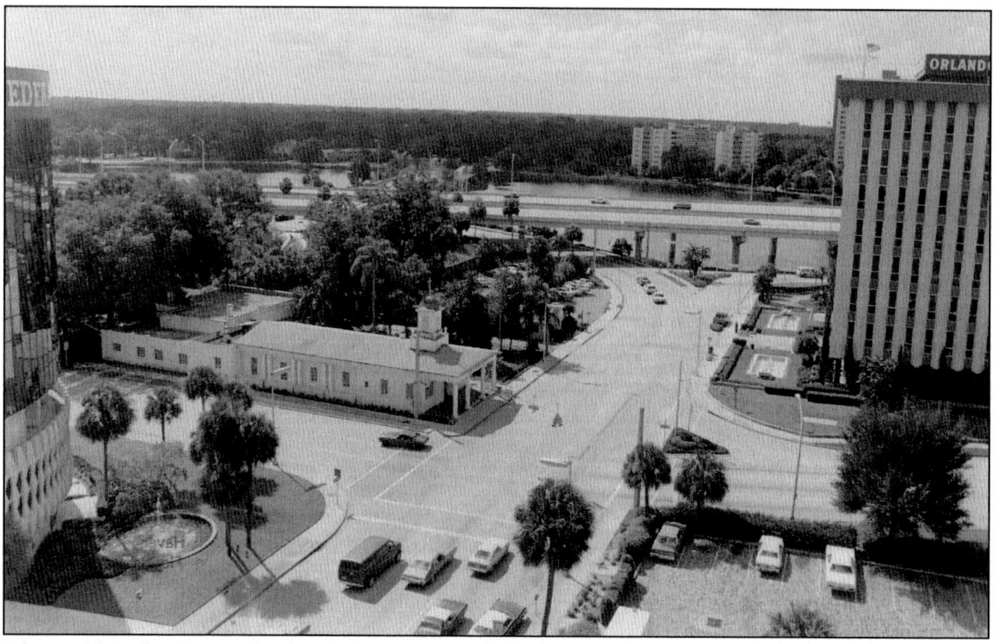

Christ Church Unity of Orlando began in 1932 with gatherings in the Tremont Hotel. Forty-two members broke ground in 1942 for their first church building at 503 South Orange Avenue. Having outgrown the small white church with its dome and front porch columns, the congregation bought land on Holden Avenue in 1992 and built a new church in 1999. The old building was demolished in 1999.

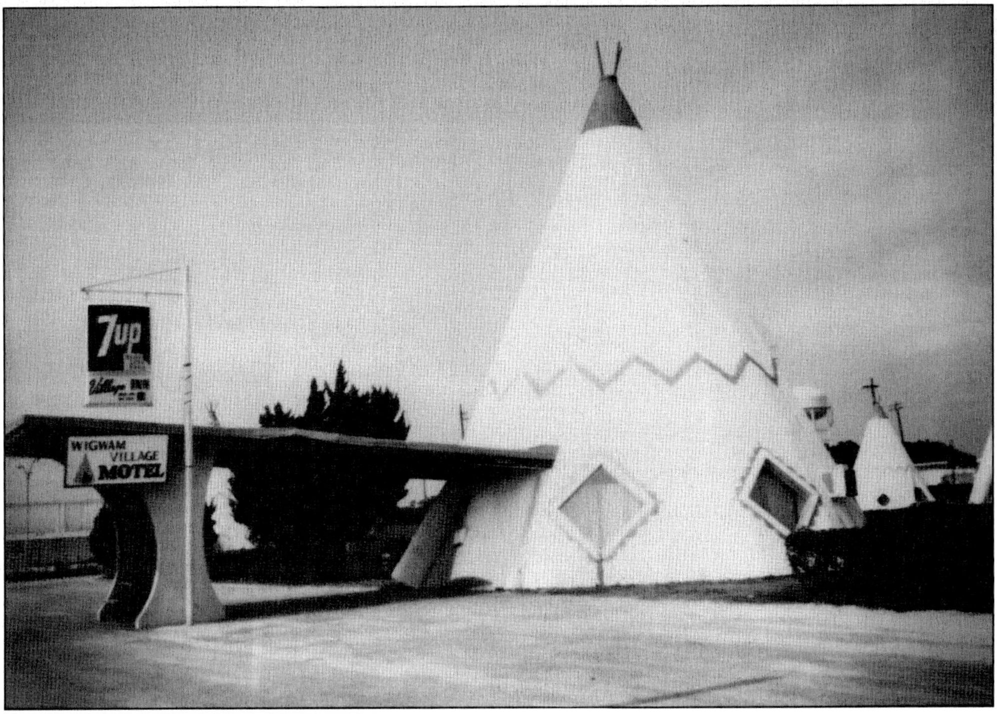

The eye-catching Wigwam Village Motel was built in 1947 at a cost of $100,000, along the South Orange Blossom Trail. Each of the 27 steel and concrete stucco cones in the horseshoe-shaped complex housed one motel unit; the interior of which, shown in this 1948 postcard, was decorated with a Native American theme. Plush for the time, each unit also featured a tile bath, radio, ceiling fan, heater, and furniture constructed of solid hickory wood. Elliott Roosevelt, son of Pres. Franklin D. Roosevelt, and his wife stayed at the motel on November 16, 1951. Orlando's Wigwam Village, the fourth of seven in six states, was demolished in 1973 to build a modern motel.

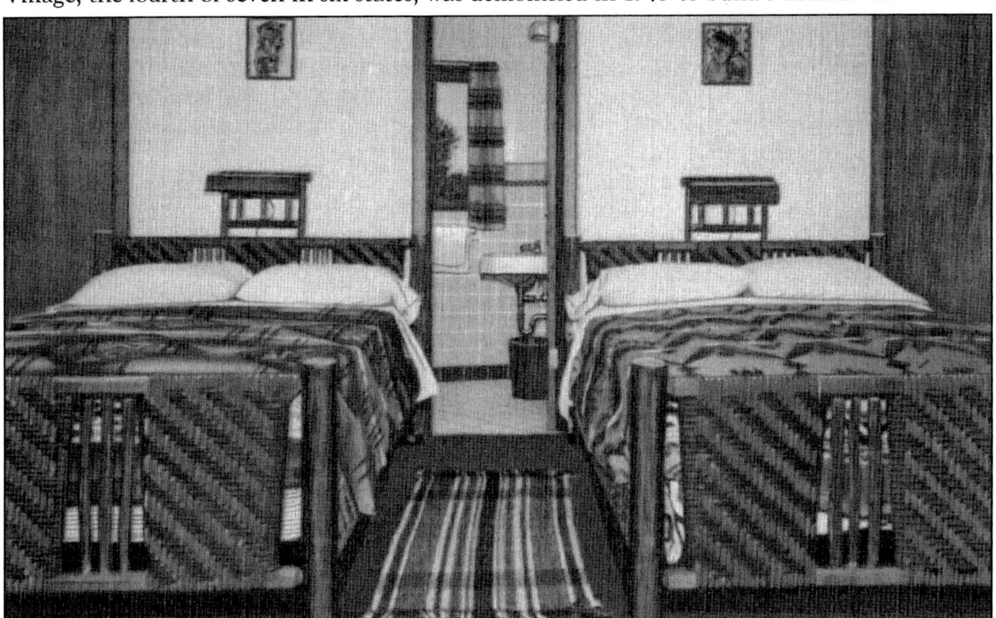

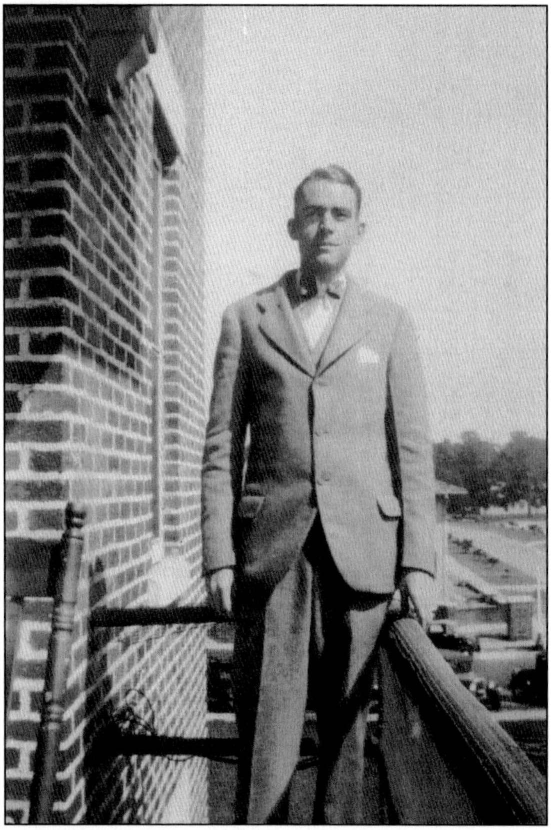

Dr. Louis Orr moved to Orlando in 1927 and became an internationally known urologist. He was the first doctor in Central Florida to use radioactive isotopes to treat certain types of cancer and introduced radioactive gold to Orange Memorial Hospital. He moved into his new clinic on South Orange Avenue in 1950. Orlando architect James Gamble Rogers II, designed the one-story brick reproduction of Jeffersonian architecture with four ionic columns and a front pediment. The massive building occupied an entire block between Copeland Drive and Underwood Avenue. Doctor Orr died in 1961, and his clinic was demolished in 1985. The Orlando Regional Medical Center Ambulatory Care now occupies the site.

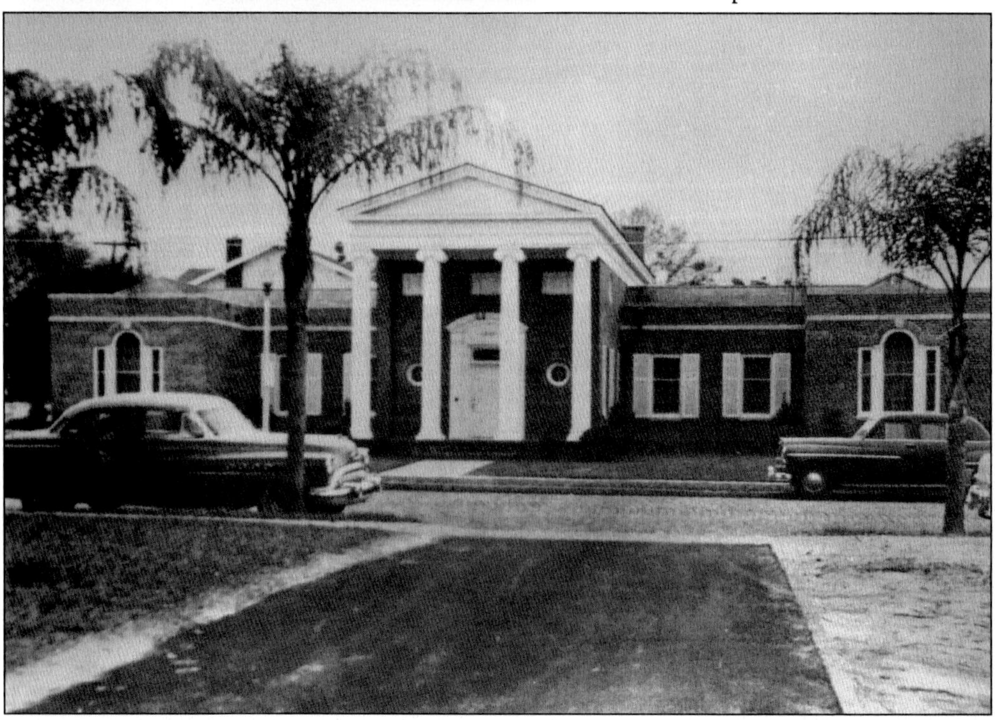

Five

1951–2011

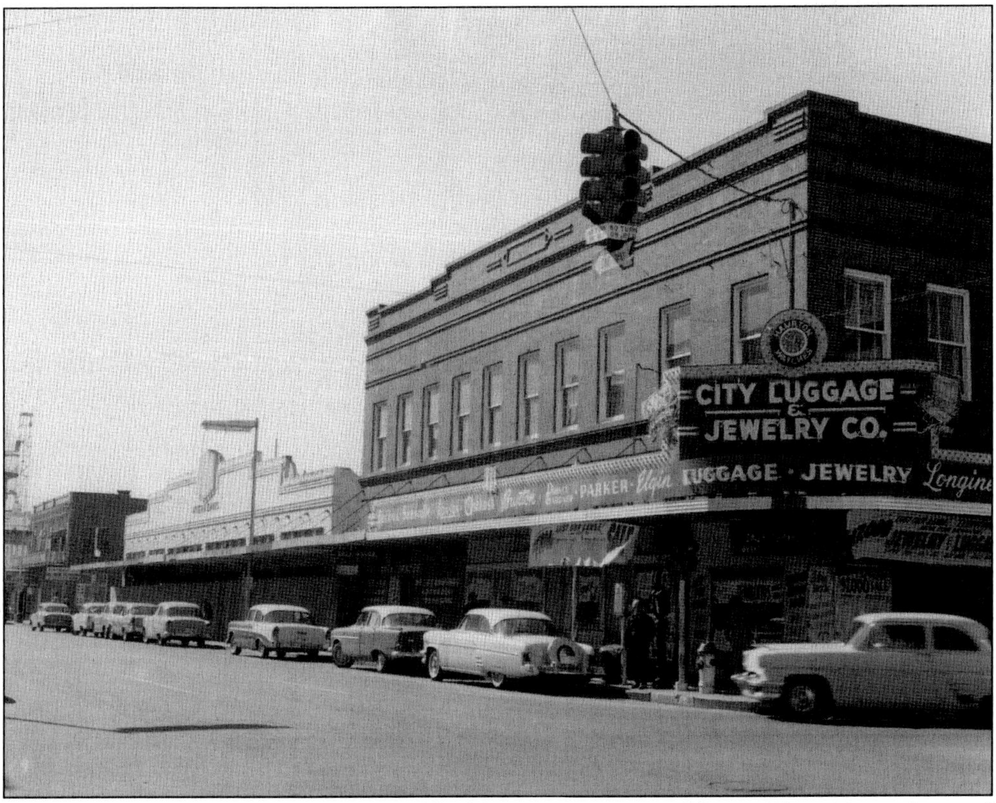

The process of building, demolishing, and building again continued from 1951 to 2011, as hospital expansions and downtown rejuvenation required mass destruction to clear whole blocks. Even relatively new structures were not immune to the wrecking ball. From its beginning, people came to Orlando to prosper and build. Now, those men and their buildings are gone, but the city's history is the richer for their having been here.

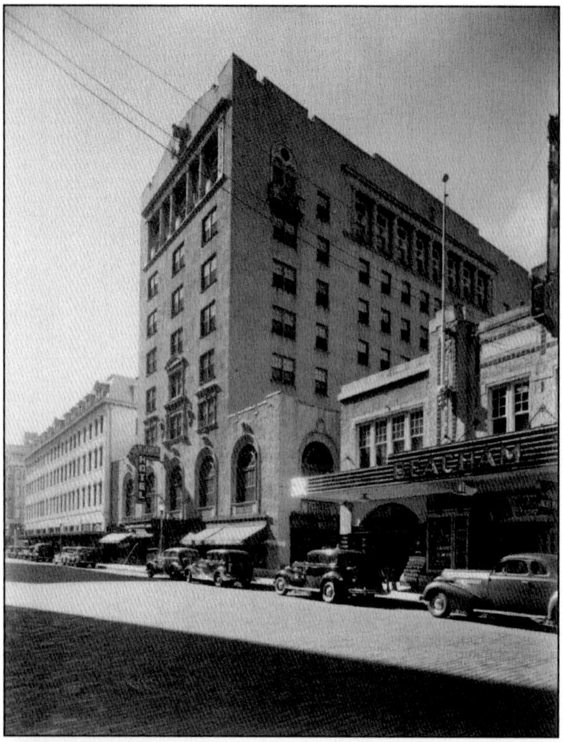

In 1921, eight stories were added to the San Juan Hotel building. The hotel underwent changes again in 1928, and the plans included rebuilding the corner of Orange Avenue and Central Boulevard along more modern lines. By the 1970s, the San Juan lost favor with the citizens of Orlando. In 1976, Orlando attorney and developer Bryan Thomas purchased the San Juan in the hopes of attracting foreign visitors. Unfortunately, his plan failed, as tourists chose to stay closer to Walt Disney World. Thomas eventually sold the building to a group of investors who renamed it Grand Central and catered to the gay community. The building caught fire in 1979 and was torn down a year later. Today, the Wachovia Building sits on the site of the once-grand hotel.

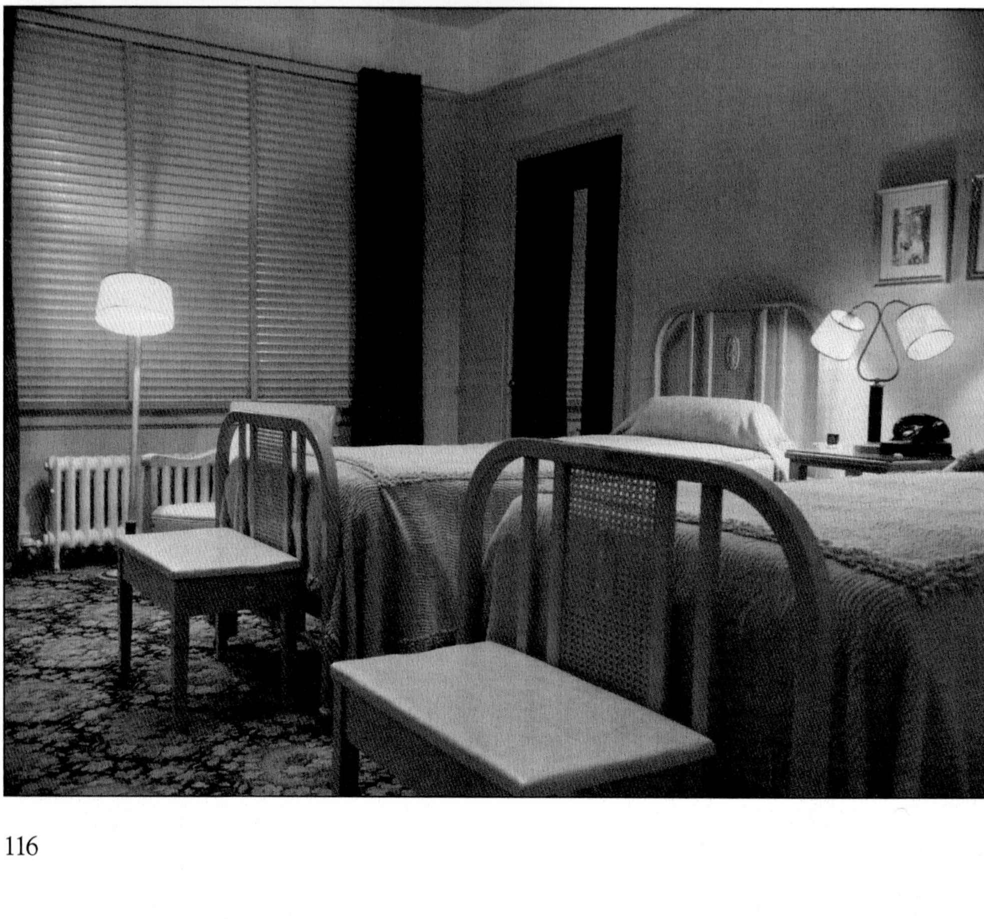

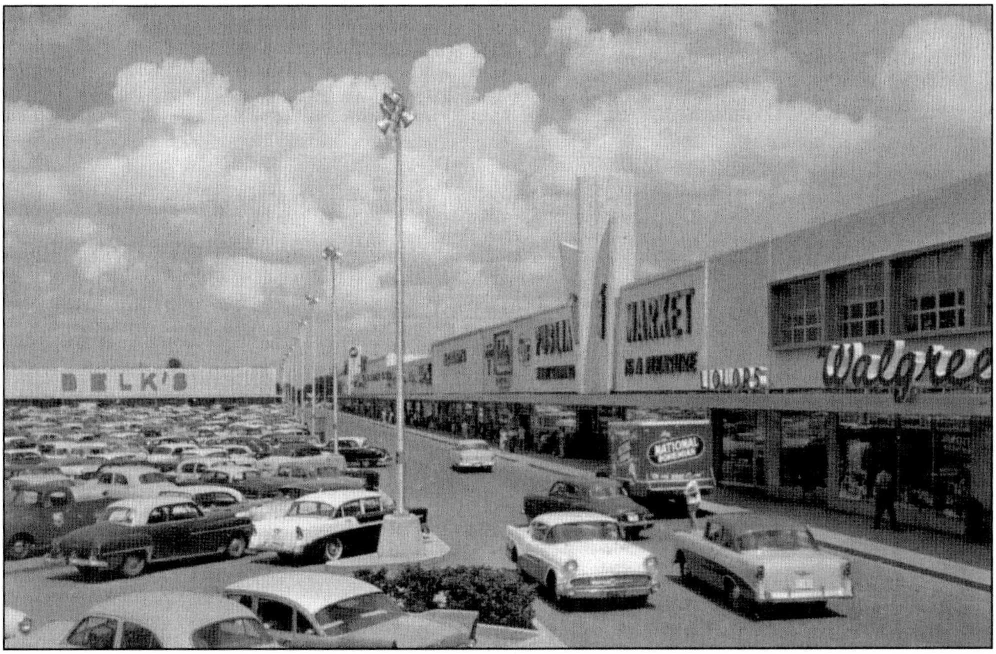

In 1953, the T.G. Lee Dairy sold 20 acres of former pastureland on Colonial Drive to an investment realty company in New York City. Colonial Plaza, Orlando's first shopping center, opened on the site in 1956, and the city changed forever. Over 20 stores and abundant free parking attracted more than 150,000 shoppers on opening day. More shopping centers followed, and finally, the downtown stores closed.

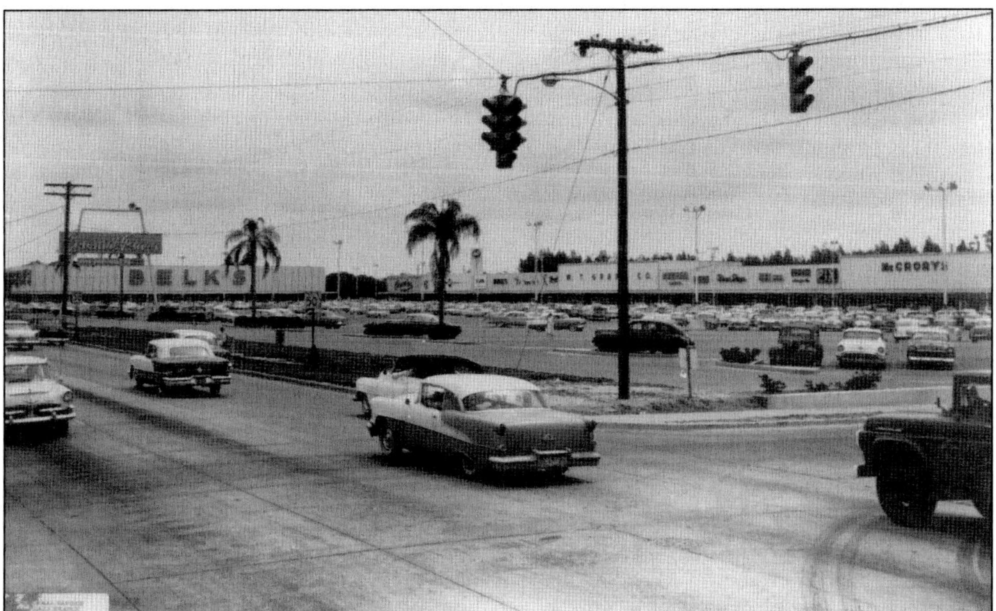

In 1956, the Belk-Lindsey store moved from its building at 129 West Church Street to the Colonial Plaza. The new freestanding store served as an anchor for a row of shops in the plaza. On October 15, 1973, a new Belk-Lindsey opened in the Colonial Plaza Mall. The structure was eventually torn down to make room for newer stores and restaurants.

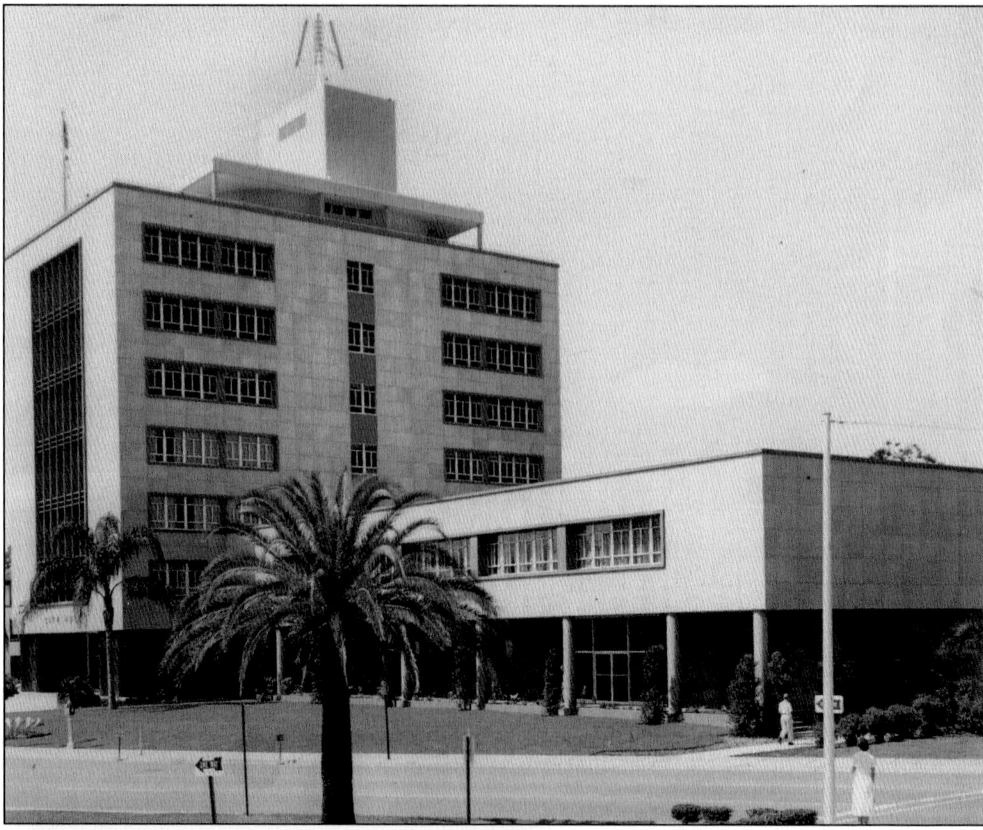

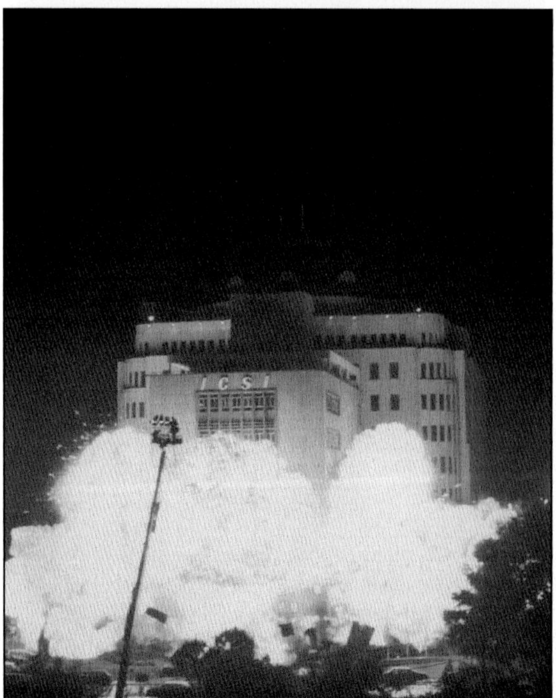

Orlando broke ground for a new city hall on the southwest corner of South Orange Avenue and South Street in 1956. City offices moved into the new $1.6 million building in 1958. In July 1991, the government moved again to a new $36 million city hall adjacent to the old one.

On October 24, 1991, the 1958 city hall building was imploded in a special effects-enhanced blast, filmed for the opening scene of the movie *Lethal Weapon 3*. Former Orlando mayor Bill Frederick had a cameo role as a policeman in the film, saying, "Bravo," to the two main characters after the explosion.

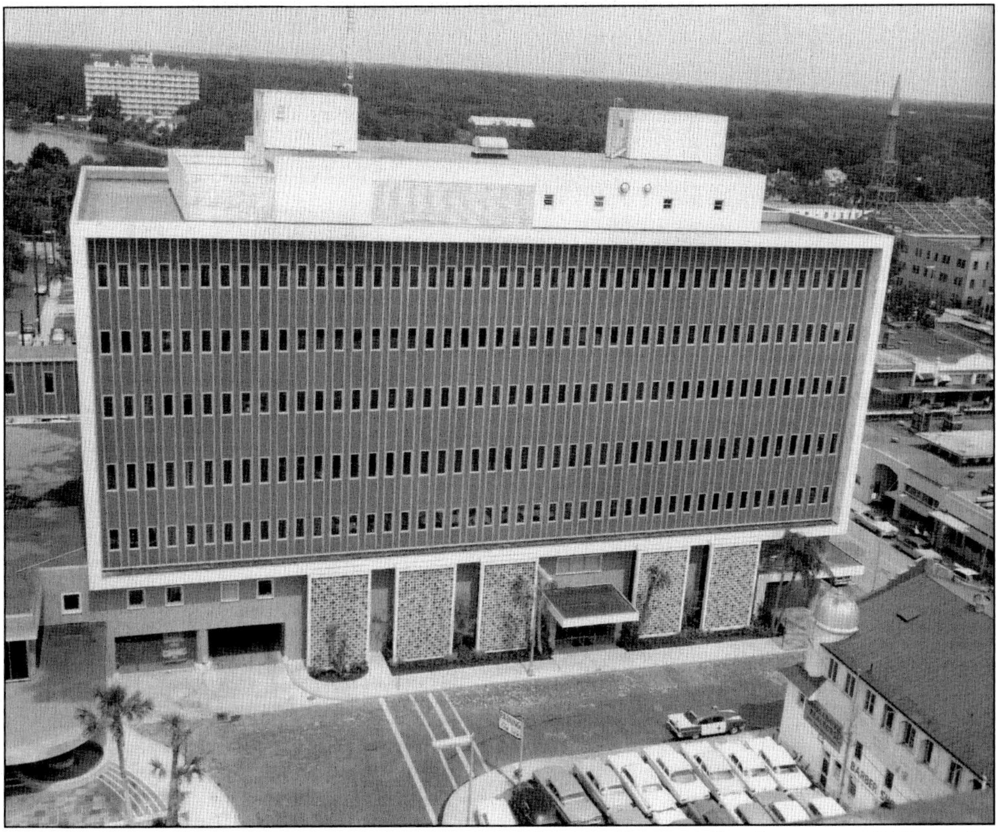

Orange County built the annex to the 1927 Courthouse on Magnolia Avenue in 1960 on the site of the former 1892 Red Brick Courthouse. Originally designed as a 14-story skyscraper with the first four floors dedicated to parking, architect James B. King scaled the building down to a seven-story structure with exterior walls covered with turquoise tile and clay blocks made in pre-Castro Cuba. The massive size of the building forced the relocation of Court Street 100 feet to the west. The Courthouse Annex was demolished in 1997, after the county built a new courthouse several blocks north on Orange Avenue. The 1927 Courthouse became home to the Orange County Regional History Center, and the site of the former Courthouse Annex became Heritage Square.

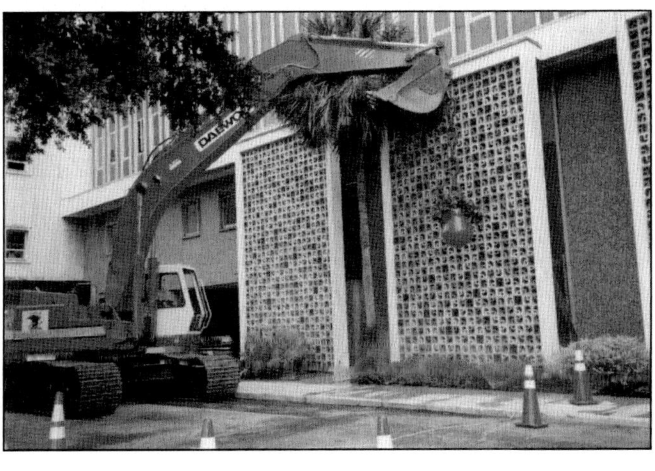

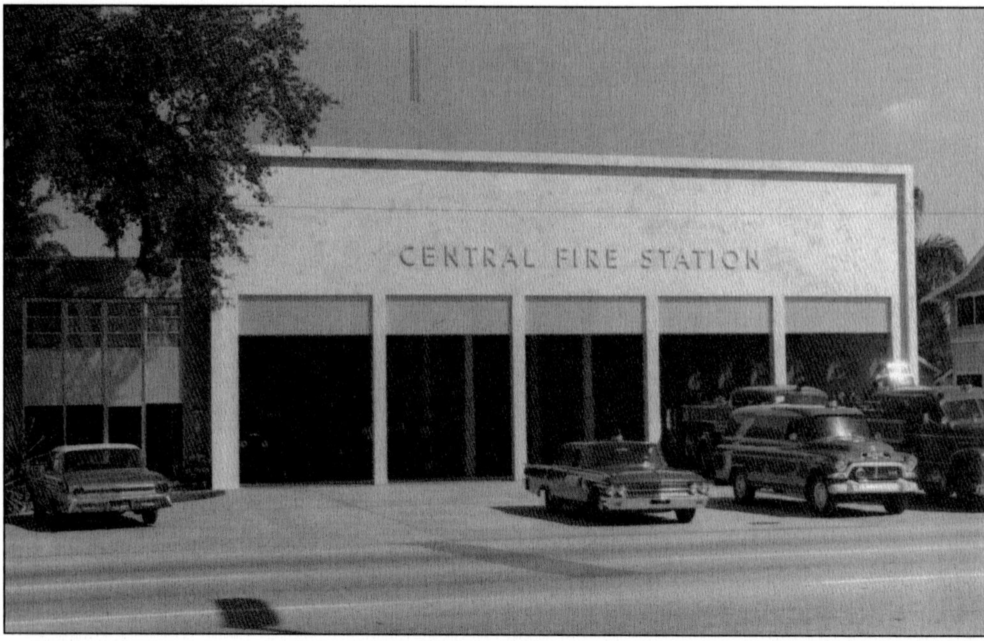

In 1960, construction started on a $292,703 central fire station on South Magnolia Avenue to replace the old one across from the courthouse. The fire department moved out of the 1960 building and into a new three-story, $21 million station in 2009. The old structure was demolished to clear the site for the Dr. Phillips Center for the Performing Arts.

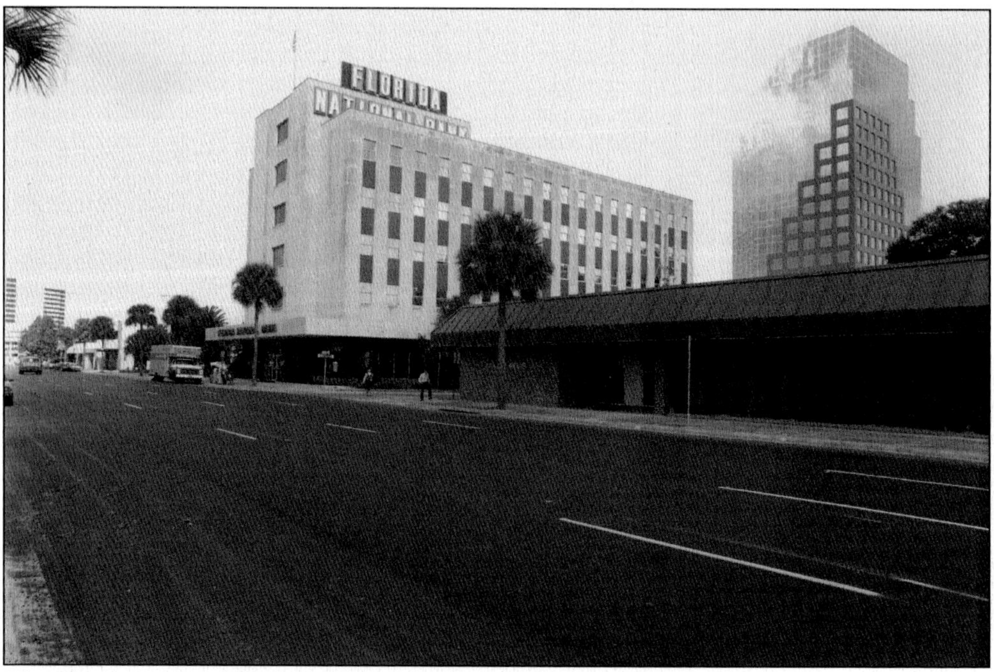

The Florida National Bank building opened in 1961 on North Orange Avenue at Park Lake Street. At that time, the six-story, steel and concrete, state-of-the-art building occupied the last undeveloped land in the downtown area. The implosion of the 28-year-old building was filmed in 1999 for a television program. Today, condominiums occupy the site.

The seven-story Downtown Motor Inn, visible at left in the foreground of the photograph, opened at 260 South Orange Avenue in 1962. Built at a cost of $1 million, the 112-room hotel included a restaurant, lounge, and banquet facilities. The owners closed it in 1974, citing a lack of business. A high-rise office building replaced it in 2000.

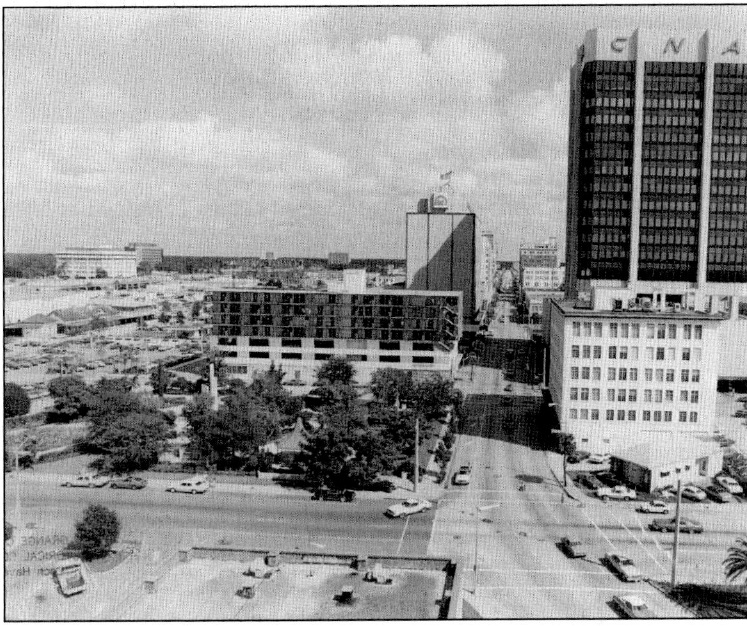

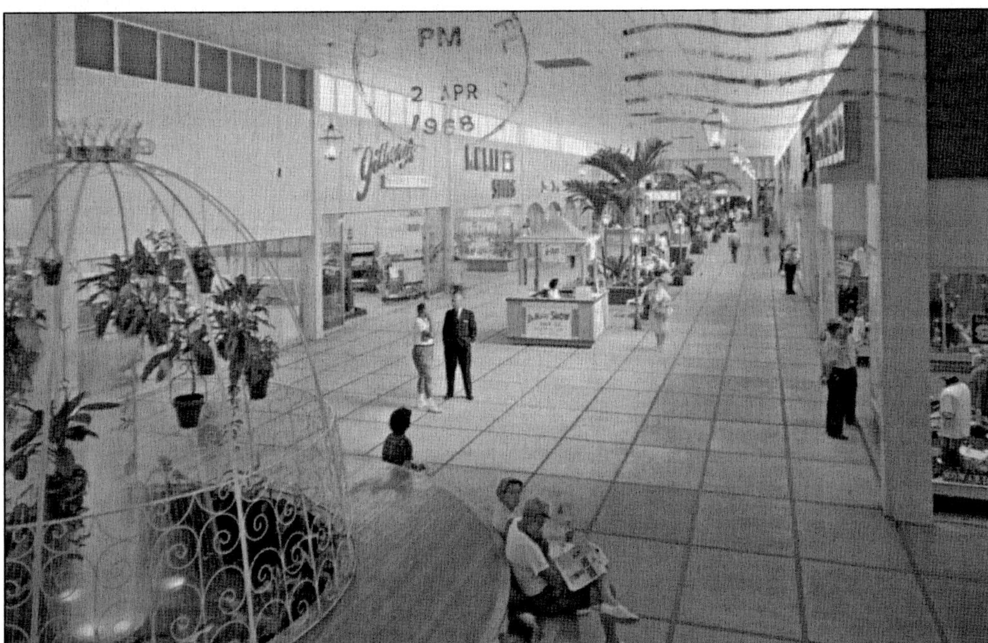

In 1962, when Jordan Marsh built a new store in Colonial Plaza, the strip shopping center expanded and converted to an enclosed mall, the first in Central Florida. By 1991, the mall competed with a growing number of newer malls, including the Fashion Square Mall, located a few blocks away. In 1995, a new owner demolished most of the mall to build a discount and specialty store shopping center.

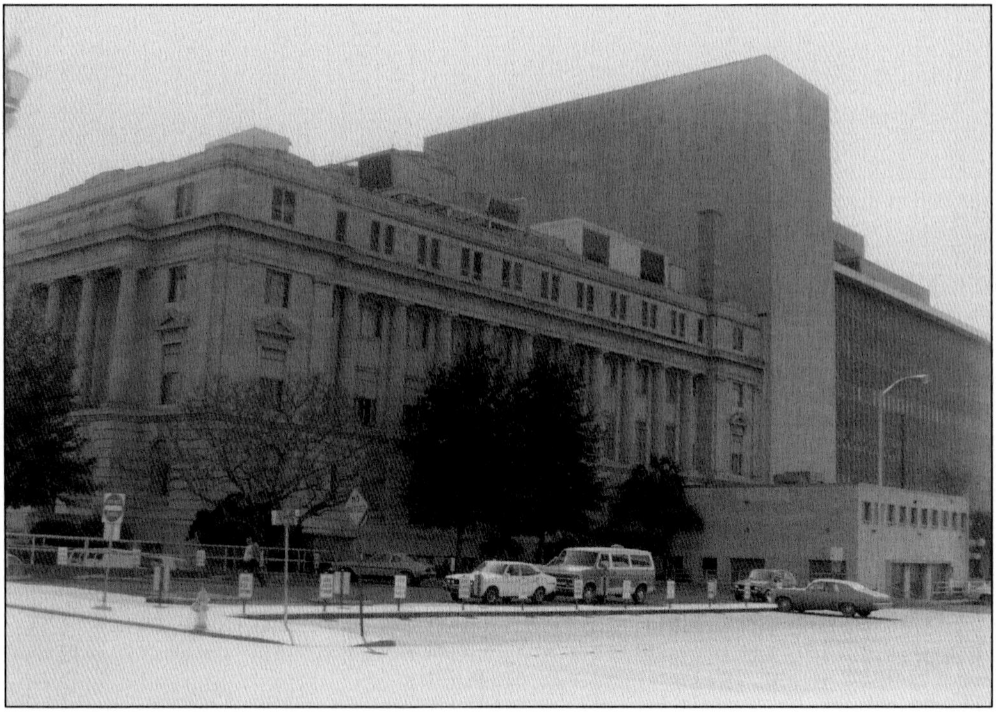

Less than a decade after the Courthouse Annex opened in 1960, Orange County officials announced that the government needed more space. A 10-story tower, completed in 1971 between the Courthouse Annex and the 1927 Courthouse, connected the two buildings. In 1989, concerns about the asbestos used in the annex led to the closing of the Courthouse Annex and the Courthouse Tower. Both were demolished in 1997 and replaced with Heritage Square.

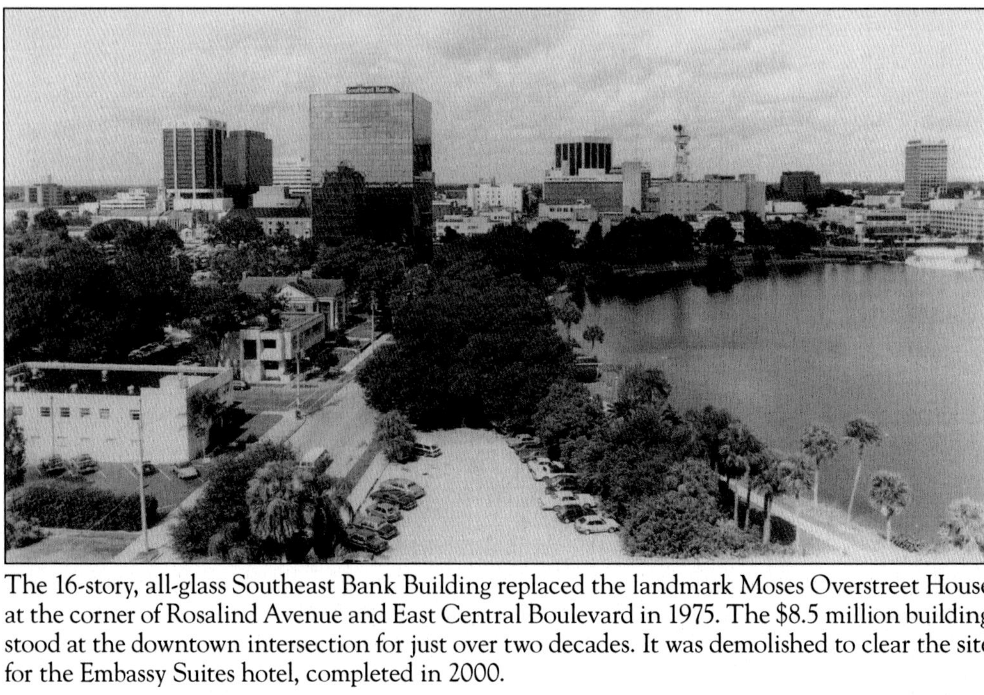

The 16-story, all-glass Southeast Bank Building replaced the landmark Moses Overstreet House at the corner of Rosalind Avenue and East Central Boulevard in 1975. The $8.5 million building stood at the downtown intersection for just over two decades. It was demolished to clear the site for the Embassy Suites hotel, completed in 2000.

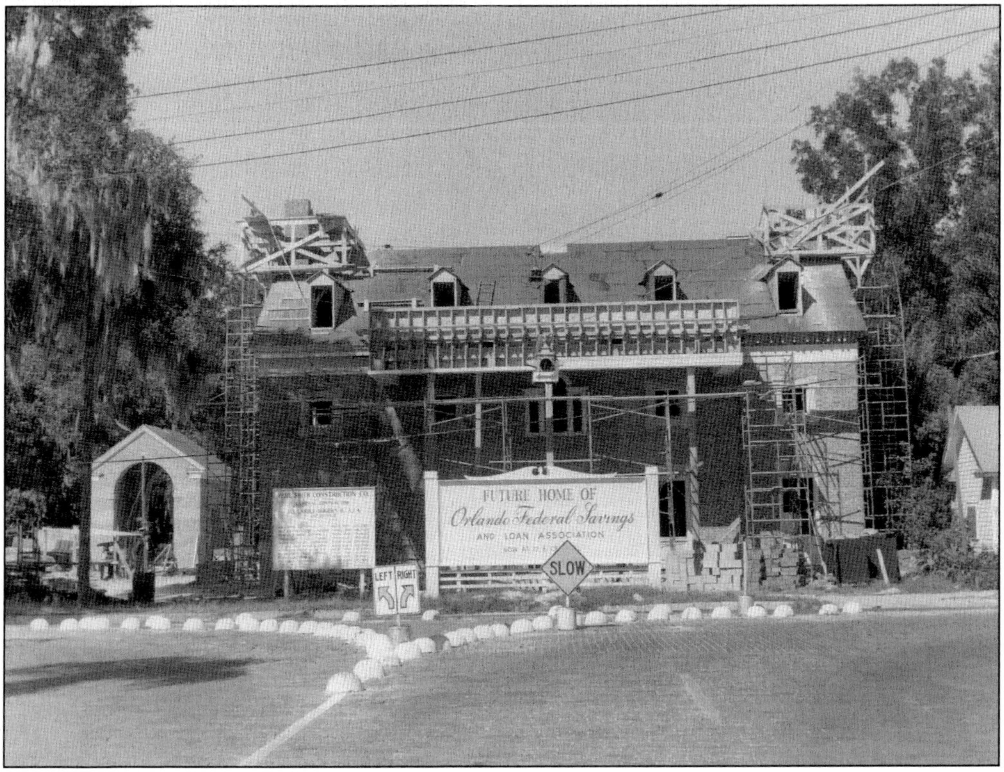

Orlando architect James Gamble Rogers II designed the Orlando Federal Savings and Loan building on East Livingston Street in 1955. Intended to become a landmark, the Colonial-style structure, built with brick from Virginia, combined aesthetic appeal with utilitarian design. The bank's founders admired Colonial Williamsburg, Virginia, as a living manifestation of the American way of life, and they built in the architectural style of Williamsburg to demonstrate that the establishment stood for those values. Colonial grandeur, historical significance, and modern convenience came together in the white-columned, redbrick bank. The bank opened with horse-drawn carriages and ladies in Colonial costumes on the lawn. The graceful structure was demolished in 1994 to clear the site for the Orange County Courthouse on North Orange Avenue.

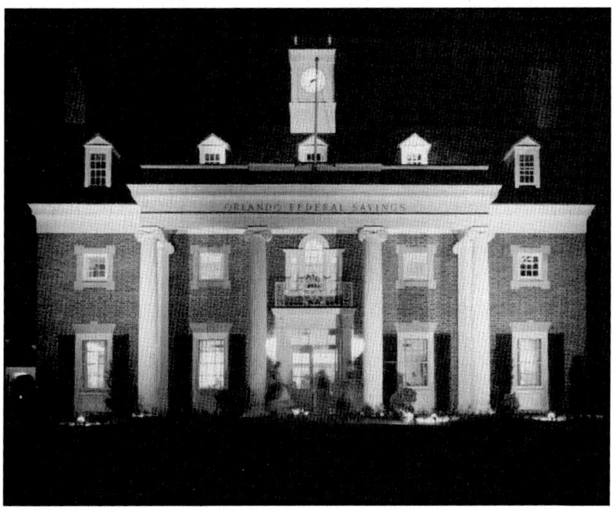

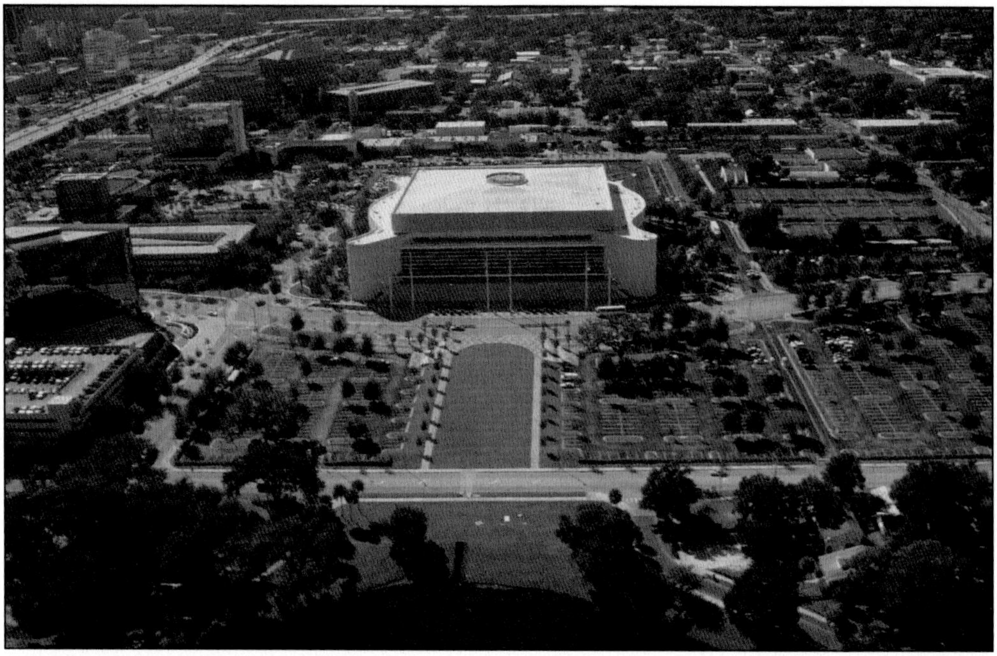

After more than a year of planning, hoping, and waiting, Orlando received the green light for an expansion basketball team in April 1987. Construction of the Amway Arena, located at 600 Amelia Street, began in early 1987 as a part of this planning process. Built at a cost of $110 million, the Amway Arena could seat over 15,000 spectators. Between its opening on January 29, 1989, and its final event on September 30, 2010, the arena was known as Orlando Arena, TD Waterhouse Centre, the arena in Orlando, and finally as the Amway Arena. The arena closed with the opening of the Amway Center, the new home of the Orlando Magic. Demolition of the building began on December 15, 2011. Slated to take its place is the new Creative Village, which will be home to high-tech companies, residences, and shopping areas.

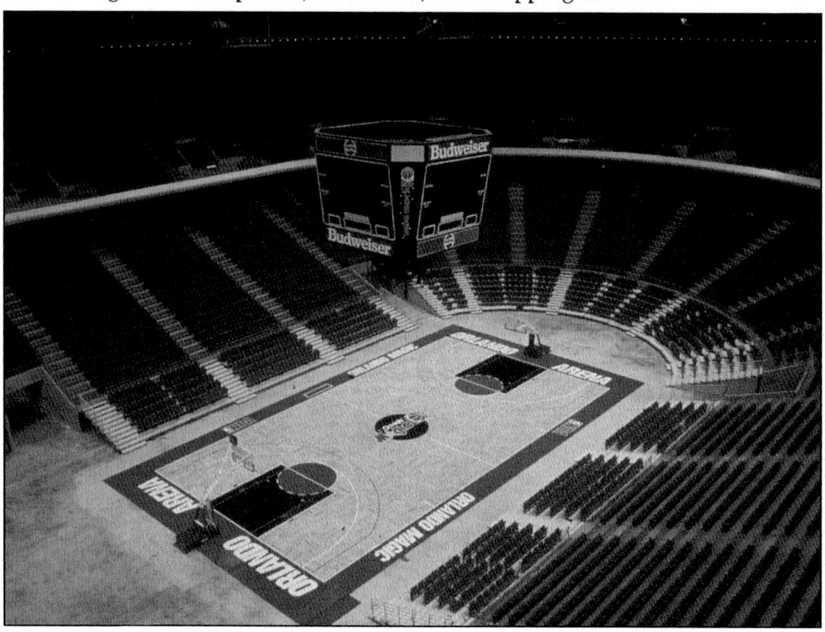

Six

ENDANGERED PROPERTIES

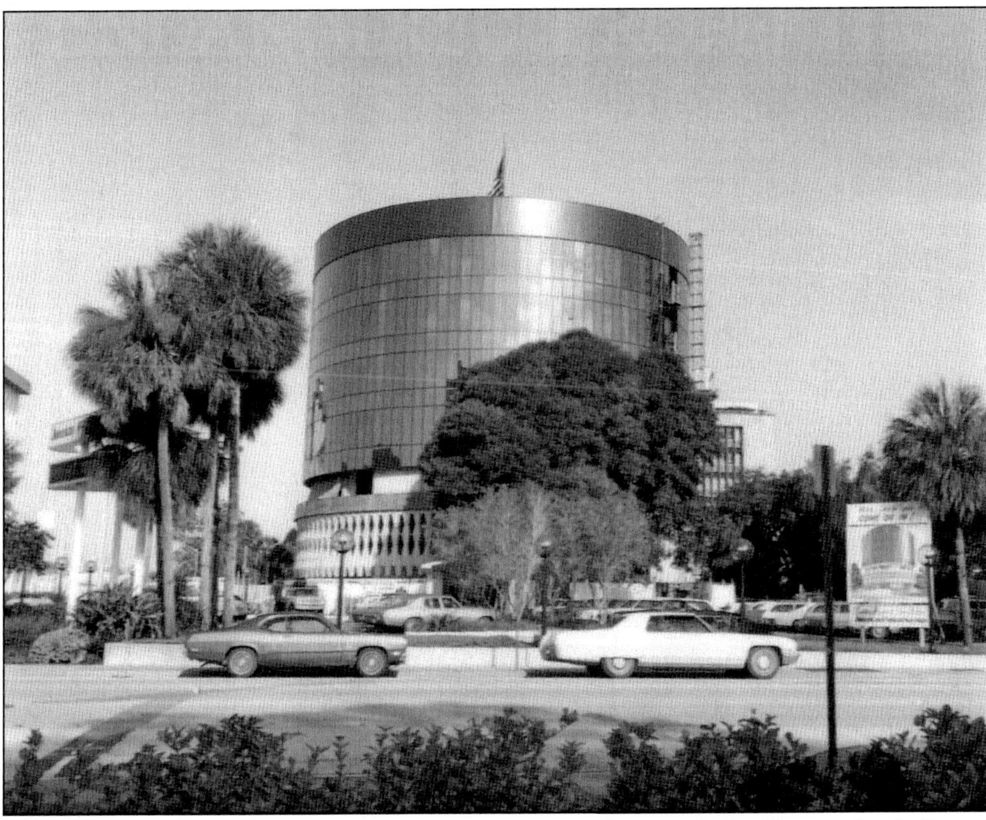

The American Federal Savings & Loan Association opened its circular building on South Orange Avenue in 1963. The American Institute of Architects protested when the demolition of the structure was scheduled for 2009 as part of the site clearance for the Dr. Phillips Center for the Performing Arts. The building remains standing while architects strive to preserve some of the exterior cement work.

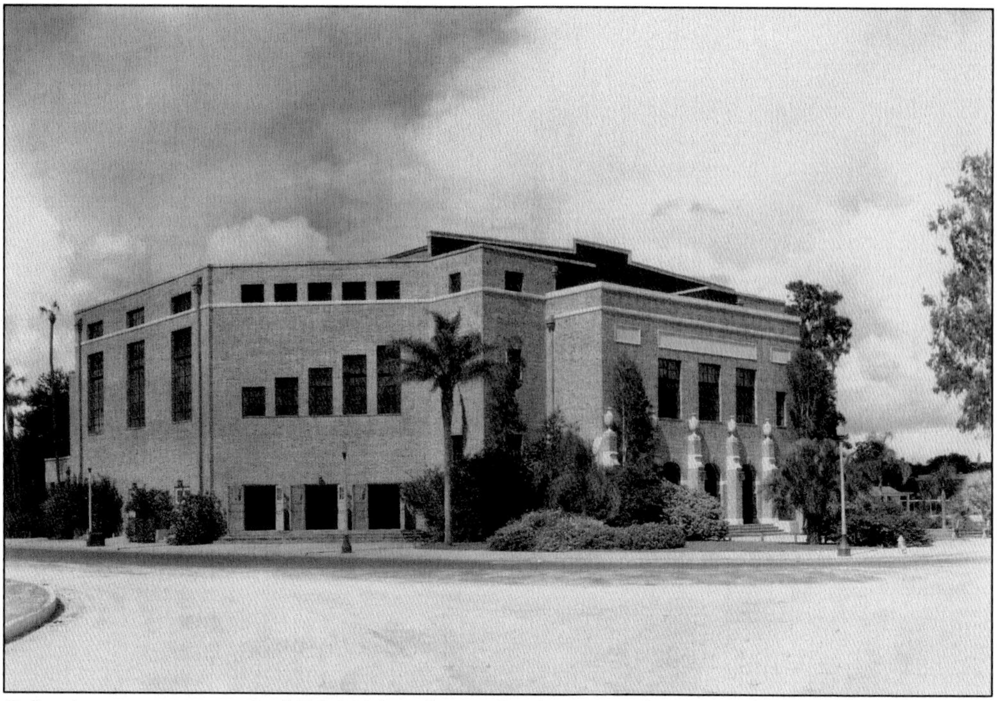

Orlando voters approved a $100,000 bond issue for the city auditorium in 1924. In a 1925 special election, voters selected the fairgrounds as the site for the new auditorium. Work started later that year. The Municipal Auditorium opened in February 1927 with a performance by the La Scala Grand Opera Company of Philadelphia. In 1976, the city started a $2.36 million project to remodel the auditorium into the Bob Carr Performing Arts Centre. The renovation included enclosing the front facade of the old building with a glass lobby. The art center's future is in limbo, as it sits on the site of the future Creative Village. In addition, the city has started construction of the Dr. Phillips Center for the Performing Arts, slated to replace the old structure.

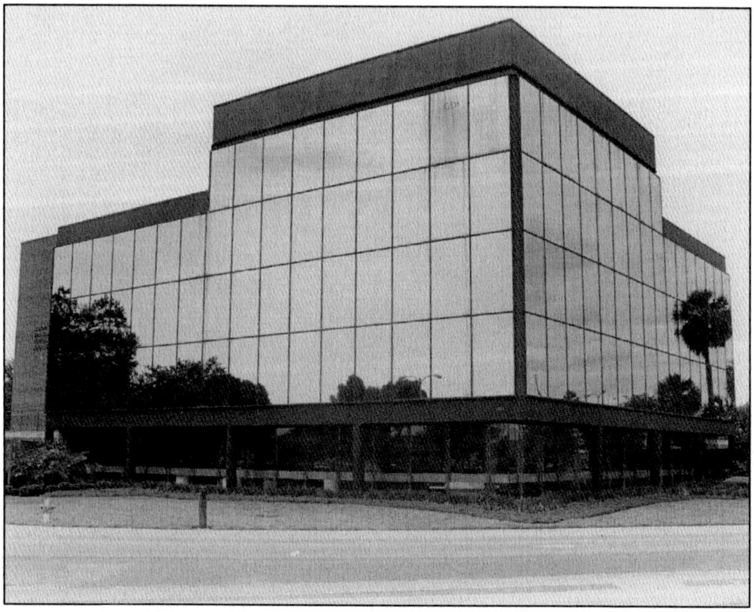

The Central Christian Church completed its Mediterranean-style building in 1928 near Lake Eola. In 1955, the congregation moved to a new church on Lake Ivanhoe. The old building was donated to the St. James Cathedral School. The Catholic diocese applied for demolition permits in 2008 and 2010. The Florida Trust for Historic Preservation added the church to its list of the state's most endangered historic sites in 2010.

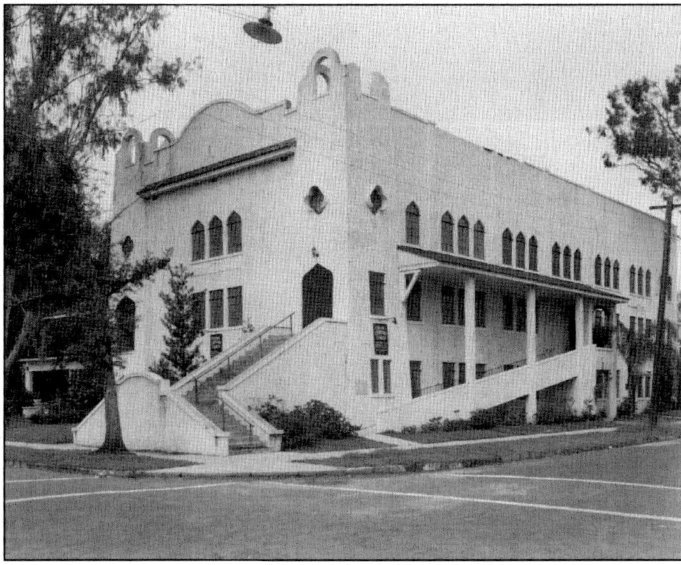

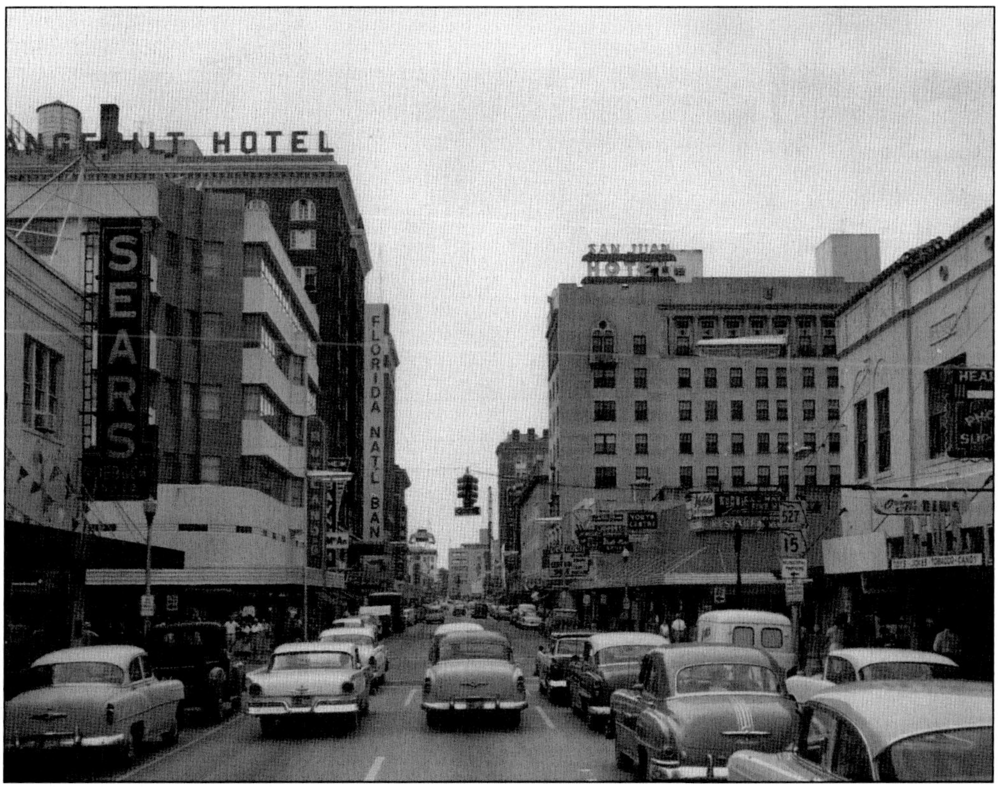

In 1991, Orlando's Historic Preservation Board denied a request to demolish the 1918 Dolive Building, seen in the right of the foreground. The city upheld the decision, the owner appealed, and the dispute went to the Orange County Circuit Court. The judge ruled the ordinance unconstitutional, and the city granted permission to demolish the building. The structure was vacated in 2005 and fell into disrepair, though it is still standing.